The Dancing Mouse

A Study in Animal Behavior

Robert M. Yerkes

Writat

This edition published in 2022

ISBN : 9789356391079

Contents

PREFACE

This book is the direct result of what, at the time of its occurrence, seemed to be an unimportant incident in the course of my scientific work— the presentation of a pair of dancing mice to the Harvard Psychological Laboratory. My interest in the peculiarities of behavior which the creatures exhibited, as I watched them casually from day to day, soon became experiment-impelling, and almost before I realized it, I was in the midst of an investigation of their senses and intelligence.

The longer I observed and experimented with them, the more numerous became the problems which the dancers presented to me for solution. From a study of the senses of hearing and sight I was led to investigate, in turn, the various forms of activity of which the mice are capable; the ways in which they learn to react adaptively to new or novel situations; the facility with which they acquire habits; the duration of habits; the roles of the various senses in the acquisition and performance of certain habitual acts; the efficiency of different methods of training; and the inheritance of racial and individually acquired forms of behavior.

In the course of my experimental work I discovered, much to my surprise, that no accurate and detailed account of this curiously interesting animal existed in the English language, and that in no other language were all the facts concerning it available in a single book. This fact, in connection with my appreciation of the exceptional value of the dancer as a pet and as material for the scientific study of animal behavior, has led me to supplement the results of my own observation by presenting in this little book a brief and not too highly technical description of the general characteristics and history of the dancer.

The purposes which I have had in mind as I planned and wrote the book are three: first, to present directly, clearly, and briefly the results of my investigation; second, to give as complete an account of the dancing mouse as a thorough study of the literature on the animal and long-continued observation on my own part should make possible; third, to provide a supplementary text-book on mammalian behavior and on methods of studying animal behavior for use in connection with courses in Comparative Psychology, Comparative Physiology, and Animal Behavior.

It is my conviction that the scientific study of animal behavior and of animal mind can be furthered more just at present by intensive special investigations than by extensive general books. Methods of research in this field are few and surprisingly crude, for the majority of investigators have been more deeply interested in getting results than in perfecting methods. In writing this account of the dancing mouse I have attempted to lay as much stress upon the development of my methods of work as upon the results which the methods yielded. In fact, I have used the dancer as a means of exhibiting a variety of methods by which the behavior and intelligence of animals may be studied. As it happens the dancer is an ideal subject for the experimental study of many of the problems of animal behavior. It is small, easily cared for, readily tamed, harmless, incessantly active, and it lends itself satisfactorily to a large number of experimental situations. For laboratory courses in Comparative Psychology or Comparative Physiology it well might hold the place which the frog now holds in courses in Comparative Anatomy.

Gratefully, and with this expression of my thanks, I acknowledge my indebtedness to Professor Hugo Münsterberg for placing at my command the resources of the Harvard Psychological Laboratory and for advice and encouragement throughout my investigation; to Professor Edwin B. Holt for valuable assistance in more ways than I can mention; to Professor Wallace C. Sabine for generous aid in connection with the experiments on hearing; to Professor Theobald Smith for the examination of pathological dancers; to Miss Mary C. Dickerson for the photographs of dancing mice which are reproduced in the frontispiece; to Mr. Frank Ashmore for additional photographs which I have been unable to use in this volume; to Mr. C. H. Toll for the drawings for Figures 14 and 20; to Doctors H. W. Rand and C. S. Berry for valuable suggestions on the basis of a critical reading of the proof sheets; and to my wife, Ada Watterson Yerkes, for constant aid throughout the experimental work and in the preparation of this volume.

R. M. Y.

CAMBRIDGE, MASSACHUSETTS,

August, 1907.

CHAPTER I

CHARACTERISTICS, ORIGIN, AND HISTORY

The variety of mouse which is known as the Japanese dancing or waltzing mouse has been of special interest to biologists and to lovers of pets because of its curious movements. Haacke in Brehm's "Life of Animals" (7 p. 337)[1] writes as follows concerning certain mice which were brought to Europe from China and Japan: "From time to time a Hamburg dealer in animals sends me two breeds of common mice, which he calls Chinese climbing mice (Chinesische Klettermäusc) and Japanese dancing mice (Japanische Tanzmäuse). It is true that the first are distinguished only by their different colors, for their climbing accomplishments are not greater than those of other mice. The color, however, is subject to many variations. Besides individuals of uniform gray, light yellow, and white color, I have had specimens mottled with gray and white, and blue and white. Tricolored mice seem to be very rare. It is a known fact that we also have white, black, and yellow mice and occasionally pied ones, and the Chinese have profited by these variations of the common mouse also, to satisfy their fancy in breeding animals. The Japanese, however, who are no less enthusiastic on this point, know how to transform the common mouse into a really admirable animal. The Japanese dancing mice, which perfectly justify their appellation, also occur in all the described colors. But what distinguishes them most is their innate habit of running around, describing greater or smaller circles or more frequently whirling around on the same spot with incredible rapidity. Sometimes two or, more rarely, three mice join in such a dance, which usually begins at dusk and is at intervals resumed during the night, but it is usually executed by a single individual."

[Footnote 1: The reference numbers, of which 7 is an example, refer to the numbers in the bibliographic list which precedes this chapter.]

As a rule the dancing mouse is considerably smaller than the common mouse, and observers agree that there are also certain characteristic peculiarities in the shape of the head. One of the earliest accounts of the animal which I have found, that of Landois (22 p. 62), states, however, that the peculiarities of external form are not remarkable. Landois further remarks, with reason, that the name dancing mouse is ill chosen, since the human dance movement is rather a rhythmic hopping motion than regular movement in a circle. As he suggests, they might more appropriately be called "circus course mice" (22 p. 63).

Since 1903 I have had under observation constantly from two to one hundred dancing mice. The original pair was presented to the Harvard Psychological Laboratory by Doctor A.G. Cleghorn of Cambridge. I have obtained specimens, all strikingly alike in markings, size, and general behavior, from animal dealers in Washington, Philadelphia, and Boston. Almost all of the dancers which I have had, and they now number about four hundred, were white with patches, streaks, or spots of black. The black markings occurred most frequently on the neck, ears, face, thighs, hind legs, about the root of the tail, and occasionally on the tail itself. In only one instance were the ears white, and that in the case of one of the offspring of a male which was distinguished from most of his fellows by the possession of one white ear. I have had a few individuals whose markings were white and gray instead of white and black.

The method by which I was able to keep an accurate record of each of my dancers for purposes of identification and reference is illustrated in Figure 1. As this method has proved very convenient and satisfactory, I may briefly describe it. With a rubber stamp[1] a rough outline of a mouse, like that of Figure 1 A, was made in my record book. On this outline I then indicated the black markings of the individual to be described. Beside this drawing of the animal I recorded its number, sex,[2] date of birth, parentage, and history. B, C, and D of Figure 1 represent typical color patterns. D indicates the markings of an individual whose ears were almost entirely white. The pattern varies so much from individual to individual that I have had no trouble whatever in identifying my mice by means of such records as these.

[Footnote 1: For the use of the plate from which this stamp was made, I am indebted to Professor W.E. Castle, who in turn makes acknowledgment to Doctor G.M. Allen for the original drawing.]

[Footnote 2: I have found it convenient to use the even numbers for the males and the odd numbers for the females. Throughout this book this usage is followed. Wherever the sex of an individual is not specially given, the reader therefore may infer that it is a male if the number is even; a female if the number is odd.]

All of my dancers had black eyes and were smaller as well as weaker than the albino mouse and the gray house mouse. The weakness indicated by their inability to hold up their own weight or to cling to an object curiously enough does not manifest itself in their dancing; in this they are indefatigable. Frequently they run in circles or whirl about with astonishing rapidity for several minutes at a time. Zoth (31 p. 173), who measured the strength of the dancer in comparison with that of the common mouse, found that it can hold up only about 2.8 times its own weight, whereas the common white mouse can hold up 4.4 times its weight. No other accurate measurements of the strength, endurance, or hardiness of the dancer are available. They are usually supposed to be weak and delicate, but my own observations cause me to regard them as exceptionally strong in certain respects and weak in others.

[Illustration: FIGURE I.—Typical markings of dancers. A, blank outline of mouse for record. B, markings of No. 2 [symbol for male], born September 7, 1905, of unknown parents, died March 30,1907. C, markings of No 43 [symbol for female], born November 10, 1906, of 212 and 211. D, markings of No. 151 [symbol for female], born February 28, 1906, of 1000 and 5, died February 26, 1907.]

What the Japanese have to say about the dancing mouse is of special importance because Japan is rather commonly supposed to be its home. For this reason, as well as because of the peculiar interest of the facts mentioned, I quote at length from Doctor Kishi (21 p. 457). "The dancing mouse has received in Europe this name which it does not bear in its own home, because of the fact that the circular movements which it makes are similar to the European (human) dance. Sometimes it is also called the Japanese or Chinese mouse; originally, however, China must have been its home, since in Japan it is mostly called '*Nankin nesumi*,' the mouse from Nankin. When this animal came from China to Japan I shall inquire at a later opportunity. There were originally in Japan two different species of mouse, the gray and the white; therefore in order to distinguish our dancing mouse from these it was necessary to use the name of its native city.

"In Japan, as in Europe, the animal lives as a house animal in small cages, but the interest which is taken in it there is shown in quite another way than in Europe, where the whirling movements, to which the name dancing mouse is due, are of chief interest. For this reason in Europe it is given as much room as possible in its cage that it may dance conveniently. In Japan also the circular movements have been known for a long time, but this has had no influence upon our interest in the animal, for the human fashion of dancing with us is quite different from that in Europe. What has lent interest to the creature for us are its prettiness, its cleverness in tricks, and its activity. It is liked, therefore, as an amusement for children. For this purpose it is kept in a small cage, usually fifteen centimeters square, sometimes in a somewhat broader wooden box one of whose walls is of wire netting. In this box are built usually a tower, a tunnel, a bridge, and a wheel. The wheel is rather broad, being made in the form of a drum and pierced with holes on one side through which the animal can slip in and out. Running around on the inside, the mouse moves the wheel often for hours at a time, especially in the evening. Moreover, there are found in the box other arrangements of different kinds which may be set in motion by the turning of the wheel. No space remains in the box in which the animal may move about freely, and therefore one does not easily or often have an opportunity to observe that the animal makes circular movements, whether voluntarily or involuntarily. This is the reason that in its home this interesting little animal has never been studied by any one in this respect."

It is odd indeed that the remarkable capacity of the dancer for the execution of quick, graceful, dextrous, bizarre, and oft-repeated movements has not been utilized in America as it has in Japan. The mice are inexhaustible sources of amusement as well as invaluable material for studies in animal behavior and intelligence.

Concerning the origin and history of this curious variety of mouse little is definitely known. I have found no mention of the animal in scientific literature previous to 1890. The fact that it is called the Chinese dancing mouse, the Japanese dancing mouse, and the Japanese waltzing mouse is indicative of the existing uncertainty concerning the origin of the race.

Thinking that Japanese literature might furnish more information bearing on the question of racial history than was available from European sources, I wrote to Professor Mitsukuri of the University of Tokyo, asking him whether any reliable records of the dancer existed in Japan. He replied as follows: "I have tried to find what is known in Japan about the history of the Japanese waltzing mice, but I am sorry to say that the results are wholly negative. I cannot find any account of the origin of this freak, either authentic or fictitious, and, strange as it may seem to you, no study of the mice in a modern sense has been made, so you may consider the literature on the mouse in the Japanese language as absolutely *nil*." In explanation of this somewhat surprising ignorance of the origin of the race in what is commonly supposed to be its native land, Professor Mitsukuri adds: "The breeders of the mice have mostly been ignorant men to whom writing is anything but easy."

In response to similar inquiries, I received the following letter, confirmatory of Professor Mitsukuri's statements, from Doctor S. Hatai of Wistar Institute, Philadelphia: "If I remember rightly the so-called Japanese dancing mouse is usually called by us *Nankin-nedzumi*. *Nankin* means anything which has been imported from China, and *nedzumi* means rat-like animal, or in this case mouse, or Chinese mouse. I referred to one of the standard Japanese dictionaries and found the following statement: 'The *Nankin-nedzumi* is one of the varieties of *Mus spiciosus* (*Hatszuka-nedzumi*), and is variously colored. It was imported from China. These mice are kept in cages for the amusement of children, who watch their play.' *Mus spiciosus*, if I remember correctly, is very much like *Mus musculus* in color, size, and several other characteristics, if not the same altogether."

In Swinhoe's list of the mammals of China, which appeared in the *Proceedings of the Zoological Society of London* for 1870, *Mus musculus L.* is mentioned as occurring in houses in South China and in Formosa. It is further stated that black and white varieties which are brought from the Straits are often kept by the Chinese (p. 637).

The statements of Kishi, Mitsukuri, and Hatai which have been quoted, taken in connection with the opinions expressed by various European scientists who have studied the dancer, make it seem highly probable that the race appeared first in China, and was thence introduced into Japan, from which country it has been brought to Europe and America. Accepting for the present this conclusion with reference to the place of origin of the dancer, we may now inquire, how and when did this curious freak, as Professor Mitsukuri has called it, come into existence? Concerning these matters there is wide divergence of opinion.

Haacke (6 p. 514), as quoted in Brehm's "Tierleben," says that an animal dealer with whom he discussed the question of the possible origin of the dancer maintained that it came from Peru, where it nests in the full cotton capsules, arranging the cotton fibers in the form of a nest by running about among them in small circles. Hence the name cotton mouse is sometimes applied to it. Haacke himself believes, however, that the race originated either in China or Japan as the result of systematic selectional breeding. Of this he has no certainty, for he states that he failed to find any literature on the "beautiful mice of China and Japan." Whether Haacke's description of the dancing mouse was published elsewhere previous to its appearance in Brehm's "Tierleben" I am unable to state; I have found nothing written on the subject by him before 1890. Zoth (31 p. 176) also thinks that the race was developed by systematic breeding, or in other words, that it is a product of the skill of the Asiatic animal breeders.

Another account of the origin of the race is that accepted by Kishi (21 p. 481) and some other Japanese biologists. It is their belief that the forms of movement acquired by the individual as the result of confinement in narrow cages are inherited. Thus centuries of subjection to the conditions which Kishi has described (p. 6) finally resulted in a race of mice which breed true to the dance movement. It is only fair to add, although Kishi does not emphasize the fact, that in all probability those individuals in which the dancing tendency was most pronounced would naturally be selected by the breeders who kept these animals as pets, and thus it would come about that selectional breeding would supplement the inheritance of an acquired character. Few indeed will be willing to accept this explanation of the origin of the dancer so long as the inheritance of acquired characters remains, as at present, unproved.

Still another mode of origin of the mice is suggested by the following facts. In 1893 Saint Loup (28 p. 85) advanced the opinion that dancing individuals appear from time to time among races of common mice. The peculiarity of movement may be due, he thinks, to an accidental nervous defect which possibly might be transmissible to the offspring of the exceptional individual. Saint Loup for several months had under observation a litter of common mice whose quick, jerky, nervous movements of the head, continuous activity, and rapid whirling closely resembled the characteristic movements of the true dancers of China. He states that these mice ran around in circles of from 1 to 20 cm. in diameter. They turned in either direction, but more frequently to the left, that is, anticlockwise. At intervals they ran in figure-eights ([Symbol: figure eight]) as do the true dancers. According to Saint Loup these exceptional individuals were healthy, active, tame, and not markedly different in general intelligence from the ordinary mouse. One of these mice produced a litter of seven young, in which, however, none of the peculiarities of behavior of the parents appeared.

In view of this proof of the occurrence of dancing individuals among common mice, Saint Loup believes that the race of dancers has resulted from the inheritance and accentuation of an "accidental" deviation from the usual mode of behavior. It is scarcely necessary to say that this opinion would be of far greater weight had he observed, instead of postulating, the inheritance of the peculiarities of movement which he has described. It might be objected, to the first of his so-called facts, that the litter resulted from the mating of mice which possessed dancer blood. Until the occurrence of dancers among varieties of mice which are known to be unmixed with true dancers is established, and further, until the inheritance of this peculiar deviation from the normal is proved, Saint Loup's account of the origin of the dancing mouse race must be regarded as an hypothesis.

The occurrence of dancing individuals among common mice has been recorded by several other observers. Kammerer (20 p. 389) reports that he found a litter of young wood mice (*Mus sylvaticus L.*) which behaved much as do the spotted dancers of China. He also observed, among a lot of true dancers, a gray individual which, instead of spinning around after the manner of the race, turned somersaults at frequent intervals. It is Kammerer's opinion, as a result of these observations, that the black and white dancers of China and Japan have been produced by selectional breeding on the basis of this occasional tendency to move in circles. Among albino mice Rawitz (25 p. 238) has found individuals which whirled about rapidly in small circles. He states, however, that they lacked the restlessness of the Chinese dancers. Some shrews (*Sorex vulgaris L.*) which exhibited whirling movements and in certain other respects resembled the dancing mouse were studied for a time by Professor Häcker of Freiburg in Baden, according to a report by von Guaita (17 p. 317, footnote). Doctor G. M. Allen of Cambridge has reported to me that he noticed among a large number of mice kept by him for the investigation of problems of heredity[1] individuals which ran in circles; and Miss Abbie Lathrop of Granby, Massachusetts, who has raised thousands of mice for the market, has written me of the appearance of an individual, in a race which she feels confident possessed no dancer blood, which whirled and ran about in small circles much as do the true dancers.

[Footnote 1: Allen, G.M. "The Heredity of Coat Color in Mice." Proc. Amer.
Academy, Vol. 40, 59-163, 1904.]

Although it is possible that some of these cases of the unexpected appearance of individuals with certain of the dancer's peculiarities of behavior may have been due to the presence of dancer blood in the parents, it is not at all probable that this is true of all of them. We may, therefore, accept the statement that dancing individuals now and then appear in various races of mice. They are usually spoken of as freaks, and, because of their inability to thrive under the conditions of life of the race in which they happen to appear, they soon perish.

Another and a strikingly different notion of the origin of the race of dancers from those already mentioned is that of Cyon (11 p. 443) who argues that it is not a natural variety of mouse, as one might at first suppose it to be, but instead a pathological variation. The pathological nature of the animals is indicated, he points out, by the exceptionally high degree of variability of certain portions of the body. According to this view the dancing is due to certain pathological structural conditions which are inherited. Cyon's belief raises the interesting question, are the mice normal or abnormal, healthy or pathological? That the question cannot be answered with certainty off-hand will be apparent after we have considered the facts of structure and function which this volume presents.

Everything organic sooner or later is accounted for, in some one's mind, by the action of natural selection. The dancing mouse is no exception, for Landois (22 p. 62) thinks that it is the product of natural selection and heredity, favored, possibly, by selectional breeding in China. He further maintains that the Chinese dancer is a variety of *Mus musculus L.* in which certain peculiarities of behavior appear because of bilateral defects in the brain. This author is not alone in his belief that the brain of the dancer is defective, but so far as I have been able to discover he is the only scientist who has had the temerity to appeal to natural selection as an explanation of the origin of the race.

Milne-Edwards, as quoted by Schlumberger (29 p. 63), is of the opinion that the Chinese dancer is not a natural wild mouse race, but instead the product of rigid artificial selection. And in connection with this statement Schlumberger describes a discovery of his own which seems to have some bearing upon the problem of origin. In an old Japanese wood carving which came into his possession he found a group of dancing mice. The artist had represented in minute detail the characteristics of the members of the group, which consisted of the parents and eight young. The father and mother as well as four of the little mice are represented as white spotted with black. Of the four remaining young mice, two are entirely black and two entirely white. The two pure white individuals have pink eyes, as has also the mother. The eyes of all the others are black. From these facts Schlumberger infers that the dancer has resulted from the crossing of a race of black mice with a race of albinos; the two original types appear among the offspring in the carving.

Experimental studies of the inheritance of the tendency to dance are of interest in their bearing upon the question of origin. Such studies have been made by Haacke (19), von Guaita (17, 18), and Darbishire (13, 14, 15, 16), and the important results of their investigations have been well summarized by Bateson (5).

By crossing dancing mice with common white mice both Haacke and von Guaita obtained gray or black mice which are very similar to the wild house mouse in general appearance and behavior. The characteristic movements of the dancers do not appear. As the result of a long series of breeding experiments, Darbishire (16 pp. 26, 27) says: "When the race of waltzing mice is crossed with albino mice which do not waltz, the waltzing habit disappears in the resulting young, so that waltzing is completely recessive in Mendel's sense; the eye-color of the hybrids is always dark; the coat-color is variable, generally a mixture of wild-gray and white, the character of the coat being distinctly correlated with characters transmitted both by the albino and by the colored parent." When hybrids produced by the cross described by Darbishire are paired, they produce dancers in the proportion of about one to five.

Bateson (5 p. 93, footnote), in discussing the results obtained by Haacke, von Guaita, and Darbishire, writes: "As regards the waltzing character, von Guaita's experiments agree with Darbishire's in showing that it was always recessive to the normal. No individual in F1 [thus the first hybrid generation is designated] or in families produced by crossing F1 with the pure normal, waltzed. In Darbishire's experiments F1 x F1 [first hybrids mated] gave 8 waltzers in 37 offspring, indicating 1 in 4 as the probable average. From von Guaita's matings in the form DR x DR the totals of families were 117 normal and 21 waltzers.... There is therefore a large excess of normals over the expected 3 to 1. This is possibly due to the delicacy of the waltzers, which are certainly much more difficult to rear than normals are. The small number in von Guaita's litters makes it very likely that many were lost before such a character as this could be determined."

Bateson does not hazard a guess at the origin of the dancer, but merely remarks (5 p. 86) that the exact physiological basis of the dancing character is uncertain and the origin of this curious variation in behavior still more obscure. "Mouse fanciers have assured me," he continues, "that something like it may appear in strains inbred from the normal type, though I cannot find an indubitable case. Such an occurrence may be nothing but the appearance of a rare recessive form. Certainly it is not a necessary consequence of inbreeding, witness von Guaita's long series of inbred albinos." (von Guaita (17 p. 319) inbred for twenty-eight generations.)

From the foregoing survey of the available sources of information concerning the origin and history of the race of dancing mice the following important facts appear. There are four theories of the origin of the race: (1) origin by selectional breeding (Haacke, Zoth, Milne- Edwards); (2) origin through the inheritance of an acquired character (Kishi); (3) origin by mutation, inheritance, and selectional breeding (Saint Loup, Kammerer, Cyon); (4) origin by natural selection, and inheritance, favored by selectional breeding (Landois). Everything indicates that the race originated in China. It is fairly certain that individuals with a tendency to move in circles appear at rare intervals in races of common mice. It seems highly probable, in view of these facts, that the Chinese took advantage of a deviation from the usual form of behavior to develop by means of careful and patient selectional breeding a race of mice which is remarkable for its dancing. Even if it should be proved that the mutation as it appears among common mice is not inherited, the view that slight deviations were taken advantage of by the breeders would still be tenable. The dancing tendency is such in nature as to unfit an individual for the usual conditions of mouse existence, hence, in all probability human care alone could have produced and preserved the race of dancers.

In answer to the question, how and when did the race of dancers originate, it may be said that historical research indicates that a structural variation or mutation which occasionally appears in *Mus musculus*, and causes those peculiarities of movement which are known as dancing, has been preserved and accentuated through selectional breeding by the Chinese and Japanese, until finally a distinct race of mice which breeds true to the dance character has been established. The age of the race is not definitely known, but it is supposed to have existed for several centuries.

CHAPTER II

FEEDING, BREEDING, AND DEVELOPMENT OF THE YOUNG

In this chapter I shall report, for the benefit of those who may wish to know how to take care of dancing mice, my experience in keeping and breeding the animals, and my observations concerning the development of the young. It is commonly stated that the dancer is extremely delicate, subject to diseases to an unusual degree and difficult to breed. I have not found this to be true. At first I failed to get them to breed, but this was due, as I discovered later, to the lack of proper food. For three years my mice have bred frequently and reared almost all of their young. During one year, after I had learned how to care for the animals, when the maximum number under observation at any time was fifty and the total number for the year about one hundred, I lost two by disease and one by an accident. I very much doubt whether I could have done better with any species of mouse. There can be no doubt, however, that the dancer is delicate and demands more careful attention than do most mice. In March, 1907, I lost almost all of my dancers from what appeared to be an intestinal trouble, but with this exception I have had remarkably good luck in breeding and rearing them.

My dancers usually were kept in the type of cage of which Figure 2 is a photograph.[1] Four of these double cages, 70 cm. long, 45 cm. wide, and 10 cm. deep in front, were supported by a frame as is shown in Figure 3. The fact that the covers of these cages cannot be left open is of practical importance. A similar type of cage, which I have used to some extent, consists of a wooden box 30 by 30 cm. by 15 cm. deep, without any bottom, and with a hinged cover made in part of 1 cm. mesh wire netting. Such a cage may be placed upon a piece of tin or board, or simply on a newspaper spread out on a table. The advantage of the loose bottom is that the box may be lifted off at any time, and the bottom thoroughly cleansed. I have had this type of cage constructed in blocks of four so that a single bottom and cover sufficed for the block. If the mice are being kept for show or for the observation of their movements, at least one side of the cages should be of wire netting, and, as Kishi suggests, such objects as a wheel, a tower, a tunnel, a bridge, and a turntable, if placed in the cage, will give the animals excellent opportunity to exhibit their capacity for varied forms of activity.

[Footnote 1: This cage was devised by Professors W.E. Castle and E.L. Mark, and has been used in the Zoological Laboratories of Harvard University for several years.]

[Illustration: FIGURE 2.—Double cage, with nest boxes and water dishes.]

The floors of the cages were covered with a thin layer of sawdust for the sake of cleanliness, and in one corner of each cage a nest box of some sort was placed. During the warm months I found it convenient and satisfactory to use berry boxes, such as appear in Figure 2, with a small entrance hole cut in one side; and during the cold months cigar boxes, with an entrance hole not more than 5 cm. in diameter at one end. In the nest box a quantity of tissue paper, torn into fragments, furnished material for a nest in which the adults could make themselves comfortable or the female care for her young. Cotton should never be used in the nest boxes, for the mice are likely to get it wound about their legs with serious results. Apparently they are quite unable to free themselves from such an incumbrance, and their spinning motion soon winds the threads so tightly that the circulation of the blood is stopped.

[Illustration: FIGURE 3.—Double cages in frame.]

The cages and nest boxes were emptied and thoroughly cleaned once a week with an emulsion made by heating together one part of kerosene and one part of water containing a little soap. This served to destroy whatever odor the cages had acquired and to prevent vermin from infesting the nests. In hot weather far greater cleanliness is necessary for the welfare of the mice than in cold weather. The animals attend faithfully to their own toilets, and usually keep themselves scrupulously clean.

For water and food dishes I have used heavy watch glasses[1] 5 cm. in diameter and 1/2 cm. deep. They are convenient because they are durable, easily cleaned, and not large enough for the young mice to drown in when they happen to spin into one which contains water. It is said that mice do not need water, but as the dancers seem very fond of a little, I have made it a rule to wash the watch glasses thoroughly and fill them with pure fresh water daily. The food, when moist, may be placed in the cages in the same kind of watch glass.

[Footnote 1: Minot watch glasses.]

There is no need of feeding the animals oftener than once a day, and as they eat mostly in the evening and during the night, it is desirable that the food should be placed in the cage late in the afternoon. For almost a year I kept a pair of dancers on "force"[1] and water. They seemed perfectly healthy and were active during the whole time, but they produced no young. If the animals are kept as pets, and breeding is not desired, a diet of "force," "eggo-see,"[1] and crackers, with some bird-seed every few days, is likely to prove satisfactory. As with other animals, a variety of food is beneficial, but it appears to be quite unnecessary. Too much rich food should not be given, and the mice should be permitted to dictate their own diet by revealing their preferences. They eat surprisingly little for the amount of their activity. I have had excellent success in breeding the mice by feeding them a mixture of dry bread- crumbs, "force," and sweet, clean oats slightly moistened with milk. The food should never be made soppy. A little milk added thus to the food every other day greatly increases fertility. About once a week a small quantity of some green food, lettuce for example, should be given. It is well, I have found, to vary the diet by replacing the bread and "force" at intervals with crackers and seeds. Usually I give the food dry every other day, except in the case of mice which are nursing litters. One person to whom I suggested that lettuce was good for the dancers lost four, apparently because of too much of what the mice seemed to consider a good thing. This suggests that it should be used sparingly.

[Footnote 1: A cereal food.]

Success in keeping and breeding dancing mice depends upon three things: cleanliness, warmth, and food supply. The temperature should be fairly constant, between 60° and 70° Fahr. They cannot stand exposure to cold or lack of food. If one obtains good healthy, fertile individuals, keeps them in perfectly clean cages with soft nesting materials, maintains a temperature of not far above or below 65°, and regularly supplies them with pure water and food which they like, there is not likely to be trouble either in keeping or breeding these delicate little creatures. Several persons who have reported to me difficulty in rearing the young or in keeping the adults for long periods have been unable to maintain a sufficiently high or constant temperature, or have given them food which caused intestinal trouble.

The males are likely to fight if kept together, and they may even kill one another. A male may be kept with one or more females, or several females may be kept together, for the females rarely, in my experience, fight, and the males seldom harm the females. Unless the male is removed from the cage in which the female is kept before the young are born, he is likely to kill the newborn animals. When a female is seen to be building a nest in preparation for a litter, it is best to place her in a cage by herself so that she may not be disturbed.

The sex of individuals may be determined easily in most cases, at the age of 10 to 12 days, by the appearance of teats in the case of females.

The period of gestation is from 18 to 21 days. The maximum number born by my dancers in any single litter was 9, the minimum number 3. In 25 litters of which I have accurate records, 135 individuals were born, an average of 5.4. The average number of males per litter was precisely the same, 2.7, as the number of females.

On the birth of a litter it is well to see that the female has made a nest from which the young are not likely to escape, for at times, if the nest is carelessly made, they get out of it or under some of the pieces of paper which are used in its construction, and perish. Several times I have observed nests so poorly built that almost all of the young perished because they got too far away to find their way back to the mother. It is surprising that the female should not take more pains to keep her young safe by picking them up in her mouth, as does the common mouse, and carrying them to a place where they can obtain warmth and nourishment. This I have never seen a dancing mouse do. For the first day or two after the birth of a litter the female usually remains in the nest box almost constantly and eats little. About the second day she begins to eat ravenously, and for the next three or four weeks she consumes at least twice as much food as ordinarily. Alexander and Kreidl (3 p. 567) state that the female does not dance during the first two weeks after the birth of a litter, but my experience contradicts their statement. There is a decreased amount of activity during this period, and usually the whirling movement appears but rarely; but in some cases I have seen vigorous and long-continued dancing within a few hours after the birth of a litter. There is a wide range of variability in this matter, and the only safe statement, in the light of my observations, is that the mother dances less than usual for a few days after a litter is born to her.

The development of the young, as I have observed it in the cases of twenty litters, for ten of which (Table I) systematic daily records were kept, may be sketched as follows. At birth the mice have a rosy pink skin which is devoid of hair and perfectly smooth; they are blind, deaf, and irresponsive to stimulation of the vibrissae on the nose. During the first week of post-natal life the members of a litter remain closely huddled together in the nest, and no dance movements are exhibited. The mother stays with them most of the time. On the fourth or fifth day colorless hairs are visible, and by the end of the week the body is covered with a coat which rapidly assumes the characteristic black and white markings of the race. For the first few days the hind legs are too weak to support the body weight, and whatever movements appear are the result of the use of the fore legs. As soon as the young mice are able to stand, circling movements are exhibited, and by the end of the second week they are pronounced. Somewhere about the tenth day the appearance of the teats in the case of the females serves to distinguish the sexes plainly. Between the tenth and fifteenth days excitability, as indicated by restless jerky movements in the presence of a disturbing condition, increases markedly; the auditory meatus opens, and, in the case of some individuals, there are signs of hearing. On or after the fifteenth day the eyes open and the efforts to escape from the nest box rapidly become more vigorous. About this time the mother resumes her dancing with customary vigor, and the young, when they have opportunity, begin to eat of the food which is given to her. They now dance essentially as do the adults. From the end of the third week growth continues without noteworthy external changes until sexual maturity is attained, between the fourth and the sixth week. For several weeks after they are sexually mature the mice continue to increase in size.

TABLE I

DEVELOPMENT OF THE YOUNG

NUMBER JERKY REACT IN HAIR TEATS MOVE- EARS TO EYES PARENTS LITTER VISIBLE VISIBLE MENTS OPEN SOUND OPEN M F APPEAR

152+151 5 0 4th day — 13th day 14th day 14th day 16th day 152+151 1 3 4th day 9th day 10th day 12th day 13th day 15th day 410+415 4 1 5th day 11th day 14th day 15th day 15th day 17th day 410+415 2 4 5th day 10th day 13th day 14th day 14th day 16th day 420+425 0 2 4th day 10th day 12th day 14th day 14th day 16th day 210+215 4 1 — — 17th day 13th day 17th day 15th day 210+215 3 3 5th day 11th day 11th day 14th day No 16th day 212+211 1 3 4th day 10th day 15th day 14th day No 15th day 220+225 2 4 4th day 10th day 16th day 14th day No 15th day 220+225 3 3 4th day 10th day 17th day 13th day No 15th day

A course of development very similar to that just described was observed by Alexander and Kreidl (3 p. 565) in three litters of dancing mice which contained 3, 5, and 7 individuals respectively. These authors, in comparing the development of the dancer with that of the common mouse, say that at birth the young in both cases are about 24 mm. in length. The young common mouse grows much more rapidly than the dancer, and by the ninth day its length is about 43 mm. as compared with 31 mm. in the case of the dancer. According to Zoth (31 p. 148) the adult dancer has a body length of from 7 to 7.5 cm., a length from tip of nose to tip of tail of from 12 to 13 cm., and a weight of about 18 grams. The movement of the dancer from the first tends to take the form of circles toward the middle of the nest; that of the common mouse has no definite tendency as to direction. When the common mouse does move in circles, it goes first in one direction, then in the other, and not for any considerable period in one direction as does the true dancer. Neither the young dancer nor the common mouse is able to equilibrate itself well for the first few days after birth, but the latter can follow a narrow path with far greater accuracy and steadiness than the former. The uncertain and irregular movements of the common mouse are due to muscular weakness and to blindness, but the bizarre movements of the young dancer seem to demand some additional facts as an explanation.

A brief account of the development of the dancer given by Zoth (31 p. 149) adds nothing of importance to the description given by Alexander and Kreidl. As my own observations disagree with their accounts in certain respects, I shall now give, in the form of a diary, a description of the important changes observed from day to day in a normal litter. The litter which I have selected as typical of the course of development in the dancer grew rapidly under favorable conditions. I have observed many litters which passed through the various stages of development mentioned in this description anywhere from a day to a week later. This was usually due to some such obviously unfavorable condition as too little food or slight digestive or bowel troubles. According to the nature of the conditions of growth the eyes of the dancer open anywhere from the fourteenth to the twentieth day. This statement may serve to indicate the degree of variability as to the time at which a given stage of development is reached by different litters.

On July 14, 1906, No. 151 (female) and No. 152 (male) were mated, and on August 3 a litter of six was born to them. The course of the development of this litter during the first three weeks was as follows:—

First day The skin is pink and hairless, several vibrissae are visible on the nose and lips, but there is no definite response when they are touched. The mice are both blind and deaf, but they are able to squeak vigorously. The mother was not seen to dance or eat during the day.

Second day. There is a very noticeable increase in size. The vibrissae are longer, but touching them still fails to cause a reaction. No hairs are visible on the body. The mother danced rapidly for periods of a minute several times while the record was being made. She ate very little to-day.

Third day. Scales began to appear on the skin to-day. The animals are rapidly increasing in strength; they can now crawl about the nest easily, but they are too weak to stand, and constantly roll over upon their sides or backs when they are placed on a smooth surface. Because of their inability to progress it is impossible to determine with certainty whether they have a tendency to move in circles. The mother was seen out of the nest dancing once to-day. She now eats ravenously.

Fourth day. One of the six young mice was found under a corner of the nest this morning dead, and the others were scattered about the nest box. I gathered them together into a nest which I made out of bits of tissue paper, and the mother immediately began to suckle them. They are very sensitive to currents of air, but they do not respond to light or sound and seldom to contact with the vibrissae.

Fifth day. When placed on a smooth surface, they tend to move in circles, frequently rolling over. When placed on their sides or backs, they immediately try to right themselves. They do not walk, for their legs are still too weak to support the weight of the body; instead they drag themselves about by the use of the fore legs. Fine colorless hairs are visible over the entire body surface. When the vibrissae are touched, the head is moved noticeably. The mother dances a great deal and eats about twice as much as she did before the birth of the litter.

Sixth day. Certain regions of the skin, which were slightly darker than the remainder on the fourth and fifth days, are now almost black. It is evident that they are the regions in which the black hair is to appear. The movement in circles is much more definite today, although most of the individuals are still too weak to stand on their feet steadily for more than a few seconds at a time. Most of their time, when they are first taken from the nest, is spent in trying to maintain or regain an upright position. The hair is now easily visible, and the skin begins to have a white appearance as a result.

Seventh day. Although they are strong enough to move about the nest readily, none of the young has attempted to leave the nest. They huddle together in the middle of it for warmth. The epidermal scales, which have increased in number since the third day, are dropping off rapidly. Contact with the vibrissae or with the surface of the body, frequently calls forth a motor reaction but neither light nor sound produces any visible change in behavior. The black and white regions of the skin are sufficiently definite now to enable one to distinguish the various individuals by their markings. The mother was seen to dance repeatedly today, and she ate all the food that was given to her.

Eighth day. A fold is plainly visible where later the eyelids will separate. The black pigment in the skin has increased markedly.

Ninth day. The eyelids are taking form rapidly, but they I have not separated. The body is covered with a thick coat of hair which is either pure white or black. Standing on the four legs is still a difficult task.

Tenth day. To-day teats are plainly visible in the case of four of the five individuals of the litter. Up to this time I had thought, from structural indications, that there were three males and two females; it is now evident that there are four females and one male. The external ear, the pinna, is well formed, and has begun to stand out from the head, but no opening to the inner portion of the ear is present. The eyelids appear to be almost fully formed.

Eleventh day. There are no very noticeable changes in appearance except in size, which continues to increase rapidly. They are able to regain their normal upright position almost immediately when they happen to roll over. The mother dances as usual.

Twelfth day. It appears to-day as if the eyes were about to open. The ears are still closed, and there is no evidence of a sense of hearing. They squeaked considerably when in the nest, but not at all when I took them out to note their development. The mother stays outside of the nest box much of the time now, probably to prevent the young ones from sucking continuously.

Thirteenth day. One of the little mice came out of the nest box while I was watching the litter this morning, and was able to find his way back directly despite the lack of sight. The mice are still dependent upon the mother for nourishment. I have not seen any of them attempt to eat the food which is given to the mother. They are extremely neat and clean. I watched one of them wash himself this morning. Each foot was carefully licked with the tongue. There seems to be special care taken to keep the toes perfectly clean.

Fourteenth day. An opening into the ear is visible to-day. When tested with the Galton whistle, all five responded with quick, jerky movements of the head and legs. They evidently hear certain tones. During the past two days the ears have changed rapidly. In one of the females, which seems to be a little in advance of the others in development, certain peculiarities of behavior appeared to-day. She jumped and squeaked sharply when touched and sprang out of my hand when I attempted to take her up. This is in marked contrast with her behavior previously.

Fifteenth day. The eyes are partly opened. All of the members of the litter came out of the nest box this morning and ran around the cage, dancing frequently and trying to eat with the mother. Three out of the five gave auditory reactions on first being stimulated; none of them responded to repetitions of the stimulus. All appeared to be less sensitive to sounds than yesterday. The quick, nervous, jerky movements are very noticeable.

Sixteenth day. The eyes of all five are fully opened. They dance vigorously and are outside the nest much of the time.

Seventeenth day. No reactions to sound could be detected to-day. The sense of sight gives evidence of being well developed. The nervous jumping movements persist.

Eighteenth day. The young mice continue to suck, although they eat of the food which is given to the mother. They are now able to take care of themselves.

Nineteenth day. There are no noteworthy changes except increase in size and strength.

Twentieth day. No auditory reactions were obtained today, but other forms of stimulation brought about unmistakable responses.

Twenty-first day. They are now about half grown and there is no other change of special interest to be recorded. Growth continues for several weeks. The statement made by Alexander and Kreidl to the effect that the dancer is almost full grown by the thirty-first day of life is false. At that age they may be sexually mature, but usually they are far from full grown.

CHAPTER III

BEHAVIOR: DANCE MOVEMENTS

The peculiarities of behavior of the dancing mouse are responsible alike for the widespread interest which it has aroused, and for its name. In a little book on fancy varieties of mice, in which there is much valuable information concerning the care of the animals, one who styles himself "An old fancier" writes thus of the behavior of the dancer: "I believe most people have an idea that the waltzing is a stately dance executed on the hind feet; this is not so. The performer simply goes round and round on all fours, as fast as possible, the head pointing inwards. The giddy whirl, after continuing for about a dozen turns, is then reversed in direction, and each performance usually occupies from one to two minutes. Whether it is voluntary or not, is difficult to determine, but I am inclined to think the mouse can refrain if it wishes to do so, because I never see them drop any food they may be eating, and begin to waltz in the midst of their meal. The dance, if such it can be called, generally seizes the mouse when it first emerges from its darkened sleeping place, and this would lead one to suppose that the light conveys an impression of shock to the brain, through the eyes, which disturbs the diseased centers and starts the giddy gyrations. The mice can walk or run in a fairly straight line when they wish to do so." Some of the old fancier's statements are true, others are mere guesses. Those who have studied the mice carefully will doubtless agree that he has not adequately described the various forms of behavior of which they are capable. I have quoted his description as an illustration of the weakness which is characteristic of most popular accounts of animal behavior. It proves that it is not sufficient to watch and then describe. The fact is that he who adequately describes the behavior of any animal watches again and again under natural and experimental conditions, and by prolonged and patient observation makes himself so familiar with his subject that it comes to possess an individuality as distinctive as that of his human companions. To the casual observer the individuals of a strange race are almost indistinguishable. Similarly, the behavior of all the animals of a particular species seems the same to all except the observer who has devoted himself whole-heartedly to the study of the subject and who has thus become as familiar with their life of action as most of us are with that of our fellow-men; for him each individual has its own unmistakable characteristics.

I shall now describe the behavior of the dancing mouse in the light of the results of the observation of scores of individuals for months at a time, and of a large number of experiments. From time to time I shall refer to points in the accounts of the subject previously given by Rawitz (25 p. 236), Cyon (9 p. 214), Alexander and Kreidl (1 p. 542), Zoth (31 p. 147), and Kishi (21 p. 479).

The most striking features of the ordinary behavior of the dancer are restlessness and movements in circles. The true dancer seldom runs in a straight line for more than a few centimeters, although, contrary to the statements of Rawitz and Cyon, it is able to do so on occasion for longer distances. Even before it is old enough to escape from the nest it begins to move in circles and to exhibit the quick, jerky head movements which are characteristic of the race. At the age of three weeks it is able to dance vigorously, and is incessantly active when not washing itself, eating, or sleeping. According to Zoth (31 p. 149) the sense of sight and especially the sense of smell of the dancer "seem to be keenly developed; one can seldom remain for some time near the cage without one or another of the animals growing lively, looking out of the nest, and beginning to sniff around in the air (*windet*). They also seem to have strongly developed cutaneous sensitiveness, and a considerable amount of curiosity, if one may call it such, in common with their cousin, the white mouse." I shall reserve what I have to say concerning the sense of sight for later chapters. As for the sense of smell and the cutaneous sensitiveness, Zoth is undoubtedly right in inferring from the behavior of the animal that it is sensitive to certain odors and to changes in temperature. One of the most noticeable and characteristic activities of the dancer is its sniffing. Frequently in the midst of its dancing it stops suddenly, raises its head so that the nose is pointed upward, as in the case of one of the mice of the frontispiece, and remains in that position for a second or two, as if sniffing the air.

The restlessness, the varied and almost incessant movements, and the peculiar excitability of the dancer have repeatedly suggested to casual observers the question, why does it move about in that aimless, useless fashion? To this query Rawitz has replied that the lack of certain senses compels the animal to strive through varied movements to use to the greatest advantage those senses which it does possess. In Rawitz's opinion the lack of hearing and orientation is compensated for by the continuous use of sight and smell. The mouse runs about rapidly, moves its head from side to side, and sniffs the air, in order that it may see and smell as much as possible. In support of this interpretation of the restlessness of the dancer, Rawitz states that he once observed similar behavior in an albino dog which was deaf. This suggestion is not absurd, for it seems quite probable that the dancer has to depend for the guidance of its movements upon sense data which are relatively unimportant in the common mouse, and that by its varied and restless movements it does in part make up for its deficiency in sense equipment.

The dancing, waltzing, or circus course movement, as it is variously known, varies in form from moment to moment. Now an individual moves its head rapidly from side to side, perhaps backing a little at the same time, now it spins around like a top with such speed that head and tail are almost indistinguishable, now it runs in circles of from 5 cm. to 30 cm. in diameter. If there are any objects in the cage about or through which it may run, they are sure to direct the expression of activity. A tunnel or a hole in a box calls forth endless repetitions of the act of passing through. When two individuals are in the same cage, they frequently dance together, sometimes moving in the same direction, sometimes in opposite directions. Often, as one spins rapidly about a vertical axis, the other runs around the first in small circles; or again, both may run in a small circle in the same direction, so that their bodies form a living ring, which, because of the rapidity of their movements, appears perfectly continuous. The three most clearly distinguishable forms of dance are (1) movement in circles with all the feet close together under the body, (2) movement in circles, which vary in diameter from 5 cm. to 30 cm., with the feet spread widely, and (3) movement now to the right, now to the left, in figure eights ([Symbol: figure eight]). For convenience of reference these types of dance may be called *whirling, circling*, and the *figure eight dance*. Zoth, in an excellent account of the behavior of the dancer (31 p. 156), describes "manège movements," "solo dances," and "centre dances." Of these the first is whirling, the second one form of circling, and the third the dancing of two individuals together in the manner described above.

Both the whirling and the circling occur to the right (clockwise) and to the left (anticlockwise). As certain observers have stated that it is chiefly to the left and others that it is as frequently to the right, I have attempted to get definite information concerning the matter by observing a number of individuals systematically and at stated intervals. My study of this subject soon convinced me that a true conception of the facts cannot be got simply by noting the direction of turning from time to time. I therefore planned and carried out a series of experimental observations with twenty dancers, ten of each sex. One at a time these individuals were placed in a glass jar, 26 cm. in diameter, and the number of circle movements executed to the right and to the left during a period of five minutes was determined as accurately as possible. This was repeated at six hours of the day: 9 and 11 o'clock A.M., and 2, 4, 6, and 8 o'clock P.M. In order that habituation to the conditions under which the counts of turning were made might hot influence the results for the group, with ten individuals the morning counts were made first, and with the others the afternoon counts. No attempt was made in the counting to keep a separate record of the whirling and circling, although had it been practicable this would have been desirable, for, as soon became evident to the observer, some individuals which whirl in only one direction, circle in both.

In Table 2 the results of the counts for the males are recorded; in Table 3 those for the females. Each number in the column headed "right" and "left" indicates the total number of circles executed by a certain dancer in a period of five minutes at the hour of the day named at the head of the column. I may point out briefly the curiously interesting and entirely unexpected new facts which this method of observation revealed to me.

First, there are three kinds of dancers: those which whirl almost uniformly toward the right, those which whirl just as uniformly toward the left, and those which whirl about as frequently in one direction as in the other. To illustrate, No. 2 of Table 2 may be characterized as a "right whirler," for he turned to the right almost uniformly. In the case of the 6 P.M. count, for example, he turned 285 times to the right, not once to the left. No. 152, on the contrary, should be characterized as a "left whirler," since he almost always turned to the left. From both of these individuals No. 210 is distinguished by the fact that he turned now to the left, now to the right. For him the name "mixed whirler" seems appropriate.

Second, the amount of activity, as indicated by the number of times an individual turns in a circle within five minutes, increases regularly and rapidly from 9 A.M. to 8 P.M. According to the general averages which appear at the bottom of Table 2, the average number of circles executed by the males at 9 A.M. was 89.8 as compared with 207.1 at 8 P.M. In other words, the mice dance more in the evening than during the day.

Third, as it appears in a comparison of the general averages of Tables 2 and 3, the females dance more than the males, under the conditions of observation. At 9 A.M. the males circled 89.8 times, the females 151.0 times; at 8 P.M. the males circled 207.1 times, the females, 279.0 times.

Fourth, according to the averages for the six counts made with each individual, as they appear in Table 4, the males turn somewhat more frequently to the left than to the right (the difference, however, is not sufficient to be considered significant); whereas, the females turn much more frequently to the right than to the left. I do not wish to emphasize the importance of this difference, for it is not improbable that counts made with a larger number of animals, or even with another group of twenty, would yield different results.

TABLE 2

NUMBER or WHIRLS TO THE RIGHT AND TO THE LEFT DURING
FIVE-MINUTE INTERVALS AS DETERMINED BY COUNTS MADE AT
SIX DIFFERENT HOURS, FOR EACH OF TEN MALE DANCERS

NUMBER 9 A.M 11 A.M. 2 P.M. OF ANIMAL RIGHT LEFT RIGHT LEFT RIGHT LEFT

2 11 2 23 4 194 1 30 20 1 134 1 109 2 34 2 16 2 48 4 92 36 194 21 180 11 143 65 152 7 48 3 171 6 79 156 63 8 53 9 27 6 210 3 9 7 41 225 21 220 168 105 39 43 47 5 410 2 67 10 27 8 103 420 15 142 5 214 16 238

Averages 48.5 41.3 45.6 56.9 77.9 61.2

Gen. Av. 89.8 102.5 139.1

NUMBER 4 P.M 6 P.M. 8 P.M. OF ANIMAL RIGHT LEFT RIGHT LEFT RIGHT LEFT

2 70 3 285 0 237 10 30 154 0 107 6 134 5 34 7 158 5 118 6 147 36 173 14 170 11 325 19 152 0 91 16 210 9 223 156 85 2 72 26 139 26 210 159 18 31 82 47 201 220 45 38 78 17 69 33 410 9 155 9 394 24 94 420 18 243 16 291 3 320

Averages 72.0 72.2 78.9 115.5 99.3 107.8

Gen. Av. 144.2 194.4 207.1

TABLE 3

NUMBER OF WHIRLS TO THE RIGHT AND TO THE LEFT DURING FIVE-MINUTE INTERVALS AS DETERMINED BY COUNTS MADE AT SIX DIFFERENT HOURS, FOR EACH OF TEN FEMALE DANCERS

NUMBER 9 A.M. 11 A.M. 2 P.M. OF ANIMAL RIGHT LEFT RIGHT LEFT RIGHT LEFT

29 9 18 17 30 7 22 33 287 0 329 1 352 3 35 48 15 198 46 208 14 151 13 88 7 75 3 167 157 57 6 50 45 53 12 211 218 21 31 55 66 5 215 67 216 33 105 37 226 225 46 39 72 49 143 44 415 23 0 156 0 34 3 425 43 296 12 201 12 210

Averages 81.1 69.9 90.5 60.7 91.5 70.6

Gen. Av. 151.0 151.2 162.1

NUMBER 4 P.M. 6 P.M. 8 P.M. OF ANIMAL RIGHT LEFT RIGHT LEFT RIGHT LEFT

29 33 114 31 36 45 99 33 436 7 408 3 364 2 35 279 6 165 24 353 10 151 3 8 2 285 2 217 157 52 15 19 125 51 104 211 190 7 86 31 67 250 215 15 292 45 336 150 232 225 133 86 48 39 177 81 415 268 3 437 7 382 8 425 12 242 19 210 4 192

Averages 142.1 78.0 126.0 109.6 159.5 119.5

Gen. Av. 220.1 235.6 279.0

The most important results of this statistical study of turning are the demonstration of the existence of individual tendencies to turn in a particular direction, and of the fact that the whirling increases in amount from morning to evening.

In order to discover whether the distribution of the dancers among the three groups which have been designated as right, left, and mixed whirlers agrees in general with that indicated by Table 4 (approximately the same number in each group) I have observed the direction of turning in the case of one hundred dancers, including those of the foregoing tables, and have classified them in accordance with their behavior as is indicated below.

RIGHT LEFT MIXED WHIRLERS WHIRLERS WHIRLERS

Males 19 19 12
Females 12 23 15

Totals 31 42 27

The left whirlers occur in excess of both the right and the mixed whirlers. This fact, together with the results which have already been considered in connection with the counts of turning, suggests that a tendency to whirl in a certain way may be inherited. I have examined my data and conducted breeding experiments for the purpose of ascertaining whether this is true. But as the results of this part of the investigation more properly belong in a special chapter on the inheritance of behavior (XVIII), the discussion of the subject may be closed for the present with the statement that the preponderance of left whirlers indicated above is due to a strong tendency to turn to the left which was exhibited by the individuals of one line of descent.

TABLE 4

AVERAGE NUMBER OF WHIRLS TO THE RIGHT AND TO THE LEFT FOR THE SIX INTERVALS OF TABLES 2 AND 3, WITH A CHARACTERIZATION OF THE ANIMALS AS RIGHT WHIRLERS, LEFT WHIRLERS, OR MIXED WHIRLERS.

AVERAGE NO. AVERAGE NO. MALES AGE OF WHIRLS OF WHIRLS CHARACTERIZATION

2 12 mo. 136.7 3.3 Right whirler
30 2 mo. 109.7 2.5 Right whirler
34 2 mo. 4.3 96.5 Left whirler
36 2 mo. 197.5 23.5 Right whirler
152 6 mo. 6.8 137.0 Left whirler
156 1 mo. 73.2 12.8 Right whirler
210 3 mo. 78.7 62.0 Mixed whirler
220 4 mo. 74.3 40.2 Mixed whirler
410 3 mo. 10.3 139.0 Left whirler
420 3 mo. 12.2 241.3 Left whirler

Average 70.4 75.8 4 Right whirlers
4 Left whirlers
2 Mixed whirlers

FEMALES

29 2 mo. 23.7 53.2 Left whirler 33 2 mo. 362.7 2.7 Right whirler 35 2 mo. 208.5 19.2 Left whirler 151 6 mo. 5.0 140.0 Right whirler 157 1 mo. 47.0 51.2 Left whirler 211 3 mo. 109.7 61.5 Right whirler 215 3 mo. 57.8 234.5 Mixed whirler 225 4 mo. 103.2 56.3 Mixed whirler 415 3 mo. 216.7 3.5 Left whirler 425 3 mo. 17.0 225.2 Left whirler

Average 115.1 84.7 3 Right whirlers 4 Left whirlers 3 Mixed whirlers

The tendency of the dancer's activity to increase in amount toward evening, which the results of Tables 2, 3, and 4 exhibit, demands further consideration. Haacke (7 p. 337) and Kishi (21 p. 458) agree that the dancing is most vigorous in the evening; but Alexander and Kreidl (i p. 544) assert, on the contrary, that the whirling of the individuals which they observed bore no definite relation to the time of day and apparently was not influenced in intensity thereby. Since the results of my own observations contradict many of the statements made by the latter authors, I suspect that they may not have watched their animals long enough to discover the truth. The systematic records which I have kept indicate that the mice remain quietly in their nests during the greater part of the day, unless they are disturbed or come out to obtain food. Toward dusk they emerge and dance with varying intensity for several hours. I have seldom discovered one of them outside the nest between midnight and daylight. The period of greatest activity is between 5 and 10 o'clock P.M.

Zoth states that he has observed the adult dancer whirl 79 times without an instant's interruption, and I have counted as many as 110 whirls. It seems rather absurd to say that an animal which can do this is weak. Evidently the dancer is exceptionally strong in certain respects, although it may be weak in others. Such general statements as are usually made fail to do justice to the facts.

The supposition that light determines the periodicity of dancing is not borne out by my observations, for I have found that the animals continue to dance most vigorously toward evening, even when they are kept in a room which is constantly illuminated. In all probability the periodicity of activity is an expression of the habits of the mouse race rather than of the immediate influence of any environmental condition. At some time in the history of the dancer light probably did have an influence upon the period of activity; but at present, as a result of the persistence of a well-established racial tendency, the periodicity of dancing depends to a greater extent upon internal than upon external conditions. During its hours of quiescence it is possible to arouse the dancer and cause it to whirl more or less vigorously by stimulating it strongly with intense light, a weak electric current, or by placing two individuals which are strangers to one another in the same cage; but the dancing thus induced is seldom as rapid, varied, or as long-continued as that which is characteristic of the evening hours.

One of the most interesting results of this study of the direction of turning, from the observer's point of view, is the demonstration of the fact that the truth concerning even so simple a matter as this can be discovered only by long and careful observation. The casual observer of the dancer gets an impression that it turns to the left more often than to the right; he verifies his observation a few times and then asserts with confidence that such is the truth about turning. That such a method of getting knowledge of the behavior of the animal is worse than valueless is clear in the light of the results of the systematic observations which have just been reported. But, however important the progress which we may have made by means of systematic observation of the phenomenon of turning, it must not for one moment be supposed that the whole truth has been discovered. Continued observation will undoubtedly reveal other important facts concerning circling, whirling, and the periodicity of dancing, not to mention the inheritance of peculiarities of dancing and the significance of the various forms of activity.

CHAPTER IV

BEHAVIOR: EQUILIBRATION AND DIZZINESS

Quite as interesting and important as the general facts of behavior which we have been considering are the results of experimental tests of the dancer's ability to maintain its position under unusual spatial conditions—to climb, cross narrow bridges, balance itself on high places. Because of its tendency to circle and whirl, to dart hither and thither rapidly and apparently without control of its movements, the study of the mouse's ability to perform movements which demand accurate and delicate muscular coördination, and to control its expressions of activity, are of peculiar scientific interest.

That observers do not entirely agree as to the facts in this field is apparent from the following comparison of the statements made by Cyon and Zoth (31 p. 174).

Cyon states that the dancer

Cannot run in a straight line,
Cannot turn in a narrow space,
Cannot run backward,
Cannot run up an incline,

Cannot move about safely when above the ground, because of fear and visual dizziness,
Can hear certain tones.

Zoth, on the contrary, maintains that the animal

Can run in a straight line for at least 20 cm.,
Can and repeatedly does turn in a narrow space,
Can run backward, for he has observed it do so,
Can run up an incline unless the surface is too smooth for it to gain a foothold,
Can move about safely when above the ground, and gives no signs of fear or dizziness,
Cannot hear, or at least gives no signs of sensitiveness to sounds.

Such contradictory statements (and unfortunately they are exceedingly common) stimulated me to the repetition of many of the experiments which have been made by other investigators to test the dancer's behavior in unusual spatial relations. I shall state very briefly the general conclusions to which these experiments have led me, with only sufficient reference to methods and details of results to enable any one who wishes to repeat the tests for himself to do so. For the sake of convenience of presentation and clearness, the facts have been arranged under three rubrics: equilibrational ability, dizziness, and behavior when blinded. To our knowledge of each of these three groups of facts important contributions have come from the experiments of Cyon (9 p. 220), Alexander and Kreidl (1 p. 545), Zoth (31 p. 157), and Kishi (21 p. 482), although, as has been stated, in many instances their results are so contradictory as to demand reexamination. All in all, Zoth has given the most satisfactory account of the behavior and motor capacity of the dancer.

If the surface upon which it is moving be sufficiently soft or rough to furnish it a foothold, the dancer is able to run up or down inclines, even though they be very steep, to cross narrow bridges, to balance itself at heights of at least 30 cm. above the ground, and even to climb up and down on rods, as is shown by certain of Zoth's photographs which are reproduced in Figure 4. Zoth himself says, and in this I am able fully to agree with him on the basis of my own observations, "that the power of equilibration in the dancing mouse, is, in general, very complete. The seeming reduction which appears under certain conditions should be attributed, not to visual dizziness, but in part to excitability and restlessness, and in part to a reduced muscular power" (31 p. 161). The dancer certainly has far less grasping power than the common mouse, and is therefore at a disadvantage in moving about on sloping surfaces. One evidence of this fact is the character of the tracks made by the animal. Instead of raising its feet from the substratum and placing them neatly, as does the common mouse (Figure 5), it tends to shuffle along, dragging its toes and thus producing on smoked paper such tracks as are seen in Figure 6. From my own observations I am confident that these figures exaggerate the differences. My dancers, unless they were greatly excited or moving under conditions of stress, never dragged their toes as much as is indicated in Figure 6. However, there can be no doubt that they possess less power of grasping with their toes than do common mice. The animal is still further incapacitated for movement on inclined surfaces or narrow places by its tendency to move in circles and zigzags. The results of my own experiments indicate that the timidity of the adult is greater than that of the immature animal when it is placed on a bridge 1 or 2 cm. wide at a distance of 20 cm. from the ground. Individuals three weeks old showed less hesitation about trying to creep along such a narrow pathway than did full-grown dancers three or four months old; and these, in turn, were not so timid apparently as an individual one year old. But the younger animals fell off more frequently than did the older ones.

[Illustration: FIGURE 4.—Zoth's photographs of dancers crossing bridges and climbing rods. Reproduced from *Pfluger's Archiv*, Bd. 86.]

[Illustration: FIGURE 5—Tracks of common mouse Reproduced from Alexander and Kreidl's figure in *Pfluger's Archiv*, Bd 82]

[Illustration: FIGURE 6—Tracks of dancing mouse Reproduced from Alexander and Kreidl's figure in *Pfluger's Archiv* Bd 82]

Additional support for these statements concerning equilibrational ability is furnished by the observations of Kishi (21 p. 482). He built a wooden bridge 60 cm. long, 1 cm. wide at one end, and 1/2 cm. at the other, and supported it at a height of 30 cm. above the ground by posts at the ends. On this bridge ten dancers were tested. Some attempted to move sidewise, others began to whirl and fell to the ground; only one of the ten succeeded in getting all the way across the bridge on the first trial. The second time he was tested this individual crossed the bridge and found the post; and the third time he crossed the bridge and climbed down the post directly. The others did not succeed in descending the post even after having crossed the bridge safely, but, instead, finally fell to the floor from awkwardness or exhaustion. On the basis of these and other similar observations, Kishi says that the dancer possesses a fair degree of ability to orient and balance itself.

Inasmuch as equilibration occurs similarly in darkness and in daylight, Zoth thinks that there is neither visual dizziness nor fear of heights. But it is doubtful whether he is right concerning fear. There is no doubt in my mind, in view of the way the mice behave when placed on an elevated surface, that they are timid; but this is due probably to the uncomfortable and unusual position rather than to perception of their distance from the ground. That they lack visual dizziness seems fairly well established.

When rotated in a cyclostat[1] the dancer, unlike the common mouse, does not exhibit symptoms of dizziness. The following vivid description of the behavior of both kinds of mice when rotated is given by Alexander and Kreidl (1 p. 548). I have not verified their observations.

[Footnote 1: An apparatus consisting of a glass cylinder with a mechanism for turning it steadily and at different speeds about its vertical axis.]

The common mouse at first runs with increasing rapidity, as the speed of rotation of the cyclostat cylinder is increased, in the direction opposite to that of the cylinder itself. This continues until the speed of rotation has increased to about 60 revolutions per minute. As the rotation becomes still more rapid the mouse begins to crawl along the floor, its body stretched out and clinging to the floor. At a speed of 250 revolutions per minute it lies flat on the floor with its limbs extended obliquely to the movement of rotation, and at times with its back bent against the axis of the cylinder; in this position it makes but few and feeble efforts to crawl forward. When the rotation is suddenly stopped, the animal pulls itself together, remains for some seconds with extended limbs lying on the floor, and then suddenly falls into convulsions and trembles violently. After several attacks of this kind, cramps appear and, despite its resistance, the animal is thrown about, even into the air at times, as if by an external force. This picture of the position assumed during rapid rotation, and of cramps after the cessation of rotation (the typical picture of rotation dizziness), is repeated with great uniformity in the case of the common mouse. Within fifteen minutes after being returned to its cage the animal recovers from the effects of its experience. This description of the symptoms of rotation dizziness in the common mouse applies equally well to the blinded and the seeing animal.

In sharp contrast with the behavior of the common mouse in the cyclostat is that of the dancer. As the cylinder begins to rotate the dancer runs about as usual in circles, zigzags, and figure-eights. As the speed becomes greater it naturally becomes increasingly difficult for the mouse to do this, but it shows neither discomfort nor fear, as does the common mouse. Finally the centrifugal force becomes so great that the animal is thrown against the wall of the cylinder, where it remains quietly without taking the oblique position. When the cyclostat is stopped suddenly, it resumes its dance movements as if nothing unusual had occurred. It exhibits no signs of dizziness, and apparently lacks the exhaustion which is manifest in the case of other kinds of mice after several repetitions of the experiment. The behavior of the blinded dancer is very similar.

If these statements are true, there is no reason to believe that the dancer is capable of turning or rotation dizziness. If it were, its daily life would be rendered very uncomfortable thereby, for its whirling would constantly bring about the condition of dizziness. Apparently, then, the dancer differs radically from most mammals in that it lacks visual and rotational dizziness. In the next chapter we shall have to seek for the structural causes for these facts.

The behavior of the blinded animal is so important in its bearings upon the facts of orientation and equilibration that it must be considered in connection with them. Cyon insists that the sense of vision is of great importance to the dancer in orienting and equilibrating itself. When the eyes are covered with cotton wads fastened by collodion, this writer states (9 p. 223) that the mice behave as do pigeons and frogs whose semicircular canals have been destroyed. They perform violent forced movements, turn somersaults forward and backward, run up inclines and fall over the edges, and roll over and over. In a word, they show precisely the kind of disturbances of behavior which are characteristic of animals whose semicircular canals are not functioning normally. Cyon, however, observed that in certain dancers these peculiarities of behavior did not appear when they were blinded, but that, instead, the animals gave no other indication of being inconvenienced by the lack of sight than do common white mice. This matter of individual differences we shall have to consider more fully later.

No other observer agrees with Cyon in his conclusions concerning vision, or, for that matter, in his statements concerning the behavior of the blind dancer. Alexander and Kreidl (1 p. 550) contrast in the following respects the behavior of the white mouse and that of the dancer when they are blinded. The white mouse runs less securely and avoids obstacles less certainly when deprived of vision. The dancer is much disturbed at first by the shock caused by the removal of its eyes, or in case they are covered, by the presence of the unusual obstruction. It soon recovers sufficiently to become active, but it staggers, swerves often from side to side, and frequently falls over. It moves clumsily and more slowly than usual. Later these early indications of blindness may wholly disappear, and only a slightly impaired ability to avoid obstacles remains.

It was noted by Kishi (21 p. 484), that the dancer when first blinded trembles violently, jumps about wildly, and rolls over repeatedly, as Cyon has stated; but Kishi believes that these disturbances of behavior are temporary effects of the strong stimulation of certain reflex centers in the nervous system. After having been blinded for only a few minutes the dancers observed by him became fairly normal in their behavior. They moved about somewhat more slowly than usually, especially when in a position which required accurately coordinated movements. He therefore fully agrees with Alexander and Kreidl in their conclusion that vision is not so important for the guidance of the movements of the dancer as Cyon believes.

In summing up the results of his investigation of this subject Zoth well says (31 p. 168), "the orientation of the positions of the body with respect to the horizontal and vertical planes seems to take place without the assistance of the sense of sight." And, as I have already stated, this excellent observer insists that the ability of the dancer to place its body in a particular position (orientation), and its ability to maintain its normal relations to its surroundings (equilibration) are excellent in darkness and in daylight, provided only the substratum be not too smooth for it to gain a foothold.

It must be admitted that the contradictions which exist in the several accounts of the behavior of the dancer are too numerous and too serious to be explained on the basis of careless observation. Only the assumption of striking individual differences among dancers or of the existence of two or more varieties of the animal suffices to account for the discrepancies. That there are individual or variety differences is rendered practically certain by the fact that Cyon himself worked with two groups of dancers whose peculiarities he has described in detail, both as to structure and behavior.

In the case of the first group, which consisted of three individuals, the snout was more rounded than in the four individuals of the second group, and there were present on the head three large tufts of bristly black hair which gave the mice a very comical appearance. The animals of the second group resembled more closely in appearance the common albino mouse. They possessed the same pointed snout and long body, and only the presence of black spots on the head and hips rendered them visibly different from the albino mouse.

In behavior the individuals of these two groups differed strikingly. Those of the first group danced frequently, violently, and in a variety of ways; they seldom climbed on a vertical surface and when forced to move on an incline they usually descended by sliding down backwards or sidewise instead of turning around and coming down head first; they gave no signs whatever of hearing sounds. Those of the second group, on the contrary, danced very moderately and in few ways; they climbed the vertical walls of their cage readily and willingly, and when descending from a height they usually turned around and came down head first; two of the four evidently heard certain sounds very well. No wonder that Cyon suggests the possibility of a different origin! It seems not improbable that the individuals of the second group were of mixed blood, possibly the result of crosses with common mice.

As I shall hope to make clear in a subsequent discussion of the dancer's peculiarities of behavior, in a chapter on individual differences, there is no sufficient reason for doubting the general truth of Cyon's description, although there is abundant evidence of his inaccuracy in details. If, for the present, we accept without further evidence the statement that there is more than one variety of dancer, we shall be able to account for many of the apparent inaccuracies of description which are to be found in the literature on the animal.

As a result of the examination of the facts which this chapter presents we have discovered at least six important peculiarities of behavior of the dancer which demand an explanation in terms of structure. These are: (1) the dance movements—whirling, circling, figure-eights, zigzags; (2) restlessness and the quick, jerky movements of the head; (3) lack of responsiveness to sounds; (4) more or less pronounced deficiency in orientational and equilibrational power; (5) lack of visual dizziness; (6) lack of rotational dizziness.

Naturally enough, biologists from the first appearance of the dancing mouse in Europe have been deeply interested in what we usually speak of as the causes of these peculiarities of behavior. As a result, the structure of those portions of the body which are supposed to have to do with the control of movement, with the phenomena of dizziness, and with the ability to respond to sounds, have been studied thoroughly. In the next chapter we shall examine such facts of structure as have been discovered and attempt to correlate them with the facts of behavior.

CHAPTER V

STRUCTURAL PECULIARITIES AND BEHAVIOR

The activities of an animal are expressions of changes which occur in its structure, and they can be explained satisfactorily only when the facts of structure are known. Such peculiarities of activity as are exhibited by the dancing mouse, as contrasted with the common mouse, suggest at once that this creature has a body which differs in important respects from that of the ordinary mouse. In this chapter I shall present what is known concerning the structural bases for the whirling, the lack of equilibrational ability and of dizziness, the quick jerky head movements, the restlessness, and the partial or total deafness of the dancing mouse.

Comparative physiologists have discovered that the ability of animals to regulate the position of the body with respect to external objects and to respond to sounds is dependent in large measure upon the groups of sense organs which collectively are called the ear. Hence, with reason, investigators who sought structural facts with which to explain the forms of behavior characteristic of the dancer turned their attention first of all to the study of the ear. But the ear of the animal is not, as might be supposed on superficial examination, a perfectly satisfactory natural experiment on the functions of this group of sensory structures, for it is extremely uncertain whether any one of the usual functions of the organ is totally lacking. Dizziness may be lacking, and in the adult hearing also, but in general the functional facts lead the investigator to expect modifications of the sense organs rather than their absence.

I shall now give an account of the results of studies concerning the structure of the ear and brain of the dancer. Since the descriptions given by different anatomists contradict one another in many important points, the several investigations which have been made may best be considered chronologically.

Bernhard Rawitz (25 p. 239) was the first investigator to describe the structure of the ear of the Japanese or Chinese dancers, as he calls them. The definite problem which he proposed to himself at the beginning of his study was, what is the structural basis of the whirling movement and of the deafness of the mice?

In his first paper Rawitz described the form of the ears of five dancers. His method of work was to make microscopic preparations of the ears, and from the sections, by the use of the Born method, to reconstruct the ear in wax. These wax models were then drawn for the illustration of the author's papers (Figures 8, 9, 10).

The principal results of the early work of Rawitz are summed up in the following quotation from his paper: "The Japanese dancing mice have only one normal canal and that is the anterior vertical. The horizontal and posterior vertical canals are crippled, and frequently they are grown together. The utriculus is a warped, irregular bag, whose sections have become unrecognizable. The utriculus and sacculus are in wide-open communication with each other and have almost become one. The utriculus opens broadly into the scala tympani, and the nervous elements of the cochlea are degenerate.

"The last-mentioned degeneration explains the deafness of the dancing mice; but in my opinion it is a change of secondary nature. The primary change is the broad opening between the utriculus and the scala tympani from which results the streaming of the endolymph from the semicircular canals into the cochlea. When, as a consequence of the rapid whirling movements, a great part of the endolymph is hurled into the scala tympani, the organ of Corti in the scala vestibuli is fixed and its parts are rendered incapable of vibration. The condition of atrophy which is observable in the sense cells and in the nerve elements is probably due to the impossibility of functional activity; it is an atrophy caused by disuse "(25 p. 242).

Ampulla externa
Ampulla anterior
Ramus utriculi

Membrana basilaris

Lagena

Canalis utriculo-saccularis

Membrana basilaris
Ampulla posterior
Macula acustica sacculi

[Illustration: FIGURE 7.—The inner ear of the rabbit. Reproduced from Selenka after Retzius.]

To render the terms which occur in this and subsequent descriptions of the ear of the dancer somewhat more intelligible to those who are not familiar with the general anatomy of the vertebrate ear, a side view of the inner ear of the rabbit is reproduced from a drawing by Retzius (Figure 7). I have chosen the ear of the rabbit for this purpose, not in preference to that of the common mouse, but simply because I failed to find any reliable description of the latter with drawings which could be reproduced. The rabbit's ear, however, is sufficiently like that of the mouse to make it perfectly satisfactory for our present purpose.

This drawing of the rabbit's ear represents the three semicircular canals, which occur in the ear of all mammals, and which are called, by reason of their positions, the anterior vertical, the posterior vertical, and the horizontal. Each of these membranous canals possesses at one end, in an enlargement called the ampulla, a group of sense cells. In Figure 7 the ampullae of the three canals are marked respectively, ampulla anterior, ampulla posterior, and ampulla externa. This figure shows also the cochlea, marked lagena, in which the organ of hearing of mammals (the organ of Corti) is located. The ear sac, of which the chief divisions are the utriculus and the sacculus, with which the canals communicate, is not shown well in this drawing.

Within a few months after the publication of Rawitz's first paper on the structure of the dancer's ear, another European investigator, Panse (23 and 24) published a short paper in which he claimed that previous to the appearance of Rawitz's paper he had sectioned and mounted ears of the common white mouse and the dancing mouse side by side, and, as the result of careful comparison, found such slight differences in structure that he considered them unworthy of mention. Panse, therefore, directly contradicts the statements made by Rawitz. In fact, he goes so far as to say that he found even greater differences between the ears of different white mice than between them and the ears of the dancer (23 p. 140).

In a somewhat later paper Panse (24 p. 498) expresses his belief that, since there are no peculiarities in the general form, sensory structures, or nerve supply of the ear of the dancer, which serve to explain the behavior of the animal, it is probable that there are unusual structural conditions in the brain, perhaps in the cerebellum, to which are due the dance movements and the deafness. The work of Panse is not very convincing, however, for his figures are poor and his descriptions meager; nevertheless, it casts a certain amount of doubt upon the reliability of the descriptions given by Rawitz.

[Illustration: FIGURE 8.—The membranous labyrinth of the dancer's ear. Type I. This figure, as well as 9 and 10, are reproduced from Rawitz's figures in the *Archiv für Anatomie und Physiologie, Physiologische Abtheilung*, 1899. *C.s.*, anterior vertical canal; *C.p.*, posterior vertical canal; *C.e.*, horizontal canal; *U.*, utriculus.]

The unfavorable light in which his report was placed by Panse's statements led Rawitz to examine additional preparations of the ear of the dancer. Again he used the reconstruction method. The mice whose ears he studied were sent to him by the physiologist Cyon.

As has been noted in Chapter IV, Cyon discovered certain differences in the structure and in the behavior of these dancers (11 p. 431), which led him to classify them in two groups. The individuals of one group climbed readily on the vertical walls of their cages and responded vigorously to sounds; those of the other group could not climb at all and gave no evidences of hearing. After he had completed his study of their behavior, Cyon killed the mice and sent their heads to Rawitz; but unfortunately those of the two groups became mixed, and Rawitz was unable to distinguish them. When he examined the structure of the ears of these mice, Rawitz did find, according to his accounts, two structural types between which very marked differences existed. Were it not for the carelessness which is indicated by the confusion of the materials, and the influence of Cyon's suggestion that there should be different structures to account for the differences in behavior, Rawitz's statements might be accepted. As matters stand there can be no doubt of individual differences in behavior, external appearance, and the structure of the ear; but until these have been correlated on the basis of thoroughgoing, careful observation, it is scarcely worth while to discuss their relations.

[Illustration: FIGURE 9.—The membranous labyrinth of the dancer's ear. Type II.]

[Illustration: FIGURE 10.—The membranous labyrinth of the dancer's ear. Type III.]

To his previous description of the conditions of the ear sacs, sense organs, and nerve elements of the dancer's ear, Rawitz adds nothing of importance in his second paper (26 p. 171). He merely reiterates his previous statements concerning the form of the canals, on the basis of his findings in the case of six additional dancers. Figures 8, 9, and 10 are reproduced from Rawitz to show the anatomical conditions which he claims that he found. As these figures indicate, the canals were found to be extremely variable, as well as unusual in form, and the sacs distorted. In the ears of some specimens there were only two canals, and in all cases they were more or less reduced in size, distorted, or grown together.

[Illustration: FIGURE 11.—Photograph of a wax model of the membranous labyrinth of the ear of the dancer. Reproduced from Baginsky's figure in the *Centralblatt für Physiologie*, Bd. 16.]

The work of Rawitz was unfavorably criticised by Alexander and Kreidl (2), Kishi (21), and Baginsky (4), as well as by Panse (23 and 24). To their criticisms Rawitz replied by insisting that the other investigators could not with right attack his statements because they had not used the reconstruction method. In order to test the value of this contention, and if possible settle the question of fact, Baginsky had a model of the ear of the dancer constructed by a skilled preparator (Herr Spitz) from sections which had been prepared by the best neurological methods. This model was made eighty times the size of the ear. It was then reduced in the process of photographic reproduction to sixteen times the natural size of the ear in the mouse. Figure 11 is a photograph of Baginsky's model. It shows beyond question the presence of three canals of the same general form and relations as those of the common mouse and of other mammals. Baginsky's paper is brief and to the point. His criticisms of the work of both Cyon and Rawitz are severe, but they are justified in all probability by the carelessness of these investigators in the fixation of their materials. Of the five skilled histologists who have examined the ear of the dancer, Rawitz alone found markedly abnormal canals. It is highly probable, therefore, that the canals in his preparations in some way became distorted before the ears were sectioned. He doubtless described accurately the conditions which he found, but the chances are that those conditions never existed in the living animals.

The conflicting statements of Rawitz and Panse stimulated interest, and as a result two other investigators, without knowledge of one another's work, began careful researches on the dancer's ear. One, Alexander (2 and 3), worked in coöperation with the physiologist Kreidl; the other, Kishi (21), worked independently. The anatomical papers of Alexander and Kishi appeared at about the same time, and since neither contains a reference to the other, it is evident that the investigations were carried on almost simultaneously. Alexander's descriptions are more detailed than those of Rawitz and Panse, and in certain respects Kishi's are even more thoroughgoing. The first paper published by Alexander and Kreidl (1) contains the results of observations on the habits and behavior of the dancers. Having examined the chief facts of function, these investigators attempted to discover the structural conditions for the peculiarities of behavior which they had observed.

As material for their anatomical work they made use of four dancers, one albino mouse, and four common gray mice. The ears of these individuals were fixed, sectioned, and examined microscopically in connection with parts of the brain. In all, eight dancer ears and six common mouse ears were studied.

Very extensive descriptions of these preparations, together with measurements of many important portions of the ear, are presented in their paper, the chief conclusions of which are the following:—

1. The semicircular canals, the ampullae, the utriculus, and the cristae acusticae of the canals are normal in their general form and relations to one

another as well as in their histological conditions (2 p. 529). This is contradictory of the statements made by Rawitz.

2. There is destruction of the macula sacculi (2 p. 534).

3. There is destruction also of the papilla basilaris cochleae, with encroachment of the surrounding tissues in varying degrees.

4. There is diminution in the number of fibers of the branches and roots of the ramus superior and ramus medius of the eighth nerve, and the fiber bundles are very loosely bound together.

5. Similarly the number of fibers in the inferior branch (the cochlear nerve) of the eighth nerve is very much reduced.

6. There is moderate reduction in the size of the two vestibular ganglia as a result of the unusually small number of nerve cells.

7. The ganglion spirale is extremely degenerate.

There is therefore atrophy of the branches, ganglia, and roots of the entire eighth nerve, together with atrophy and degeneration of the pars inferior labyrinthii. The nerve endings are especially degenerate (2 p. 534).

The above structural deviations of the ear of the dancer from that of the common mouse may be considered as primary or secondary according as they are inherited or acquired. Since, according to Alexander and Kreidl, the dancers' peculiarities of behavior and deafness are directly and uniformly inherited, it is obvious that certain primary structural deviations must serve as a basis for these functional facts. But it is equally clear, in the opinion of Alexander and Kreidl (2 p. 536), that other structural peculiarities of the dancer are the result of the primary changes, and in no way the conditions for either the dancing or the deafness. These authors feel confident that the facts of behavior which are to be accounted for are almost certainly due to the pathological changes which they have discovered in the nerves, ganglia, and especially in the peripheral nerve endings of the ear of the mouse (2 p. 537).

It is further claimed by Alexander and Kreidl that there are very marked individual differences among the dancers in the structure of the ear. In some cases the otoliths and the sensory hairs are lacking; in others, they are present in the state of development in which they are found in other varieties of mouse. Sometimes the cochlea is much reduced in size; at other times it is found to be of normal size (2 p. 538). These variations in structure, if they really exist, go far toward justifying the tendency of Cyon and Alexander and Kreidl, as well as many other investigators, to regard the dancer as abnormal or even pathological.

The functions of the ear as at present known to the comparative physiologist are grouped as the acoustic and the non-acoustic. The cochlea is supposed on very good grounds to have to do with the acoustic functions, and the organs of the semicircular canals on equally good evidence are thought to have to do with such of the non-acoustic functions as equilibration and orientation. Just what the functions of the organs of the ear sacs are is not certainly known. These facts are of importance when we consider the attempts made by Alexander and Kreidl to correlate the various peculiarities of behavior shown by the dancer with the structural facts which their work has revealed. This correlation is indicated schematically below. The physiological facts to be accounted for in terms of structure are presented in the first column, and the anatomical facts which are thought to be explanatory, in the second (2 p. 539).

FUNCTION

1 Lack of sensitiveness to auditory stimuli. {Structure 1,2,3 below}

2 Defective equilibrational ability. {Structure 4,5,6 below}

3 Lack of turning dizziness. {Structure 4,5,6 below}

4 Normal reactions to galvanic stimulation. (not related in table to any Structure)

STRUCTURE

1 Destruction of the papilla basilaris cochleae, etc.

2 Diminution of the inferior branch of the eighth nerve.

3 Marked degeneration of the ganglion spirale.

4 Destruction of the macula sacculi.

5 Diminution of the branches and roots of the superior and middle branches of the eighth nerve.

6 Diminution of both ganglia vestibulii and of the nerve cells.

Alexander and Kreidl themselves believe that the partial deafness of the dancers (for they admit that the total lack of hearing has not been satisfactorily proved) is due to the defective condition of the cochlea. They account for the imperfect equilibrational ability of the animals by pointing out the structural peculiarities of the sacculus, the vestibular ganglia, and the peripheral nerves. Similarly, the lack of dizziness they suppose to be due to the diminution of the fibers of the nerves which supply the canal organs, the atrophied condition of the vestibular ganglia, and a disturbance of the peripheral sense organs. Furthermore, there are no anatomical facts which would indicate a lack of galvanic dizziness (2 p. 552).

Despite the fact that they seem to explain all the functional peculiarities of the dancer, the statements made by Alexander and Kreidl are neither satisfying nor convincing. Their statements concerning the structure of the ear have not been verified by other investigators, and their correlation of structural with functional facts lacks an experimental basis.

In this connection it may be worth while to mention that a beautiful theory of space perception which Cyon (9) had constructed, largely on the basis of the demonstration by Rawitz that the dancers have only one normal canal, is totally destroyed by Panse, Baginsky, Alexander and Kreidl, and Kishi, for all of these observers found in the dancer three canals of normal shape. Cyon had noted that the most abnormal of the voluntary as well as of the forced movements of the dancer occur in the plane of the canal which Rawitz found to be most strikingly defective. This fact he connected with his observation that the fish Petromyzon, which possesses only two canals, moves in only two spatial dimensions. The dancer with only one functional canal in each ear moves in only one plane, and neither it nor Petromyzon is able to move far in a straight line (11 p. 444). From these and similar surmises, which his eagerness to construct an ingenious theory led him to accept as facts quite uncritically, Cyon concluded that the perception of space depends upon the number and arrangement of the semicircular canals, and that the dancer behaves as it does because it possesses canals of unusual shape and relations to one another. The absurdity of Cyon's position becomes obvious when it is shown that the structural conditions of which he was making use do not exist in the dancer.

The results obtained by Kishi in his study of the ear of the dancer differ in many important respects from those of all other investigators, but especially from those of Rawitz and Alexander and Kreidl.

Kishi's work was evidently done with admirable carefulness. His methods in the preparation of his materials, so far as can be judged from his report, were safe and satisfactory, and his descriptions of results are minute and give evidence of accuracy and conscientious thoughtfulness. The material for his histological work he obtained from three different animal dealers. It consisted of fifteen adult and nineteen young dancers, and, as material for comparison, ten common gray mice. The animals were studied first biologically, that their habits and behavior might be described accurately and so far as possible accounted for in the light of whatever histological results might be obtained subsequently; then they were studied physiologically, that the functional importance of various organs which would naturally be supposed to have to do with the peculiarities of the mouse might be understood; and, finally, they were killed and their ears and portions of their brains were studied microscopically, that structural conditions for the biological and physiological facts might be discovered.

The ear, which was studied by the use of several series of sections, as well as in gross dissections, is described by Kishi under three headings:—

(1) The sound-receiving apparatus (auditory organs).

(2) The static apparatus (equilibrational organs).

(3) The sound-transmitting apparatus (ear drum, ear bones, etc.).

The chief results of his structural investigation may be stated briefly under these three headings. In the sound-receiving or auditory apparatus, Kishi failed to find the important deviations from the usual structure of the mammalian ear which had been described by Rawitz. The latter distinctly says that although the organ of Corti is present in all of the whirls of the cochlea, the auditory cells in it are noticeably degenerate. Kishi does not agree with Panse's statement (21 p. 476) that the auditory organ of the dancer differs in no important respects from that of the common mouse, for he found that in certain regions the hair cells of the organ of Corti were fewer and smaller in the dancer. He therefore concludes that the auditory organ is not entirely normal, but at the same time he emphasizes the serious discrepancy between his results and those of Rawitz. In not one of the ears of the twelve dancers which he studied did Kishi find the direct communication between the utriculus and the scala tympani which Rawitz described, and such differences as appeared in the organ of Corti were in the nature of slight deviations rather than marked degenerations.

In the outer wall of the ductus cochlearis of the dancer the stria vasculosa is almost or totally lacking, while in the gray mouse it is prominent. This condition of the stria vasculosa Kishi was the first to notice in the dancer; Alexander and Kreidl had previously described a similar condition in an albino cat. If, as has been supposed by some physiologists, the stria vasculosa is really the source of the endolymph, this state of affairs must have a marked influence on the functions of the auditory apparatus and the static apparatus, for pressure differences between the endolymph and the perilymph spaces must be present. And, as Kishi points out, should such pressure differences be proved to exist, the functional disturbance in the organ of hearing which the lack of responses to sounds seems to indicate might better be ascribed to them than to the streaming of the endolymph from the canals into the cochlea as assumed by Rawitz (21 p. 477). Kishi merely suggests that the condition of the stria may account for the deafness of the mouse; he does not feel at all confident of the truth of his explanation, and he therefore promises in his first paper a continuation of his work in an investigation of the functions of the stria. This, however, he seems not to have accomplished thus far.

[Illustration: FIGURE 12.—The inner ear of the dancer. Reproduced from Kishi's figure in the *Zeitschrift für wissenschaftliche Zoölogie*, Bd. 71. *c.c.* crus simplex; o.b. anterior vertical canal; *h.b.* posterior vertical canal; *a.b.* horizontal canal.]

The static apparatus Kishi describes as closely similar in form to that of the gray mouse. In none of his twelve preparations of the ear of the dancer did he find such abnormalities of form and connections in the semicircular canals as Rawitz's figures and descriptions represent. Rawitz states that the anterior canal is normal except in its lack of connection with the posterior and that the posterior and horizontal are much reduced in size. Kishi, on the contrary, insists that all of the three canals are normal in shape and that the usual connection between the anterior and the posterior canals, the crus simplex, exists. He justifies these statements by presenting photographs of two dancer ears which he carefully removed from the head. Comparison of these photographs (Figures 12 and 13) with Rawitz's drawings of the conditions of the canals and sacs as he found them (Figures 8, 9, and 10), and of both with the condition in the typical mammalian ear as shown by Figure 7, will at once make clear the meaning of Kishi's statements. That Rawitz's descriptions of the canals are not correct is rendered almost certain by the fact that Panse, Baginsky, Alexander and Kreidl, and Kishi all agree in describing them as normal in form.

The only important respects in which Kishi found the membranous labyrinth, that is, the canals and the ear sacs, of the dancer to differ from that of the gray mouse are the following. In the dancer the cupola of the crista acustica is not so plainly marked and not so highly developed, and the raphae of the ampullae and canals, which frequently are clearly visible in the gray mouse, are lacking (21 p. 478).

[Illustration: FIGURE 13.—The inner ear of the dancer, showing the spiral form of the cochlea. After Kishi.]

The sound-transmitting apparatus of the dancer, according to Kishi, differs only very slightly from that of the gray mouse, and there is no reason to consider the differences which appear as important (21 p. 478).

Almost as amusing as the way in which Cyon's theory of space perception disappears in the light of critical research is Panse's explanation of the deafness of the dancer. Failing to find any defects in the auditory apparatus of the inner ear which seemed adequate to account for the obvious lack of responsiveness to sounds, this investigator concluded that plugs of wax which he had noticed in the auditory meatus of the dancer excluded sounds or in some way interfered with the functioning of the tympanic membrane. Kishi reports that he found such plugs of wax in the ears of one gray mouse, but in none of the dancers which he examined did he discover them (21 p. 479). Panse's explanation of the defective hearing of the dancer neither needs nor deserves further comment.

As one result of his investigation, Kishi is convinced that the dance movements are not due to peculiarities in the semicircular canals and their sense organs, as Rawitz claimed, for the general form and finer structure of these organs in the dancer is practically the same as in the common mouse. Kishi is just as certain that the whirling is not due to defects in the canal organs, as Rawitz is that it is due to such structural conditions! It is rather surprising that any one should feel confident of the power of the microscope to reveal all those structural conditions which are important as conditions of function. Probably there are histological differences between the ear of the dancer and that of the gray mouse, which, although undetectable by scientific means at present, furnish the structural basis for the marked differences in behavior. As has been set forth already (p. 9), Kishi accounts for the dance movements by assuming the inheritance of an acquired character of behavior. This inherited tendency to dance, he thinks, has been accentuated by the confinement of the mice in narrow cages and their long-continued movement in the wheels which are placed in the cages (21 p. 481).

Rawitz, Cyon, and Alexander and Kreidl felt themselves under the necessity of finding peculiarities of behavior in the dancer which could be referred to the various abnormalities of structure which they had either seen or accepted on faith; Kishi found himself in a very different predicament, for he had on his hands the commonly accepted statement that the animals are deaf, without being able to find any structural basis for this defect. To avoid the difficulty he questions the existence of deafness! If perchance they are deaf, he thinks that it is possibly because of the defect in the stria vasculosa. This suggestion Kishi makes despite the fact that our ignorance of the function of the stria renders it impossible for us to do otherwise than guess at its relation to hearing.

We have now briefly reviewed the results of the various important investigations of the behavior and structure of the dancer.

The observations of Cyon, Zoth, and the writer establish beyond doubt the existence of important individual differences in behavior if not of distinct divisions within the species of mouse, and the general results of the several anatomical investigations make it seem highly probable that the structure of the ear, as well as the externally visible structural features of the animals, vary widely. Unfortunately, the lack of agreement in the descriptions of the ear given by the different students of the subject renders impossible any certain correlation of structural and functional facts. That the whirling and the lack of dizziness and of hearing have their structural bases no one doubts, but whether it is in the brain itself, in the sense organs, or in the labyrinth, our knowledge does not permit us to say. With this statement Rawitz, Cyon, and Alexander and Kreidl would not agree, for they believe that they have discovered structural peculiarities which fully explain the behavior of the dancer. Panse and Kishi, on the other hand, contend that the ear gives no structural signs of such peculiarities as the dancing and deafness suggest; they therefore look to the cerebellum for the seat of the disturbance. With the same possibility in mind the author of "Fancy Varieties of Mice" writes: "These quaint little creatures make amusing pets for any one who is not scientific, or very fond of knowing 'the reason why.' In their case, the reason of the peculiarity which gives them their name is rather a sad one. It is now pretty conclusively established that they are no more Japanese than they are of any other country in particular, but that the originators of the breed were common fancy mice which were suffering from a disease of the brain analogous to the 'gid' in sheep. In the latter, the complaint is caused by a parasite in the brain; in the case of the Waltzing Mouse, it is probably due to an hereditary malformation therein. Be this as it may, the breed is now a firmly established one, and the children of waltzing mice waltz like their parents" (32 p. 45). Although it is quite possible that peculiarities in the central nervous system, rather than in the peripheral nervous system, may be responsible for the forms of behavior exhibited by the dancer, it must be remembered that no such peculiarities have been revealed by the examination of the central nervous system. The old fancier has neither better nor worse grounds for his belief than have Panse and Kishi.

So far as the reliability of the anatomical work which has been discussed is in question, it would seem that Rawitz's results are rendered somewhat unsatisfactory by the carelessness of Cyon in fixing the materials; that Panse's descriptions and comparisons are neither careful nor detailed enough to be convincing; that the work of Alexander and Kreidl, as well as that of Kishi, gives evidence of accuracy and trustworthiness. The fact that the statements of Alexander and Kreidl frequently do not agree with those of Kishi proves that there are serious errors in the work of one or another of these investigators. Cyon's discussion of the anatomy of the dancer is not to be taken too seriously, for by his theory of space perception and of a sixth sense he was unduly biased in favor of the structural peculiarities described by Rawitz. Nevertheless, his discussion is not without interest, for the way in which he succeeded in making every structural fact which Rawitz suggested fit into his theories and help to account for the functional peculiarities which he had himself observed, is extremely clever and indicates a splendid scientific imagination.

To sum up: All the facts of behavior and physiology which have been established lead us to expect certain marked structural differences between the dancer and the common mouse. The bizarre movements, lack of equilibrational ability, and the nervous shaking of the head suggest the presence of peculiar conditions in the semicircular canals or their sense organs; and the lack of sensitiveness to sounds indicates defects in the cochlea. Yet, strange as it may seem to those who are not familiar with the difficulties of the study of the minute structure of these organs, no structural conditions have been discovered which account satisfactorily for the dancer's peculiarities of behavior. That the ear is unusual in form is highly probable, since three of the four investigators who have studied it carefully agree that it differs more or less markedly from that of the common mouse. But, on the other hand, the serious lack of agreement in their several descriptions of the conditions which they observed renders their results utterly inconclusive and extremely unsatisfactory. The status of our knowledge of the structure of the central nervous system is even less satisfactory, if possible, than that of our knowledge of those portions of the peripheral nervous system which would naturally be supposed to have to do with such functional peculiarities as the dancer exhibits. So far as I have been able to learn, no investigator has carefully examined the brain and spinal cord in comparison with those of the common mouse, and only those who have failed to find any structural basis for the facts of behavior in the organs of the ear have attempted to account for the dancer's whirling and deafness by assuming that the cerebellum is unusual in structure. We are, therefore, forced to conclude that our knowledge of the nervous system of the dancing mouse does not at present enable us to explain the behavior of the animal.

It seems highly probable to me, in the light of my observation of the dancer and my study of the entire literature concerning the animal, that no adequate explanation of its activities can be given in terms of the structure of the peripheral or the central nervous system, or of both, but that the structure of the entire organism will have to be taken into account. The dancer's physiological characteristics, in fact, suggest multitudinous structural peculiarities. I have confined my study to its behavior, not because the problems of structure seemed less interesting or less important, but simply because I found it necessary thus to limit the field of research in order to accomplish what I wished within a limited period.

That there are structural bases for the forms of behavior which this book describes is as certain as it could be were they definitely known; that they, or at least some of them, are discoverable by means of our present- day histological methods is almost as certain. It is, therefore, obvious that this is an excellent field for further research. It is not an agreeable task to report inconclusive and contradictory results, and I have devoted this chapter to a brief account of the work that has been done by others on the structure of the ear of the dancer rather for the sake of presenting a complete account of the animal as it is known to-day than because of the value of the facts which could be stated.

CHAPTER VI

THE SENSE OF HEARING

Repeatedly in the foregoing chapters mention has been made of the dancer's irresponsiveness to sounds, but it has not been definitely stated whether this peculiarity of behavior is due to deafness or to the inhibition of reaction. This chapter is concerned with the evidence which bears upon the problem of the existence of a sense of hearing. Again I may be permitted to call attention to the observations of other investigators before presenting the results of my own experiments and stating the conclusions which I have reached through the consideration of all available facts.

By the results of various simple tests which he made, Rawitz (25 p. 238) was convinced that the adult dancer is totally deaf. He did not experiment with the young, but he says he thinks they may be able to hear, since the necessary structural conditions are present. This guess which Rawitz made on the basis of very indefinite and uncertain knowledge of the histology of the ear of the young dancer is of special interest in the light of facts revealed by my own experiments. Unfortunately the study of hearing made by Rawitz is casual rather than thorough, and although it may turn out that all of his statements are justified by his observations, the reader is not likely to get much satisfaction from his discussion of the subject.

Inasmuch as he could discover no structural basis for deafness, Panse (23 p. 140) expressed himself as unwilling to believe that the mice are deaf, and this despite the fact that he observed no responses to the sounds made by a series of tuning forks ranging from C5 to C8. He believes rather that they are strangely irresponsive to sounds and that their sensitiveness is dulled, possibly, by the presence of plugs of wax in the ears. Since another investigator, Kishi, has observed the presence of similar plugs of wax in the ears of common mice which could hear, there is but slight probability that Panse is right in considering the plugs of wax as the cause of the dancer's irresponsiveness to sounds.

Far more thoroughgoing tests than those of Rawitz or Panse were made by Cyon (9 p. 218), who holds the unique position of being the only person on record who has observed the adult dancer give definite reactions to sounds. To a König Galton whistle so adjusted that it gave a tone of about 7000 complete vibrations per second, which is said to be about the pitch of the voice of the dancer, some of the animals tested by Cyon responded unmistakably, others not at all. In one group of four mice, two not only reacted markedly to the sound of the whistle but apparently listened intently, for as soon as the whistle was blown they ran to the side of the cage and pressed their noses against the walls as if attempting to approach the source of the stimulus. The remaining two mice gave not the slightest indication that the sound acted as a stimulus. By the repetition of this sound from eight to twelve times Cyon states that he was able to arouse the mice from sleep. When thus disturbed, the female came out of the nest box before the male. Similarly when the mice were disturbed by the whistle in the midst of their dancing, the female was first to retreat into the nest box. There is thus, according to Cyon, some indication of sex, as well as individual, differences in sensitiveness to the sound of the whistle. Cyon's statement that in order to evoke a response the whistle must be held above the head of the dancer suggests at once the possibility that currents of air or odors instead of sounds may have been responsible for the reactions which he observed. The work of this investigator justifies caution in the acceptance of his statements. Neither the conditions under which the auditory tests were made nor the condition of the animals is described with sufficient accuracy to make possible the comparison of Cyon's work with that of other investigators. As will appear later, it is of the utmost importance that the influence of other stimuli than sound be avoided during the tests and that the age of the mouse be known. The conclusion reached by Cyon is that some dancers are able to hear sounds of about the pitch of their own cries.

The fact, emphasized by Cyon, that the mice respond to tones of about the pitch of their own voice is of peculiar interest in its relation to the additional statements made by the same author to the effect that the female dancer is more sensitive to sounds than the male, and that the males either do not possess a voice or are much less sensitive to disagreeable stimuli than the females. In the case of the dancers which he first studied (9 p. 218), Cyon observed that certain strong stimuli evoked pain cries; but later in his investigation he noticed that four individuals, all of which were males, never responded thus to disagreeable stimulation (11 p.431). He asks, therefore, does this mean that the males lack a voice or that they are less sensitive than the females? The fact that he did not succeed in getting a definite answer to this simple question is indicative of the character of Cyon's work. My dancers have provided me with ample evidence concerning the matter. Both the males and the females, among the dancers which I have studied, possess a voice.

The females, especially during periods of sexual excitement, are much more likely to squeak than the males. At such times they give their shrill cry whenever they are touched by another mouse or by the human hand. A slight pinching of the tail will frequently cause the female to squeak, but the male seldom responds to the same stimulus by crying out. The most satisfactory way to demonstrate the existence of a voice in the male is to subject him to the stimulating effect of an induced current, so weak that it is barely appreciable to the human hand. To this unexpected stimulus even the male usually responds by a sudden squeak. There can be no doubt, then, of the possession of a voice by both males and females. The males may be either less sensitive or less given to vocal expression, but they are quite able to squeak when favorable conditions are presented. The possession of a voice by an animal is presumptive evidence in favor of a sense of hearing, but it would scarcely be safe to say that the mice must be able to hear their own voices. Cyon, however, thinks that some dancers can. What further evidence is to be had?

Although they obtained no visible motor reactions to such noises as the clapping of the hands, the snapping of the fingers, or to the tones of tuning forks of different pitches and the shrill tones of the Galton whistle, Alexander and Kreidl (1 p. 547) are not convinced of the total deafness of the dancer, for, as they remark, common mice which undoubtedly hear do not invariably respond visibly to sounds. Furthermore, the anatomical conditions revealed by their investigation of the ear of the dancer are not such as to render sensitiveness to sounds impossible. They recognize also that the existence of the ability to produce sounds is an indication of hearing. They have no confidence in the results reported by Cyon, for they feel that he did not take adequate precautions to guard against the action of other than auditory stimuli.

Zoth (31 p. 170) has pointed out with reason and force that testing the sensitiveness of the mice is especially difficult because of their restlessness. They are almost constantly executing quick, jerky movements, starting, stopping, or changing the direction of movement, and it is therefore extremely difficult to tell with even a fair degree of certainty whether a given movement which occurs simultaneously with a sound is a response to the sound or merely coincident with it. With great care in the exclusion of the influence of extraneous stimuli, Zoth tried a large number of experiments to test the hearing of both young and adult dancers. Not once did he observe an indubitable auditory reaction. As he says, "I have performed numerous experiments with the Galton whistle, with a squeaking glass stopper, with caps and cartridges, without being able to come to any certain conclusion. With reference to the Galton whistle and particularly to the tone which was said to have been heard extremely well by Cyon's mice, I believe I am rather safe in asserting that my mice, young (12-13 days) as well as old, do not react to the König Galton whistle (7210 Vs.). They could not be awakened out of sleep by repetitions of the sound, nor enticed out of their nests, and their dancing could not be interrupted" (31 p. 170). Zoth's experiments appear to be the most careful and critical of those thus far considered.

Last to be mentioned, but in many respects of greatest interest and value, is the work of Kishi (21 p. 482) on the problem of hearing. To this acute observer belongs the credit of calling attention emphatically to the ear movements which are exhibited by the dancer. Frequently, as he remarks, the ears move as if the animal were listening or trying to determine the direction whence comes a sound, yet usually the mouse gives no other sign of hearing. That the absence of ordinary reactions to sounds is due to deafness, Kishi, like Panse, is led to doubt because his anatomical studies have not revealed any defects in the organs of hearing which would seem to indicate the lack of this sense.

This historical survey of the problem of hearing has brought out a few important facts. No one of the several investigators of the subject, with the exception of Cyon, is certain that the dancer can hear, and no one of them, with the exception of Rawitz, is certain that it cannot hear! Cyon almost certainly observed two kinds of dancing mice. Those of his dancers which exhibited exceptional ability to climb in the vertical direction and which also gave good evidence of hearing certain sounds may have been hybrids resulting from the crossing of the dancer with a common mouse, or they may have been exceptional specimens of the true dancer variety. A third possibility is suggested by Rawitz's belief in the ability of the young dancer to hear. Cyon's positive results may have been obtained with immature individuals. I am strongly inclined to believe that Cyon did observe two types of dancer, and to accept his statement that some of the mice could hear, whereas others could not. It is evident, in the light of our examination of the experimental results thus far obtained by other investigators, that neither the total lack of sensitiveness to sounds in the adult nor the presence of such sensitiveness in the young dancer has been satisfactorily proved.

I shall now report in detail the results of my own study of the sense of hearing in the dancer. As the behavior of the young differs greatly from that of the adult, by which is meant the sexually mature animal, I shall present first the results of my experiments with adults and later, in contrast, the results obtained with mice from one to twenty-eight days old.

My preliminary tests were made with noises. While carefully guarding against the interference of visual, tactual, temperature, and olfactory stimuli, I produced noises of varying degrees of loudness by clapping the hands together suddenly, by shouting, whistling, exploding pistol caps, striking steel bars, ringing an electric bell, and causing another mouse to squeak. To these sounds a common mouse usually responds either by starting violently, or by trembling and remaining perfectly quiet for a few seconds, as if frightened. The adult dancers which I have tested, and I have repeated the experiment scores of times during the last three years with more than a hundred different individuals, have never given unmistakable evidence of hearing. Either they are totally deaf or there is a most surprising lack of motor reactions.

Precisely the same results were obtained in tests made with the Galton whistle throughout its range of pitches, and with Appuun whistles which, according to their markings, ranged from 2000 Vs. (C_4) to 48,000 (G_9), but which undoubtedly did not correspond at all exactly to this range, and with a series of König tuning forks which gave tones varying in pitch from 1024 to 16,382 complete vibrations.

I am willing to trust these experimental results the more fully because during all the time I have had adult dancers under observation I have never once seen a reaction which could with any fair degree of certainty be referred to an auditory stimulus. Never once, although I have tried repeatedly, have I succeeded in arousing a dancer from sleep by producing noises or tones, nor have I ever been able to observe any influence of sounds on the dance movements. All of Cyon's signs have failed with my mice. Occasionally what looked like a response to some sound appeared, but critical observation invariably proved it to be due to some other cause than the auditory stimulus. A sound produced above the animal is very likely to bring about a motor reaction, as Cyon claims; but I have always found it to be the result of the currents of air or odors, which usually influence the animal when the experimenter is holding any object above it. I do not wish to maintain that Cyon's conclusions are false; I merely emphasize the necessity for care in the exclusion of other stimuli. The mice are extremely sensitive to changes in temperature, such, for example, as are produced by the breath of the experimenter, and one must constantly guard against the misinterpretation of behavior.

In a single experiment with mice over a month old, I observed what might possibly indicate sensitiveness to sound. While holding a mouse, thirty- five days old, in my hand I pursed my lips and made a very shrill sound by drawing in air; the mouse seemed to start perceptibly according to the indications given by my sense of touch. I repeated the stimulus several times and each time I could see and feel the animal start slightly. With two other individuals which I tested the reaction was less certain, and with several others I failed to get any indication of response. This would seem to prove that the three individuals which responded happened to be sensitive to that particular tone at the age of five weeks. The test is unsatisfactory because the vibrations from my own body may have brought about the reaction instead of the air vibrations produced by my lips, and I therefore merely mention it in the enumeration of the various experimental tests which I have made.

If we should conclude from all the negative evidence that is available, or that could be obtained, that the dancer is totally deaf, it might fairly be objected that the conclusion is unsafe, since an animal does not necessarily respond to stimuli by a visible change in the position or relations of its body. Death feigning may fairly be considered a response to a stimulus or stimulus complex, yet there may be no sign of movement. The green frog when observed in the laboratory usually gives no indication whatever, by movements that are readily observable, that it hears sounds which occur about it, but I have been able to show by means of indirect methods of study that it is stimulated by these same sounds.[1] Its rate of respiration is changed by the sounds, and although a sound does not bring about a bodily movement, it does very noticeably influence movements in response to other stimuli which occur simultaneously with the sound. I discovered that under certain rather simple experimental conditions the green frog would regularly respond to a touch on the back by drawing its hind leg up toward the body. Under the same conditions the sound of an electric bell caused no visible movement of the leg, but if at the instant the back was touched the bell was rung, the leg movement was much greater than that brought about by the touch alone. This suggests at once the desirability of studying the sense of hearing in the dancer by some indirect method. The animal may be stimulated, and yet it may not give any visible sign of the influence of the auditory stimulus.

[Footnote 1: "The Sense of Hearing in Frogs." *Journal of Comparative Neurology and Psychology*, Vol. XV, p. 288, 1905.]

Were not the dancing so extremely variable in rapidity and duration, it might be used as an index of the influence of auditory stimuli. Cyon's statements would indicate that sounds interfere with the dancing, but as I obtained no evidence of this, I worked instead with the following indirect method, which may be called the method of auditory choice.

The apparatus which was used is described in detail in Chapter VII. Figures 14 and 15 will greatly aid the reader in understanding its essential features. Two small wooden boxes, identical in form and as closely similar as possible in general appearance, were placed in a larger box in such positions that a mouse was forced to enter and pass through one of them in order to get to the nest-box. On the bottom of each of these small boxes was a series of wires through which an electric current could be made to pass at the will of the experimenter. The boxes could readily be interchanged in position. At one side of the large wooden box and beyond the range of vision of the mouse was an electric bell which could be caused to ring whenever the mouse approached the entrance to one of the small boxes. The point of the experiment was to determine whether the dancer could learn to avoid the box-which-rang when it was approached. The method of conducting the tests was as follows. Each day at a certain hour the mouse was placed in that part of the large box whence it could escape to the nest-box only by passing through one of the small boxes. If it approached the wrong box (whether it happened to be the one on the right or the one on the left depended upon the experimenter's decision), the bell began to ring as a warning against entering; if it approached the other box, all was silent. As motives for the choice of the box-which-did- not-ring both reward and punishment were employed. The reward consisted of freedom to return to the nest-box *via* the passage which led from the box-which-did-not-ring; the punishment, which consisted of a disagreeable electric shock, was given whenever the mouse entered the wrong box, that is, the one which had the sound as a warning. Entering the wrong box resulted in a disagreeable stimulus and in the necessity of returning to the large box, for the exit to the nest-box by way of the passage from this box was closed. My assumption, on the basis of extended study of the ability of the dancer to profit by experience, was that if it could hear the sound of the bell it would soon learn to avoid the box-that-rang and enter instead the one which had no sound associated with it.

Systematic tests were made with No. 4 from the 3d to the 12th of February, inclusive, 1906. Each day the mouse was permitted to find his way to the nest-box through one of the small boxes ten times in succession. Usually the experimenter rang the bell alternately for the box on the left and the box on the right. The time required for such a series of experiments varied, according to the rapidity with which the mouse made his choice, from ten to thirty minutes. If in these experiments the animal approached and entered the right, or soundless box, directly, the choice indicated nothing so far as ability to hear is concerned; if it entered the wrong, or sounding box, despite the ringing of the bell, it indicated either the lack of the influence of experience or inability to hear the sound; but if it regularly avoided the box-which-sounded it thus gave evidence of ability to hear the sound of the bell. The purpose of the test was to determine, not whether the mouse could learn, but whether it could hear.

For ten successive days this experiment was carried on with No. 4 without the least indication of increasing ability to avoid the wrong box by the association of the sound of the bell with the disagreeable electric shock and failure to escape to the nest-box. In fact, the experiment was discontinued because it became evident that an impossible task had been set for the mouse. Day by day as the tests were in progress I noticed that the animal became increasingly afraid of the entrances to the small boxes; it seemed absolutely helpless in the face of the situation. Partly because of the definiteness of the negative results obtained with No. 4 and partly because of the cruelty of subjecting an animal to disagreeable conditions which it is unable to avoid, the experiment was not repeated with other individuals. I have never conducted an experiment which gave me as much discomfort as this; it was like being set to whip a deaf child because it did not learn to respond to stimuli which it could not feel.

By a very similar method No. 18 was tested for his sensitiveness to the noise and jar from the induction apparatus which was used in connection with many of my experiments on vision and the modifiability of behavior. In this experiment the wrong box was indicated by the buzzing sound of the apparatus and the slight vibrations which resulted from it. Although No. 18 was tested, as was No. 4, for ten successive days, ten trials each day, it gave no evidence of ability to avoid the box-which-buzzed.

Since both direct and indirect methods of testing the hearing of the dancer have uniformly given negative results, in the case of mice more than five weeks old, I feel justified in concluding that they are totally deaf and not merely irresponsive to sounds.

Rawitz's statements, and the fact that what may have been auditory reactions were obtained with a few individuals of five weeks of age, suggest that the mice may be able to hear at certain periods of life. To discover whether this is true I have tested the young of twenty different litters from the first day to the twenty-eighth, either daily or at intervals of two or three days. In these tests König forks, steel bars, and a Galton whistle were used. The results obtained are curiously interesting.

During the first two weeks of life none of the mice which I tested gave any visible motor response to the various sounds used. During the third week certain of the individuals responded vigorously to sudden high tones and loud noises. After the third week I have seen only doubtful signs of hearing. I shall now describe in detail the method of experimentation, the condition of the animals, and the nature of the auditory reactions.

Between the twelfth and the eighteenth day the auditory canal becomes open to the exterior. The time is very variable in different litters, for their rate of growth depends upon the amount of nourishment which the mother is able to supply. Without exception, in my experience, the opening to the ear appears before the eyes are open. Consequently visual stimuli usually are not disturbing factors in the auditory tests with mice less than sixteen days old. There is also a sudden and marked change in the behavior of the mice during the third week. Whereas, for the first fourteen or eighteen days they are rather quiet and deliberate in their movements when removed from the nest, some time in the third week their behavior suddenly changes and they act as if frightened when taken up by the experimenter. They jump out of his hand, squeak, and sometimes show fight. This is so pronounced that it has attracted my attention many times and I have studied it carefully to determine, if possible, whether it is due to some profound change in the nervous system which thus suddenly increases the sensitiveness of the animal or to the development of the sexual organs. I am inclined to think that it is a nervous phenomenon which is intimately connected with the sexual condition. Within a day or two after it appears the mice usually begin to show auditory reactions and continue to do so for three to five days.

I shall now describe the results obtained with a few typical litters. A litter born of Nos. 151 and 152 gave uniformly negative results in all auditory tests up to the fourteenth day. On that day the ears were open, and the following observations were recorded. The five individuals of the litter, four females and one male, were taken from the nest one at a time at 7 A.M. and placed on a piece of paper in the bright sunlight. The warmth of the sun soon quieted them so that auditory tests could be made to advantage. As soon as an individual had become perfectly still, the Galton whistle was held at a distance of about four inches from its head in such a position that it could not be seen nor the currents of air caused by it felt, and suddenly blown. Each of the five mice responded to the first few repetitions of this stimulus by movements of the ears, twitchings of the body, and jerky movements of the legs. The most violent reactions resulted when the individual was lying on its back with its legs extended free in the air. Under such circumstances the four legs were often drawn together suddenly when the whistle was sounded. Similar responses were obtained with the lip sound already mentioned. Two other observers saw these experiments, and they agreed that there can be no doubt that the mice responded to the sound. The sounds which were effective lay between 5000 and 10,000 complete vibrations.

On the fifteenth day the eyes were just beginning to open. Three of the mice responded definitely to the sounds, but the other two slightly, if at all. On the sixteenth day they were all too persistently active for satisfactory auditory tests, and on the seventeenth, although they were tested repeatedly under what appeared to be favorable conditions, no signs of sensitiveness were noted. Although I continued to test this litter, at intervals of three or four days, for two weeks longer, I did not once observe a response to sound.

This was the first litter with which I obtained perfectly definite, clear- cut responses to sounds. That the reactive ability had not been present earlier than the fourteenth day I am confident, for I had conducted the tests in precisely the same manner daily up to the time of the appearance of the reactions. To argue that the mice heard before the fourteenth day, but were unable to react because the proper motor mechanism had not developed sufficiently would be short-sighted, for if the response depended upon the development of such a mechanism, it is not likely that it would disappear so quickly. I am therefore satisfied that these reactions indicate hearing.

With another litter the following results were obtained. On the thirteenth day each of the eight members of the litter responded definitely and uniformly to the Galton whistle, set at 5 (probably about 8000 complete vibrations), and to a König steel bar of a vibration rate of 4096 Vs. The largest individuals, for almost always there are noticeable differences in size among the members of a litter, appeared to be most sensitive to sounds.

On the fifteenth day and again on the seventeenth unmistakable responses to sound were observed; on the eighteenth the responses were indefinite, and on the nineteenth none were obtained. I continued the tests up to the twenty-eighth day without further indications of hearing.

Certain individuals in this litter reacted so vigorously to the loud sound produced by striking the steel bar a sharp blow and also to the Galton whistle, during a period of five days, that I have no hesitation in saying that they evidently heard during that period of their lives. Other members of the litter seemed to be less sensitive; their reactions were sometimes so indefinite as to leave the experimenter in doubt about the presence of hearing.

A third litter, which developed very slowly because of lack of sufficient food, first showed unmistakable reactions to sound on the twenty-first day. On this day only two of the five individuals reacted. The reactions were much more obvious on the twenty-second day, but thereafter they became indefinite.

Still another litter, which consisted of one female and four males, began to exhibit the quick, jerky movements, already mentioned, on the fourteenth day. On the morning of the fifteenth day three members of the litter definitely reacted to the tone of the steel bar, and also to the hammer blow when the bar was held tightly in the hand of the experimenter. My observations were verified by another experimenter. Two individuals which appeared to be very sensitive were selected for special tests. Their reactions were obvious on the sixteenth, seventeenth, and eighteenth days; on the nineteenth day they were indefinite, and on the twentieth none could be detected. Some individuals of this litter certainly had the ability to hear for at least five days.

A sixth litter of four females and two males first gave indications of the change in behavior which by this time I had come to interpret as a sign of the approach of the period of auditory sensitiveness, on the seventeenth day. I had tested them almost every day previous to this time without obtaining evidence of hearing. The tests with the steel bar and the Galton whistle were continued each day until the end of the fourth week without positive results. To all appearances the individuals of this litter were unable to hear at any time during the first month of life.

Practically the same results were obtained with another litter of four females. The change in their behavior was obvious on the eighteenth day, but at no time during the first month did they give any satisfactory indications of hearing.

In the accompanying table, I have presented in condensed form the results of my auditory tests in the case of twelve litters of young dancers.

TABLE 5

PERIOD OF AUDITORY REACTION IN YOUNG DANCERS

PARENTS	No. in Litter	Change in Behavior	Ears Open	Auditory Reactions Appear	Auditory Reactions Disappear
152+151	5	13th day	14th day	14th day	16th day
152+15l	8 (?)	13th day	13th day	13th day	17th day
152+151	5	13th day	13th day	13th day	17th day
152+151	4	10th day	12th day	13th day	15th day
410+415	5	14th day	15th day	15th day	19th day
410+415	6	13th day	14th day	14th day	18th day
420+425	2	12th day	14th day	14th day	17th day
210+215	5	17th day	13th day	17th day	19th day
210+215	6	11th day	14th day	No reactions	
220+225	6	16th day	14th day	No reactions	
220+225	6	17th day	13th day	No reactions	
212+211	4	15th day	14th day	No reactions	

Certain of the litters tested responded definitely to sounds, others gave no sign of hearing at any time during the first four weeks of life. Of the twelve litters for which the results of auditory tests are presented in Table 5, eight evidently passed through an auditory period. It is important to note that all except one of these were the offspring of Nos. 151 and 152, or of their descendants Nos. 410 and 415 and Nos. 420 and 425. In fact every one of the litters in this line of descent which I have tested, and they now number fifteen, has given indications of auditory sensitiveness. And, on the other hand, only in a single instance have the litters born of Nos. 210 and 215, or of their descendants, given evidence of ability to hear.

These two distinct lines of descent may be referred to hereafter as the 400 and the 200 lines. I have observed several important differences between the individuals of these groups in addition to the one already mentioned. The 200 mice were sometimes gray and white instead of black and white; they climbed much more readily and danced less vigorously than those of the 400 group. These facts are particularly interesting in connection with Cyon's descriptions of the two types of dancer which he observed.

In criticism of my conclusion that the young dancers are able to hear certain sounds for a few days early in life, and then become deaf, it has been suggested that they cease to react because they rapidly become accustomed to the sounds. That this is not the case, is evident from the fact that the reactions often increase in definiteness during the first two or three days and then suddenly disappear entirely. But even if this were not true, it would seem extremely improbable that the mouse should become accustomed to a sudden and startlingly loud sound with so few repetitions as occurred in these tests. On any one day the sounds were not made more than five to ten times. Moreover, under the same external condition, the common mouse reacts unmistakably to these sounds day after day when they are first produced, although with repetition of the stimulus at short intervals, the reactions soon become indefinite or disappear.

The chief results of my study of hearing in the dancer may be summed up in a very few words. The young dancer, in some instances, hears sounds for a few days during the third week of life. The adult is totally deaf. Shortly before the period of auditory sensitiveness, the young dancer becomes extremely excitable and pugnacious.

CHAPTER VII

THE SENSE OF SIGHT: BRIGHTNESS VISION

The sense of sight in the dancer has received little attention hitherto. In the literature there are a few casual statements to the effect that it is of importance. Zoth, for example (31 p. 149), remarks that it seems to be keenly developed; and other writers, on the basis of their observation of the animal's behavior, hazard similar statements. The descriptions of the behavior of blinded mice, as given by Cyon, Alexander and Kreidl, and Kishi (p.47), apparently indicate that the sense is of some value; they do not, however, furnish definite information concerning its nature and its role in the daily life of the animal.

The experimental study of this subject which is now to be described was undertaken, after careful and long-continued observation of the general behavior of the dancer, in order that our knowledge of the nature and value of the sense of sight in this representative of the Mammalia might be increased in scope and definiteness. The results of this study naturally fall into three groups: (1) those which concern brightness vision, (2) those which concern color vision, and (3) those which indicate the role of sight in the life of the dancer.

Too frequently investigators, in their work on vision in animals, have assumed that brightness vision and color vision are inseparable; or, if not making this assumption, they have failed to realize that the same wave-length probably has markedly different effects upon the retinal elements of the eyes of unlike organisms. In a study of the sense of sight it is extremely important to discover whether difference in the quality, as well as in the intensity, of a visual stimulus influences the organism; in other words, whether color sensitiveness, as well as brightness sensitiveness, is present. If the dancer perceives only brightness or luminosity, and not color, it is evident that its visual world is strikingly different from that of the normal human being. The experiments now to be described were planned to show what the facts really are.

[Illustration: Figure 14.—Discrimination box. *W*, electric-box with white cardboards; B, electric-box with black cardboards. Drawn by Mr. C.H. Toll.]

As a means of testing the ability of the dancer to distinguish differences in brightness, the experiment box represented by Figures 14 and 15 was devised. Figure 14 is the box as seen from the position of the experimenter during the tests. Figure 15 is its ground plan. This box, which was made of wood, was 98 cm. long, 38 cm. wide, and 17 cm. deep, as measured on the outside. The plan of construction and its significance in connection with these experiments on vision will be clear from the following account of the experimental procedure. A mouse whose brightness vision was to be tested was placed in the nest-box, A (Figure 15). Thence by pushing open the swinging door at *I*, it could pass into the entrance chamber, *B*. Having entered *B* it could return to *A* only by passing through one of the electric-boxes, marked *W*, and following the alley to *O*, where by pushing open the swing door it could enter the nest-box. The door at *I* swung inward, toward *B*, only; those at *O*, right and left, swung outward, toward *A*, only. It was therefore impossible for the mouse to follow any other course than *A-I-B-L-W-E-O* or *A-I-B-R-W-E-O*. The doors at *I* and *O* were pieces of wire netting of 1/2 cm. mesh, hinged at the top so that a mouse could readily open them, in one direction, by pushing with its nose at any point along the bottom. On the floor of each of the electric-boxes, *W*, was an oak board 1 cm. in thickness, which carried electric wires by means of which the mouse could be shocked in *W* when the tests demanded it. The interrupted circuit constituted by the wires in the two electric-boxes, in connection with the induction apparatus, *IC*, the dry battery, *C*, and the hand key, *K*, was made by taking two pieces of No. 20 American standard gauge copper wire and winding them around the oak board which was to be placed on the floor of each electric-box. The wires, which ran parallel with one another, 1/2 cm. apart, fitted into shallow grooves in the edges of the board, and thus, as well as by being drawn taut, they were held firmly in position. The coils of the two pieces of wire alternated, forming an interrupted circuit which, when the key *K* was closed, was completed if the feet of a mouse rested on points of both pieces of wire. Since copper wire stretches easily and becomes loose on the wooden base, it is better to use phosphor bronze wire of about the same size, if the surface covered by the interrupted circuit is more than three or four inches in width. The phosphor bronze wire is more difficult to wind satisfactorily, for it is harder to bend than the copper wire, and it has the further disadvantage of being more brittle. But when once placed properly, it forms a far more lasting and satisfactory interrupted circuit for such experiments as those to be described than does copper wire. In the case of the electric-boxes under consideration, the oak boards which carried the interrupted circuits were separate, and the two circuits were joined by the union of the wires between the boxes. The free ends of the two pieces of wire which constituted the interrupted circuit were connected with the secondary coil of a Porter inductorium whose primary coil was in circuit with a No. 6 Columbia dry battery. In the light of preliminary experiments, made in preparation for the tests of vision, the strength of the induced current received by the mouse was so regulated, by changing the position of the secondary coil with reference to the primary, that it was disagreeable but not injurious to the animal. What part the disagreeable shock played in the test of brightness vision will now be explained.

[Illustration: FIGURE 15.—Ground plan of discrimination box. *A*, nest-box; *B*, entrance chamber; *W,W*, electric-boxes; *L*, doorway of left electric-box; *R*, doorway of right electric-box; *E*, exit from electric- box to alley; *I*, swinging door between *A* and *B*; *O*, swinging door between alley and *A*; *IC*, induction apparatus; *C*, electric cell; *K*, key in circuit.]

An opportunity for visual discrimination by brightness difference was provided by placing dead black cardboard at the entrance and on the inside of one of the electric-boxes, as shown in Figure 14, *B*, and white cardboard similarly in the other box. These cardboards were movable and could be changed from one box to the other at the will of the experimenter. The test consisted in requiring the mouse to choose a certain brightness, for example, the white cardboard side, in order to return to the nest-box without receiving an electric shock. The question which the experimenter asked in connection with this test really is, Can a dancer learn to go to the white box and thus avoid discomfort? If we assume its ability to profit by experience within the limits of the number of experiences which it was given, such a modification of behavior would indicate discrimination of brightness. Can the dancer distinguish white from black; light gray from dark gray; two grays which are almost of the same brightness? The results which make up the remainder of this and the following chapter furnish a definite answer to these questions.

To return to the experimental procedure, the mouse which is being tested is placed by the experimenter in the nest-box, where frequently in the early tests food and a comfortable nest were attractions. If it does not of its own accord, as a result of its abundant random activity, pass through *I* into *B* within a few seconds, it is directed to the doorway and urged through. A choice is now demanded of the animal; to return to the nest-box it must enter either the white electric-box or the black one. Should it choose the white box, it is permitted to return directly to *A* by way of the doorway *E*, the alley, and the swinging door at *O*, and it thus gets the satisfaction of unobstructed activity, freedom to whirl, to feed, and to retreat for a time to the nest. Should it choose to attempt to enter the black box, as it touches the wires of the interrupted circuit it receives a shock as a result of the closing of the key in the circuit by the experimenter, and further, if it continues its forward course instead of retreating from the "stinging" black box, its passage through *E* is blocked by a barrier of glass temporarily placed there by the experimenter, and the only way of escape to the nest-box is an indirect route by way of *B* and the white box. Ordinarily the shock was given only when the mouse entered the wrong box, not when it retreated from it; it was never given when the right box was chosen. The box to be chosen, whether it was white, gray, or black, will be called the right box. The electric shock served as a means of forcing the animal to use its discriminating ability. But the question of motives in the tests is not so simple as might appear from this statement.

The reader will wonder why the mouse should have any tendency to enter *B*, and why after so doing, it should trouble to go further, knowing, as it does from previous experiences, that entering one of the electric-boxes may result in discomfort. The fact is, a dancer has no very constant tendency to go from *A* to *B* at the beginning of the tests, but after it has become accustomed to the box and has learned what the situation demands, it shows eagerness to make the trip from *A* to *B*, and thence by way of either the right or the left route to *A*. That the mouse should be willing to enter either of the electric-boxes, after it has experienced the shock, is even more surprising than its eagerness to run from *A* to *B*. When first tested for brightness discrimination in this apparatus, a dancer usually hesitated at the entrance to the electric-boxes, and this hesitation increased rapidly unless it were able to discriminate the boxes by their difference in brightness and thus to choose the right one. During the period of increasing hesitancy in making the choice, the experimenter, by carefully moving from *I* toward the entrances to the electric-boxes a piece of cardboard which extended all the way across *B*, greatly increased the mouse's desire to enter one of the boxes by depriving it of dancing space in *B*. If an individual which did not know which entrance to choose were permitted to run about in *B*, it would often do so for minutes at a time without approaching the entrance to the boxes; but the same individual, when confined to a dancing space 4 or 5 cm. wide in front of the entrances, would enter one of the electric-boxes almost immediately. This facilitation of choice by decrease in the amount of space for whirling was not to any considerable extent the result of fear, for all the dancers experimented with were tame, and instead of forcing them to rush into one of the boxes blindly and without attempt at discrimination, the narrowing of the space simply increased their efforts to discriminate. The common mouse when subjected to similar experimental conditions is likely to be frightened by being forced to approach the entrances to the boxes, and fails to choose; it rushes into one box directly, and in consequence it is as often wrong as right. The dancer always chooses, but its eagerness to choose is markedly increased by the restriction of its movements to a narrow space in front of the entrances between which it is required to discriminate. It is evident that the animal is uncomfortable in a space which is too narrow for it to whirl in freely. It must have room to dance. This furnished a sufficiently strong motive for the entering of the electric-boxes. It must avoid disagreeable and unfavorable stimuli. This is a basis for attempts to choose, by visual discrimination, the electric-box in which the shock is not given. It may safely be said that the success of the majority of the experiments of this book depended upon three facts: (1) the dancer's tendency to avoid disagreeable external conditions, (2) its escape-from-confinement- impelling need of space in which to dance freely, and (3) its abundant and incessant activity.

Of these three conditions of success in the experiments, the second and third made possible the advantageous use of the first. For the avoidance of a disagreeable stimulus could be made use of effectively in the tests just because the mice are so restless and so active. In fact their eagerness to do things is so great that the experimenter, instead of having to wait for them to perform the desired act, often is forced to make them wait while he completes his observation and record. In this respect they are unlike most other animals.

My experiments with the dancer differ from those which have been made by most students of mammalian behavior in one important respect. I have used punishment instead of reward as the chief motive for the proper performance of the required act. Usually in experiments with mammals hunger has been the motive depended upon. The animals have been required to follow a certain devious path, to escape from a box by working a button, a bolt, a lever, or to gain entrance to a box by the use of teeth, claws, hands, or body weight and thus obtain food as a reward. There are two very serious objections to the use of the desire for food as a motive in animal behavior experiments—objections which in my opinion render it almost worthless in the case of many mammals. These are the discomfort of the animal and the impossibility of keeping the motive even fairly constant. However prevalent the experience of starvation may be in the life of an animal, it is not pleasant to think of subjecting it to extreme hunger in the laboratory for the sake of finding out what it can do to obtain food. Satisfactory results can be obtained in an experiment whose success depends chiefly upon hunger only when the animal is so hungry that it constantly does its best to obtain food, and when the desire for food is equally strong and equally effective as a spur to action in the repetitions of the experiment day after day. It is easy enough to get almost any mammal into a condition of utter hunger, but it is practically impossible to have the desire for food of the same strength day after day. In short, the desire for food is unsatisfactory as a motive in animal behavior work, first, because a condition of utter hunger, as has been demonstrated with certain mammals, is unfavorable for the performance of complex acts, second, because it is impossible to control the strength of the motive, and finally, because it is an inhumane method of experimentation.

In general, the method of punishment is more satisfactory than the method of reward, because it can be controlled to a greater extent. The experimenter cannot force his subject to desire food; he can, however, force it to discriminate between conditions to the best of its knowledge and ability by giving it a disagreeable stimulus every time it makes a mistake. In other words, the conditions upon which the avoidance of a disagreeable factor in the environment depends are far simpler and much more constant than those upon which the seeking of an agreeable factor depends. Situations which are potentially beneficial to the animal attract it in varying degrees according to its internal condition; situations which are potentially disagreeable or injurious repel it with a constancy which is remarkable. The favorable stimulus solicits a positive response; the unfavorable stimulus demands a negative response.

Finally, in connection with the discussion of motives, it is an important fact that forms of reward are far harder to find than forms of punishment. Many animals feed only at long intervals, are inactive, do not try to escape from confinement, cannot be induced to seek a particular spot, in a word, do not react positively to any of the situations or conditions which are employed usually in behavior experiments. It is, however, almost always possible to find some disagreeable stimulus which such an animal will attempt to avoid.

As it happens, the dancer is an animal which does not stand the lack of food well enough to make hunger a possible motive. I was driven to make use of the avoiding reaction, and it has proved so satisfactory that I am now using it widely in connection with experiments on other animals. The use of the induction shock, upon which I depended almost wholly in the discrimination experiments with the dancer, requires care; but I am confident that no reasonable objection to the conduct of the experiments could be made on the ground of cruelty, for the strength of the current was carefully regulated and the shocks were given only for an instant at intervals. The best proof of the humaneness of the method is the fact that the animals continued in perfect health during months of experimentation.

The brightness discrimination tests demanded, in addition to motives for choice, adequate precautions against discrimination by other than visual factors, and, for that matter, by other visual factors than that of brightness. The mouse might choose, for example, not the white or the black box, but the box which was to the right or to the left, in accordance with its experience in the previous test. This would be discrimination by position. As a matter of fact, the animals have a strong tendency at first to go uniformly either to the right or to the left entrance. This tendency will be exhibited in the results of the tests. Again, discrimination might depend upon the odors of the cardboards or upon slight differences in their shape, texture, or position. Before conclusive evidence of brightness discrimination could be obtained, all of these and other possibilities of discrimination had to be eliminated by check tests. I shall describe the various precautions taken in the experiments to guard against errors in interpretation, in order to show the lengths to which an experimenter may be driven in his search for safely interpretable results.

To exclude choice by position, the cardboards were moved from one electric-box to the other. When the change was made regularly, so that white was alternately on the right and the left, the mouse soon learned to go alternately to the right box and the left without stopping to notice the visual factor. This was prevented by changing the position of the cardboards irregularly.

Discrimination by the odor, texture, shape, and position of the cardboards was excluded by the use of different kinds of cardboards, by changing the form and position of them in check tests, and by coating them with shellac.

The brightness vision tests described in this chapter were made in a room which is lighted from the south only, with the experiment box directed away from the windows. The light from the windows shone upon the cardboards at the entrances to the electric-boxes, not into the eyes of the mouse as it approached them. Each mouse used in the experiments was given a series of ten tests in succession daily. The experiment was conducted as follows. A dancer was placed in *A*, where it usually ran about restlessly until it happened to find its way into *B*. Having discovered that the swing door at *I* could be pushed open, the animal seemed to take satisfaction in passing through into *B* as soon as it had been placed in or had returned to *A*. In *B*, choice of two entrances, one of which was brighter than the other, was forced by the animal's need of space for free movement. If the right box happened to be chosen, the mouse returned to *A* and was ready for another test; if it entered the wrong box, the electric shock was given, and it was compelled to retreat from the box and enter the other one instead. In the early tests with an individual, a series sometimes covered from twenty to thirty minutes; in later tests, provided the condition of discrimination was favorable, it did not occupy more than ten minutes.

To exhibit the methods of keeping the records of these experiments and certain features of the results, two sample record sheets are reproduced below. The first of these sheets, Table 6, represents the results given by No. 5, a female,[1] in her first series of white-black tests. Table 7 presents the results of the eleventh series of tests given to the same individual.

[Footnote 1: It is to be remembered that the even numbers always designate males; the odd numbers, females.]

In the descriptions of the various visual experiments of this and the following chapters, the first word of the couplet which describes the condition of the experiment, for example, white-black, always designates the visual condition which the animal was to choose, the second that which it was to avoid on penalty of an electric shock. In the case of Tables 6 and 7, for example, white cardboard was placed in one box, black in the other, and the animal was required to enter the white box. In the tables the first column at the left gives the number of the test, the second the positions of the cardboards, and the third and fourth the result of the choice. The first test of Table 6 was made with the white cardboard on the box which stood at the left of the mouse as it approached from *A*, and, consequently, with the black cardboard on the right. As is indicated by the record in the "wrong" column, the mouse chose the black instead of the white. The result of this first series was choice of the white box four times as compared with choice of the black box six times. On the eleventh day, that is, after No. 5 had been given 100 tests in this brightness vision experiment, she made no mistakes in a series of ten trials (Table 7).

TABLE 6

BRIGHTNESS DISCRIMINATION

White-Black, Series 1

Experimented on No. 5 January 15, 1906
POSITION OF
TEST CARDBOARDS RIGHT WRONG

1 White left — Wrong 2 White right — Wrong 3 White left — Wrong 4 White right — Wrong 5 White left Right — 6 White right Right — 7 White left — Wrong 8 White right Right — 9 White left — Wrong 10 White right Right —

Totals 4 6

Before tests, such as have been described, can be presented as conclusive proof of discrimination, it must be shown that the mouse has no preference for the particular brightness which the arrangement of the test requires it to select. That any preference which the mouse to be tested might have for white, rather than black, or for a light gray rather than a dark gray, might be discovered, what may be called preference test series were given before the discrimination tests were begun. These series, two of which were given usually, consisted of ten tests each, with the white alternately on the left and on the right. The mouse was permitted to enter either the white or the black box, as it chose, and to pass through to the nest-box without receiving a shock and without having its way blocked by the glass plate. The conditions of these preference tests may be referred to hereafter briefly as "No shock, open passages." The preference tests, which of course would be valueless as such unless they preceded the training tests, were given as preliminary experiments, in order that the experimenter might know how to plan his discrimination tests, and how to interpret his results.

TABLE 7

BRIGHTNESS DISCRIMINATION

White-Black, Series II

Experimented on No. 5 February 2, 1906

POSITION TEST OF CARDBOARDS RIGHT WRONG

1 White left Right —
2 White left Right —
3 White right Right —
4 White right Right —
5 White right Right —
6 White left Right —
7 White left Right —
8 White left Right —
9 White right Right —
10 White right Right —

Totals 10 0

The results given in the white-black preference tests by ten males and ten females are presented in Table 8. Three facts which bear upon the brightness discrimination tests appear from this table: (1) black is preferred by both males and females, (2) this preference is more marked in the first series of tests than in the second, and (3) it is slightly stronger for the first series in the case of females than in the case of males.

TABLE 8

WHITE-BLACK PREFERENCE TESTS

MALES FIRST SERIES SECOND SERIES WHITE BLACK WHITE BLACK

No. 10 3 7 3 7 18 5 5 5 5 20 2 8 4 6 152 4 6 6 4 210 4 6 4 6 214 6 4 3 7 220 5 5 3 7 230 4 6 2 8 410 4 6 5 5 420 4 6 9 1

Averages 4.1 5.9 4.4 5.6

FEMALES FIRST SERIES SECOND SERIES WHITE BLACK WHITE BLACK

No. 11 5 5 4 6 151 6 4 5 5 215 2 8 2 8 213 2 8 5 5 225 4 6 2 8 227 4 6 6 4 235 6 4 4 6 415 2 8 4 6 425 5 5 8 2 229 2 8 5 5

Averages 3.8 6.2 4.5 5.5

That the dancers should prefer to enter the dark rather than the light box is not surprising in view of the fact that the nests in which they were kept were ordinarily rather dark. But whatever the basis of the preference, it is clear that it must be taken account of in the visual discrimination experiments, for an individual which strongly preferred black might choose correctly, to all appearances, in its first black-white series. Such a result would demonstrate preference, and therefore one kind of discrimination, but not the formation of a habit of choice by discrimination. The preference for black is less marked in the second series of tests because the mouse as it becomes more accustomed to the experiment box tends more and more to be influenced by other conditions than those of brightness. The record sheets for both series almost invariably indicate a strong tendency to continue to go to the left or the right entrance according to the way by which the animal escaped the first time. This cannot properly be described as visual choice, for the mouse apparently followed the previous course without regard to the conditions of illumination. We have here an expression of the tendency to the repetition of an act. It is only after an animal acquires considerable familiarity with a situation that it begins to vary its behavior in accordance with relatively unimportant factors in the situation. It is this fact, illustrations of which may be seen in human life, as well as throughout the realm of animal behavior, that renders it imperative that an animal be thoroughly acquainted with the apparatus for experimentation and with the experimenter before regular experiments are begun. Any animal will do things under most experimental conditions, but to discover the nature and scope of its ability it is necessary to make it thoroughly at home in the experimental situation. As the dancer began to feel at home in the visual discrimination apparatus it began to exercise its discriminating ability, the first form of which was choice according to position.

Since there appears to be a slight preference on the part of most dancers' for the black box in comparison with the white box, white-black training tests were given to fifty mice, and black-white to only four. The tests with each individual were continued until it had chosen correctly in all of the tests of three successive series (thirty tests). As the reproduction of all the record sheets of these experiments would fill hundreds of pages and would provide most readers with little more information than is obtainable from a simple statement of the number of right and wrong choices, only the brightness discrimination records of Tables 6 and 7 are given in full.

As a basis for the comparison of the results of the white-black tests with those of the black-white tests, two representative sets of data for each of these conditions of brightness discrimination are presented (Tables 9 and 10). In these tables only the number of right and wrong choices for each series of ten tests appears.

Tables 9 and 10 indicate—if we grant that the precautionary tests to be described later exclude the possibility of other forms of discrimination—that the dancer is able to tell white from black; that it is somewhat easier, as the preference tests might lead us to expect, for it to learn to go to the black than to the white, and that the male forms the habit of choosing on the basis of brightness discrimination more quickly than the female.

TABLE 9 WHITE-BLACK TESTS

		No. 210 AGE, 28 DAYS		No. 215 AGE, 28 DAYS	
SERIES	DATE	RIGHT (WHITE)	WRONG (BLACK)	RIGHT (WHITE)	WRONG (BLACK)
A	June 22	4	6	2	8
B	23	4	6	2	8
1	24	4	6	3	7
2	25	6	4	5	5
3	26	7	3	7	3
4	27	5	5	8	2
5	28	7	3	9	1
6	29	8	2	8	2
7	30	9	1	9	1
8	July 1	10	0	10	0
9	2	10	0	9	1
10	3	10	0	10	0
11	4	—	—	10	0
12	5	—	—	10	0

TABLE 10 WHITE-BLACK TESTS

SERIES	DATE	No. 14 AGE, 32 DAYS		No. 13 AGE, 32 DAYS	
		RIGHT (WHITE)	WRONG (BLACK)	RIGHT (WHITE)	WRONG (BLACK)
1	May 13[1]	5	5	7	3
2	14	8	2	6	4
3	15	7	3	9	1
4	16	9	1	9	1
5	17	10	0	10	0
6	18	10	0	9	1
7	19	10	0	10	0
8	20	—	—	10	0
9	21	—	—	10	0

[Footnote 1: No preference tests were given.]

It is now necessary to justify the interpretation of these results as evidence of brightness discrimination by proving that all other conditions for choice except brightness difference may be excluded without interfering with the animal's ability to select the right box. We shall consider in order the possibility of discrimination by position, by odor, and by texture and form of the cardboards.

The tendency which the dancer has in common with many, if not all, animals to perform the same movement or follow the same path under uniform conditions is an important source of error in many habit-formation experiments. This tendency is evident even from casual observation of the behavior of the dancer. The ease with which the habit of choosing the box on the left or the box on the right is formed in comparison with that of choosing the white box or the black box is strikingly shown by the following experiment. Five mice were given one series of ten trials each in the discrimination box of Figure 14 without the presence of cardboards or of other means of visual discrimination. The electric shock was given whenever the box on the left was entered. Thus without other guidance than that of direction, for the boxes themselves were interchanged in position, and, as was proved by additional tests, the animals were utterly unable to tell one from the other, the mouse was required to choose the box on its right. Only one of the five animals went to the box on the left after once experiencing the electric shock. The results of the series are given in Table 11.

TABLE 11

CHOICE BY POSITION

	Choices of Box on Right	Choices of Box on Left
First mouse	9	1
Second mouse	8	2
Third mouse	9	1
Fourth mouse	9	1
Fifth mouse	9	1

This conclusively proves that the habit of turning in a certain direction or of choosing by position can be formed more readily than a habit which depends upon visual discrimination. A rough comparison justifies the statement that it takes from six to ten times as long for the dancer to learn to choose the white box as it does to learn to choose the box on the right. Since this is true, it is exceedingly important that the possibility of choice by position or direction of movement be excluded in the case of tests of brightness discrimination. To indicate how this was effectively accomplished in the experiments, the changes in the position of the cardboards made in the case of a standard set of white-black series are shown in Table 12. The number of the series, beginning at the top of the table with the two lettered preference series, is given in the first column at the left, the number of the tests at the top of the table, and the position of the white cardboard, left or right, is indicated below by the letters l (left) and r (right).

TABLE 12

POSITION OF WHITE CARDBOARDS FOR A SET OF 150 TESTS

SERIES	1	2	3	4	5	6	7	8	9	10
Preference										
A	l	r	l	r	l	r	l	r	l	r
B	r	l	r	l	r	l	r	l	r	l
1	r	l	r	l	r	l	r	l	r	l
2	l	l	r	r	l	r	l	l	r	r
3	r	r	l	r	l	l	r	l	r	l
4	l	l	l	r	r	r	l	r	r	l
5	r	l	r	l	r	l	r	l	r	l
6	l	l	r	l	r	r	l	r	l	r
7	r	l	l	l	r	r	r	l	r	l
8	r	r	l	l	r	l	r	l	r	l
9	r	r	r	l	l	l	r	l	r	l
10	l	l	l	l	r	r	r	r	l	r
11	r	l	r	r	r	l	l	l	r	l
12	r	l	r	l	r	r	l	l	r	l
13	r	l	r	l	l	l	r	r	r	l
14	l	l	l	l	r	r	r	r	l	r
15	r	l	r	r	r	l	l	l	r	l

It is to be noted that in the case of each series of ten tests the white cardboard was on the left five times and on the right five times. Thus the establishment of a tendency in favor of one side was avoided. The irregularity of the changes in position rendered it impossible for the mouse to depend upon position in its choice. It is an interesting fact that the dancer quickly learns to choose correctly by position if the cardboards are alternately on the left box and on the right.

The prevalent, although ill-founded, impression that mice have an exceedingly keen sense of smell might lead a critic of these experiments to claim that discrimination in all probability was olfactory rather than visual. As precautions against this possibility the cardboards were renewed frequently, so that no odor from the body of the mouse itself should serve as a guiding condition, different kinds of cardboard were used from time to time, and, as a final test, the cardboards were coated with shellac so that whatever characteristic odor they may have had for the dancer was disguised if not totally destroyed. Despite all these precautions the discrimination of the boxes continued. A still more conclusive proof that we have to do with brightness discrimination, and that alone, in these experiments is furnished by the results of white- black tests made with an apparatus which was so arranged that light was transmitted into the two electric-boxes through a ground glass plate in the end of each box. No cardboards were used. The illumination of each box was controlled by changes in the position of the sources of light. Under these conditions, so far as could be ascertained by critical examination of the results, in addition to careful observation of the behavior of the animals as they made their choices, there was no other guiding factor than brightness difference. Nevertheless the mice discriminated the white from the black perfectly. This renders unnecessary any discussion of the possibility of discrimination by the texture or form of the cardboards.

Since a variety of precautionary tests failed to reveal the presence, in these experiments, of any condition other than brightness difference by which the mice were enabled to choose correctly, and since evidence of ability to discriminate brightness differences was obtained by the use of both reflected light (cardboards) and transmitted light (lamps behind ground glass), it is necessary to conclude that the dancer possesses brightness vision.

CHAPTER VIII

THE SENSE OF SIGHT: BRIGHTNESS VISION (Continued)

Since the ability of the dancer to perceive brightness has been demonstrated by the experiments of the previous chapter, the next step in this investigation of the nature of vision is a study of the delicacy of brightness discrimination, and of the relation of the just perceivable difference to brightness value. Expressed in another way, the problems of this portion of the investigation are to determine how slight a difference in brightness enables the dancer to discriminate one light from another, and what is the relation between the absolute brightnesses of two lights and that amount of difference which is just sufficient to render the lights distinguishable. It has been discovered in the case of the human being that a stimulus must be increased by a certain definite fraction of its own value if it is to seem different. For brightness, within certain intensity limits, this increase must be about one one-hundredth; a brightness of 100 units, for example, is just perceivably different from one of 101 units. The formulation of this relation between the amount of a stimulus and the amount of change which is necessary that a difference be noted is known as Weber's law. Does this law, in any form, hold for the brightness vision of the dancing mouse?

Two methods were used in the study of these problems. For the first problem, that of the delicacy of brightness discrimination, I first used light which was reflected from gray papers, according to the method of Chapter VII. For the second, the Weber's law test, transmitted light was used, in an apparatus which will be described later. Either of these methods might have been used for the solution of both problems. Which of them is the more satisfactory is definitely decided by the results which make up the material of this chapter, Under natural conditions the dancer probably sees objects which reflect light more frequently than it does those which transmit it; it would seem fairer, therefore, to require it to discriminate surfaces which differ in brightness. This the use of gray papers does. But, on the other hand, gray papers are open to the objections that they may not be entirely colorless (neutral), and that their brightness values cannot be changed readily by the experimenter. As will be made clear in the subsequent description of the experiments with transmitted light, neither of these objections can be raised in connection with the second method of experimentation.

To determine the delicacy of discrimination with reflected light it is necessary to have a series of neutral grays (colorless) whose adjacent members differ from one another in brightness by less than the threshold of discrimination of the animal to be tested. A series which promised to fulfill these conditions was that of Richard Nendel of Berlin. It consists of fifty papers, beginning with pure white, numbered 1, and passing by almost imperceptible steps of decrease in brightness through the grays to black, which is numbered 50. For the present we may assume that these papers are so nearly neutral that whatever discrimination occurs is due to brightness. The differences between successive papers of the series are perceptible to man. The question is, can they, under favorable conditions of illumination, be perceived by the dancer?

On the basis of the fact that the dancer can discriminate between white and black, two grays which differed from one another in brightness by a considerable amount were chosen from the Nendel series; these were numbers 10 and 20. It seemed certain, from the results of previous experiments, that the discrimination of these papers by brightness difference would be possible, and that therefore the use of papers between these two extremes would suffice to demonstrate the delicacy of discrimination. In Figure 16 we have a fairly accurate representation of the relative brightness of the Nendel papers Nos. 10, 15, and 20.

[Illustration: FIGURE 16. Three of Nendel's gray papers: Nos. 10, 15, and 20. To exhibit differences in brightness.]

Pieces of the gray papers were pasted upon cardboard carriers so that they might be placed in the discrimination box as were the white and black cardboards in the tests of brightness vision previously described. Mice which had been trained to choose the white box by series of white-black tests were now tested with light gray (No. 10) and dark gray (No. 20), my assumption being that they would immediately choose the brighter of the two if they were able to detect the difference. As a matter of fact this did not always occur; some individuals had to be trained to discriminate gray No. 10 from gray No. 20. As soon as an individual had been so trained that the ability to choose the lighter of these grays was perfect, it was tested with No. 10 in combination with No. 15. If these in turn proved to be discriminable, No. 10 could be used with No. 14, with No. 13, and so on until either the limit of discrimination or that of the series had been reached.

That it was not necessary to use other combinations than 10 with 20, and 10 with 15 is demonstrated by the results of Table 13. Mouse No. 420, whose behavior was not essentially different from that of three other individuals which were tested for gray discrimination, learned with difficulty to choose gray No. 10 even when it was used with No. 20. Two series of ten tests each were given to this mouse daily, and not until the twentieth of these series (200 tests) did he succeed in making ten correct choices in succession. Immediately after this series of correct choices, tests with grays No. 10 and No. 15 were begun. In the case of this amount of brightness difference twenty series failed to reveal discrimination. The average number of right choices in the series is slightly in excess of the mistakes, 5.8 as compared with 4.2.

From the experiments with gray papers we may conclude that under the conditions of the tests the amount by which Nendel's gray No. 10 differs in brightness from No. 20 is near the threshold of discrimination, or, in other words, that the difference in the brightness of the adjacent grays of Figure 16 is scarcely sufficient to enable the dancer to distinguish them.

TABLE 13

GRAY DISCRIMINATION

The Delicacy of Brightness Discrimination

No. 420

GRAYS NOS. 10 GRAYS NOS. 20 AND 20 AND 15 SERIES DATE DATE NO. 10 NO. 2 NO. 10 NO. 15 (RIGHT) (WRONG) (RIGHT) (WRONG)

1	Jan. 26	5	5	Feb. 6	8	2
2	27	8	2	6	5	5
3	28	6	4	7	9	1
4	28	2	8	7	7	3
5	29	1	9	8	5	5
6	29	6	4	8	6	4
7	30	9	1	9	5	5
8	30	7	3	9	6	4
9	31	6	4	10	8	2
10	31	4	6	10	3	7
11	Feb. 1	7	3	11	4	6
12	1	8	2	11	4	6
13	2	7	3	12	7	3
14	2	8	2	12	7	3
15	3	9	1	13	6	4
16	3	9	1	13	4	6
17	4	6	4	14	4	6
18	4	9	1	14	5	5
19	5	6	4	15	5	5
20	5	10	0	15	8	2
Averages		6.6	3.4		5.8	4.2

This result of the tests with gray papers surprised me very much at the time of the experiments, for all my previous observation of the dancer had led me to believe that it is very sensitive to light. It was only after a long series of tests with transmitted light, in what is now to be described as the Weber's law apparatus, that I was able to account for the meager power of discrimination which the mice exhibited in the gray tests. As it happened, the Weber's law experiment contributed quite as importantly to the solution of our first problem as to that of the second, for which it was especially planned.

For the Weber's law experiment a box similar to that used in the previous brightness discrimination experiments (Figure 14) was so arranged that its two electric-boxes could be illuminated independently by the light from incandescent lamps directly above them. The arrangements of the light-box and the lamps, as well as their relations to the other important parts of the apparatus, are shown in Figure 17. The light-box consisted of two compartments, of which one may be considered as the upward extension of the left electric-box and the other of the right electric-box. The light- box was pivoted at A and could be turned through an angle of 180° by the experimenter. Thus, by the turning of the light-box, the lamp which in the case of one test illuminated the left electric-box could be brought into such a position that in the case of the next test it illuminated the right electric-box. The practical convenience of this will be appreciated when the number of times that the brightnesses of the two boxes had to be reversed is considered. The light-box was left open at the top for ventilation and the prevention of any considerable increase in the temperature of the experiment box. In one side of each of the compartments of the light-box a slit (B, B of the figure) was cut out for an incandescent lamp holder. A strip of leatherette, fitted closely into inch grooves at the edges of the slit, prevented light from escaping through these openings in the sides of the light-box. By moving the strips of leatherette, one of which appears in the figure, C, the lamps could be changed in position with reference to the bottom of the electric-box. A scale, S, at the edge of each slit enabled the experimenter to determine the distance of the lamp from the floor of the electric-box. The front of the light-box was closed, instead of being open as it appears in the figure.

[Illustration: Figure 17.—Weber's law apparatus for testing brightness discrimination. Lower part, discrimination box similar to that of Figure 14. Upper part, rotatory light-box, pivoted at A, and divided into two compartments by a partition P in the middle. L, L, incandescent lamps movable in slits, B, B, in which a narrow strip of leatherette, C, serves to prevent the escape of light. S, scale.]

This apparatus has the following advantages. First, the electric-boxes, between which the mouse is expected to discriminate by means of their difference in brightness, are illuminated from above and the light therefore does not shine directly from the lamps into the eyes of the animal, as it approaches the entrances to the boxes. Choice is required, therefore, between illuminated spaces instead of between two directly illuminated surfaces. Second, the amount of illumination of each electric- box can be accurately measured by the use of a photometer. Third, since the same kind of lamp is used in each box, and further, since the lamps may be interchanged at any time, discrimination by qualitative instead of quantitative difference in illumination is excluded. And finally, fourth, the tests can be made expeditiously, conveniently, and under such simple conditions that there should be no considerable error of measurement or of observation within the range of brightness which must be used.

It was my purpose in the experiment with this apparatus to ascertain how great the difference in the illumination of the two electric-boxes must be in order that the mouse should be able to choose the brighter of them. This I attempted to do by fixing an incandescent lamp of a certain known illuminating power at such a position in one compartment of the light-box that the electric-box below it was illuminated by what I call a standard value, and by moving the incandescent lamp in the other compartment of the light-box until the illumination of the electric-box below it was just sufficiently less than that of the standard to enable the dancer to distinguish them, and thereby to choose the brighter one. The light which was changed from series to series I shall call the *variable*, in contrast with the *standard*, which was unchanged.

The tests, which were made in a dark-room under uniform conditions, were given in series of fifty each; usually only one such series was given per day, but sometimes one was given in the morning and another in the afternoon of the same day. To prevent choice by position the lights were reversed in position irregularly, first one, then the other, illuminating the right electric-box. For the fifty tests of each initial series the order of the changes in position was as follows: standard (brighter light) on the *l* (left), *l*, *r* (right), *r*, *l*, *l*, *r*, *r*, *l*, *r*, *l*, *r*, *l*, *l*, *r*, *r*, *l*, *l*, *r*, *r*, *l*, *l*, *l*, *r*, *r*, *r*, *l*, *r*, *l*, *r*, *r*, *r*, *l*, *l*, *l*, *r*, *r*, *r*, *l*, *l*, *r*, *l*, *r*, *l*, *r*, *l*, *r*, *l*, *r*, *l*. Twenty-five times in fifty the standard light illuminated the right electric-box, and the same number of times it illuminated the left electric-box. When a second series was given under the same conditions of illumination, a different order of change was followed.

In order to discover whether Weber's law holds in the case of the brightness vision of the dancer it was necessary for me to determine the just perceivable difference between the standard and the variable lights for two or more standard values. I chose to work with three values, 5, 20, and 80 hefners, and I was able to discover with a fair degree of accuracy how much less than 5, 20, or 80 hefners, as the case might be, the variable light had to be in order that it should be discriminable from the other. For the work with the 5 hefner standard I used 2-candle-power lamps,[1] for the 20, 4-candle-power, and for the 80, 16-candle-power.

[Footnote 1: I give merely the commercial markings of the lamps. They had been photometered carefully by two observers by means of a Lummer-Brodhun photometer and a Hefner amyl acetate lamp previous to their use in the experiment. For the photometric measurements in connection with the Weber's law tests I made use of the Hefner lamp with the hope of attaining greater accuracy than had been possible with a standard paraffine candle, in the case of measurements which I had made in connection with the experiments on color vision that are reported in Chapters IX and X. The Hefner unit is the amount of light produced by an amyl acetate lamp at a flame height of 40 mm. (See Stine's "Photometrical Measurements.") A paraffine candle at a flame height of 50 mm. is equal to 1.2 Hefner units.]

For reasons which will soon appear, Weber's law tests were made with only one dancer. This individual, No. 51, had been thoroughly trained in white-black discrimination previous to the experiments in the apparatus which is represented in Figure 17. Having given No. 51 more than two hundred preliminary tests in the Weber's law apparatus with the electric-boxes sufficiently different in brightness to enable her to discriminate readily, I began my experiments by trying to ascertain how much less the value of the illumination of one electric-box must be in order that it should be discriminable from a value of 20 hefners in the other electric- box. In recording the several series of tests and their results hereafter, I shall state in Hefner units the value of the fixed or standard light and the value of the variable light, the difference between the two in terms of the former, and the average number of wrong choices in per cent.

With the lamps so placed that the difference in the illumination of the two electric-boxes was .53 of the value of the standard, that is about one half, No. 51 made twenty wrong choices in one hundred, or 20 per cent. When the difference was reduced to .36 (one third) the number of errors increased to 36 per cent, and with an intermediate difference of .48 there were 26 per cent of errors (see Table 14).

Are these results indicative of discrimination, or are the errors in choice too numerous to justify the statement that the dancer was able to distinguish the boxes by their difference in brightness? Evidently this question cannot be answered satisfactorily until we have decided what the percentage of correct choices should be in order that it be accepted as evidence of ability to discriminate, or, to put it in terms of errors, what percentage of wrong choices is indicative of the point of just perceivable difference in brightness. Theoretically, there should be as many mistakes as right choices, 50 per cent of each, when the two electric-boxes are equally illuminated (indiscriminable), but in practice this does not prove to be the case because the dancer tends to return to that electric-box through which in the previous test it passed safely, whereas it does not tend in similar fashion to reënter the box in which it has just received an electric shock. The result is that the percentage of right choices, especially in the case of series which have the right box in the same position two, three, or four times in succession, rises as high as 60 or 70, even when the visual conditions are indiscriminable. Abundant evidence in support of this statement is presented in Chapters VII and IX, but at this point I may further call attention to the results of an experiment in the Weber's law apparatus which was made especially to test the matter. The results appear under the date of May 27 in Table 14. In this experiment, despite the fact that both boxes were illuminated by 80 hefners, the mouse chose the standard (the illumination in which it was not shocked) 59 times in 100. In other words the percentage of error was 41 instead of 50. It is evident, therefore, that as low a percentage of errors as 40 is not necessarily indicative of discrimination. Anything below 40 per cent is likely, however, to be the result of ability to distinguish the brighter from the darker box. To be on the safe side we may agree to consider 25 wrong choices per 100 as indicative of a just perceivable difference in illumination. Fewer mistakes we shall consider indicative of a difference in illumination which is readily perceivable, and more as indicative of a difference which the mouse cannot detect. The reader will bear in mind as he examines Table 14 that 25 per cent of wrong choices indicates the point of just perceivable difference in brightness.

TABLE 14

RESULTS OF WEBER'S LAW EXPERIMENTS
Brightness vision

DATE	NUMBER OF TESTS	STANDARD LIGHT	VARIABLE LIGHT	DIFFERENCE	% OF ERRORS
May 13	100	20	9.4	.53	20
15	100	20	12.8	.36	36
16	100	20	10.8	.46	26
20	50	80	37.6	.53	6
21	50	80	51.3	.36	10
22	100	80	71.1	.11	35
24	100	80	60.0	.25	21
25	100	80	65.0	.19	25
27	100	80	80	0	41
28	50	5	2.5	.50	18
29	50	5	4.0	.20	14
29	100	5	4.5	.10	25
31	50	5	4.25	.15	20
June 1	50	5	4.85	.03	48
2	50	20	15.0	.25	16
3	50	20	17.4	.13	22
3	100	20	18.0	.10	22
4	100	80	72.0	.10	18
5	100	5	4.5	.10	12
7	100	5	4.67	.067	46
8	50	80	74.67	.067	56
9	50	20	18.67	.067	44

If we apply this rule to the results of the first tests, reported above, it appears that a standard of 20 hefners was distinguished from a variable of 9.4 hefners (.53 difference), for the percentage of errors was only 20. But in the case of a difference of .36 in the illuminations lack of discrimination is indicated by 36 per cent of errors. A difference of .46 gave a frequency of error so close to the required 25 (26 per cent) that I accepted the result as a satisfactory determination of the just perceivable difference for the 20 hefner standard and proceeded to experiment with another standard value.

The results which were obtained in the case of this second standard, the value of which was 80 hefners, are strikingly different from those for the 20 hefner standard. Naturally I began the tests with this new standard by making the differences the same as those for which determinations had been made in the case of the 20 standard. Much to my surprise only 6 per cent of errors resulted when the difference in illumination was .53. I finally discovered that about .19 difference (about one fifth) could be discriminated with that degree of accuracy which is indicated by 25 per cent of mistakes.

So far as I could judge from the results of determinations for the 20 and the 80 hefner standards, Weber's law does not hold for the dancer. With the former a difference of almost one half was necessary for discrimination; with the latter a difference of about one fifth could be perceived. But before presenting additional results I should explain the construction of Table 14, and comment upon the number of experiments which constitutes a set.

The table contains the condensed results of several weeks of difficult experimentation. From left to right the columns give the date of the initial series of a given set of experiments, the number of experiments in the set, the value of the standard light in hefners, the value of the variable light, the difference between the lights in terms of the standard (the variable was always less than the standard), and the percentage of errors or wrong choices. Very early in the investigation I discovered that one hundred tests with any given values of the lights sufficed to reveal whatever discriminating ability the mouse possessed at the time. In some instances either the presence or the lack of discrimination was so clear, as the result of 50 tests (first series), that the second series of 50 was not given. Consequently in the table the number of tests for the various values of the lights is sometimes 100, sometimes 50.

After finishing the experiments with the 80 standard on May 27 (see table) I decided, in spite of the evidence against Weber's law, to make tests with 5 as the standard, for it seemed not impossible that the lights were too bright for the dancer to discriminate readily. I even suspected that I might have been working outside of the brightness limits in which Weber's law holds, if it holds at all. The tests soon showed that a difference of one tenth made discrimination possible in the case of this standard. If the reader will examine the data of the table, he will note that a difference of .20 gave 14 per cent of mistakes; a difference of .03, 48 per cent. Evidently the former difference is above the threshold, the latter below it. But what of the interpretation of the results in terms of Weber's law? The difference instead of being one half or one fifth, as it was in the cases of the 20 and 80 standards respectively, has now become one tenth. Another surprise and another contradiction!

Had these three differences either increased or decreased regularly with the value of the standard I should have suspected that they indicated a principle or relationship which is different from but no less interesting than that which Weber's law expresses. But instead of reading 5 standard, difference one tenth; 20 standard, difference one fifth; 80 standard, difference one half: or 5 standard, difference one half; 20 standard, difference one fifth; 80 standard, difference one tenth: they read 5 standard, difference one tenth; 20 standard, difference one half; 80 standard, difference one fifth. What does this mean? I could think of no other explanation than that of the influence of training. It seemed not impossible, although not probable, that the mouse had been improving in ability to discriminate day by day. It is true that this in itself would be quite as interesting a fact as any which the experiment might reveal.

To test the value of my supposition, I made additional experiments with the 20 standard, the results of which appear under the dates June 2 and 3 of the table. These results indicate quite definitely that the animal had been, and still was, improving in her ability to discriminate. For instead of requiring a difference of about one half in order that she might distinguish the 20 standard from the variable light she was now able to discriminate with only 22 per cent of errors when the difference was one tenth.

As it seemed most improbable that improvement by training should continue much longer, I next gave additional tests with the 80 standard. Again a difference of one tenth was sufficient for accurate discrimination (18 per cent of errors). These series were followed immediately by further tests with the 5 standard. As the results indicated greater ease of discrimination with a difference of one tenth in the case of this standard than in the case of either of the others I was at first uncertain whether the results which I have tabulated under the dates June 3, 4, and 5 of the table should be interpreted in terms of Weber's law.

Up to this point the experiments had definitely established two facts: that the dancer's ability to discriminate by means of brightness differences improves with training for a much longer period and to a far greater extent than I had supposed it would; and that a difference of one tenth is sufficient to enable the animal to distinguish two lights in the case of the three standard values, 5, 20, and 80 hefners. The question remains, is this satisfactory evidence that Weber's law holds with respect to the brightness vision of the dancer, or do the results indicate rather, that this difference is more readily detected in the case of 5 as a standard (12 per cent error) than in the case of 20 as a standard (22 per cent error)?

For the purpose of settling this point I made tests for each of the three standards with a difference of only one fifteenth. In no instance did I obtain the least evidence of ability to discriminate. These final tests, in addition to establishing the fact that the limit of discrimination for No. 51, after she had been subjected to about two thousand tests, lay between one tenth and one fifteenth, proved to my satisfaction, when taken in connection with the results already discussed, that Weber's law does hold for the brightness vision of the dancer.

In concluding this discussion of the Weber's law experiment I wish to call attention to the chief facts which have been revealed, and to make a critical comment. In my opinion it is extremely important that the student of animal behavior should note the fact that the dancer with which I worked week after week in the Weber's law investigation gradually improved in her ability to discriminate on the basis of brightness differences until she was able to distinguish from one another two boxes whose difference in illumination was less than one tenth[1] that of the brighter box. At the beginning of the experiments a difference of one half did not enable her to choose as certainly as did a difference of one tenth after she had chosen several hundred times. Evidently we are prone to underestimate the educability of our animal subjects.

[Footnote 1: Under the conditions of the experiment I was unable to distinguish the electric-boxes when they differed by less than one twentieth.]

The reason that the experiments were carried out with only one mouse must now be apparent. It was a matter of time. The reader must not suppose that my study of this subject is completed. It is merely well begun, and I report it here in its unfinished state for the sake of the value of the method which I have worked out, rather than for the purpose of presenting the definite results which I obtained with No. 51.

The critical comment which I wish to make for the benefit of those who are working on similar problems is this. The phosphor bronze wires, on the bottom of the electric-boxes, by means of which an electric shock could be given to the mouse when it chose the wrong box, are needless sources of variability in the illumination of the boxes. They reflect the light into the eyes of the mouse too strongly, and unless they are kept perfectly clean and bright, serious inequalities of illumination appear. To avoid these undesirable conditions I propose hereafter to use a box within a box, so that the wires shall be hidden from the view of the animal as it attempts to discriminate.

A brief description of the behavior of the dancer in the brightness discrimination experiments which have been described may very appropriately form the closing section of this chapter. For the experimenter, the incessant activity and inexhaustible energy of the animal are a never-failing source of interest and surprise. When a dancer is inactive in the experiment box, it is a good indication either of indisposition or of too low a temperature in the room. In no animal with which I am familiar is activity so much an end in itself as in this odd species of mouse. With striking facility most of the mice learn to open the wire swing doors from either side. They push them open with their noses in the direction in which they were intended by the experimenter to work, and with almost equal ease they pull them open with their teeth in the direction in which they were not intended to work. In the rapidity with which this trick is learned, there are very noticeable individual differences. The pulling of these doors furnished an excellent opportunity for the study of the imitative tendency.

When confronted with the two entrances of the electric-boxes, the dancer manifested at first only the hesitation caused by being in a strange place. It did not seem much afraid, and usually did not hesitate long before entering one of the boxes. The first choice often determined the majority of the choices of the preference series. If the mouse happened to enter the left box, it kept on doing so until, having become so accustomed to its surroundings that it could take time from its strenuous running from *A* by way of the left box to the alley and thence to *A*, to examine things in *B* a little, it observed the other entrance and in a seemingly half-curious, half-venturesome way entered it. In the case of other individuals, the cardboards themselves seemed to determine the choices from the first.

The electric shock, as punishment for entering the wrong box, came as a surprise. At times an individual would persistently attempt to enter, or even enter and retreat from the wrong box repeatedly, in spite of the shock. This may have been due in some instances to the effects of fright, but in others it certainly was due to the strength of the tendency to follow the course which had been taken most often previously. The next effect of the shock was to cause the animal to hesitate before the entrances to the boxes, to run from one to the other, poking its head into each and peering about cautiously, touching the cardboards at the entrances, apparently smelling of them, and in every way attempting to determine which box could be entered safely. I have at times seen a mouse run from one entrance to the other twenty times before making its choice; now and then it would start to enter one and, when halfway in, draw back as if it had been shocked. Possibly merely touching the wires with its fore paws was responsible for this simulation of a reaction to the shock. The gradual waning of this inhibition of the forward movement was one of the most interesting features of the experiment. Could we but discover what the psychical states and the physiological conditions of the animal were during this period of choosing, comparative psychology and physiology would advance by a bound.

If the conditions at the entrances of the two boxes were discriminable, the mouse usually learned within one hundred experiences to choose the right box without much hesitation. Three distinct methods of choice were exhibited by different individuals, and to a certain extent by the same individual from time to time. These methods, which I have designated *choice by affirmation*, *choice by negation*, and *choice by comparison*, are of peculiar interest to the psychologist and logician.

When an individual runs directly to the entrance of the right box, and, after stopping for an instant to examine it, enters, the choice may be described as recognition of the right box. I call it choice by affirmation because the act of the animal is equivalent to the judgment—"this is it." If instead it runs directly to the wrong box, and, after examining it, turns to the other box and enters without pause for examination, its behavior may be described as recognition of the wrong box. This I call choice by negation because the act seems equivalent to the judgment—"this is not it." Further, it seems to imply the judgment—"therefore the other is it." In the light of this fact, this type of choice might appropriately be called choice by exclusion. Finally, when the mouse runs first to one box and then to the other, and repeats this anywhere from one to fifty times, the choice may be described as comparison of the boxes; therefore, I call it choice by comparison. Certain individuals choose first by comparison, and later almost uniformly by affirmation and negation. Whenever the conditions are difficult to discriminate, choice by comparison occurs most frequently and persistently. If, however, the conditions happen to be absolutely indiscriminable, as was true, for example, in the case of the sound tests, in certain of the Weber's law tests, and in the plain electric-box tests, the period of hesitation rapidly increases during the first three or four series of tests, then the mouse seems to lessen its efforts to discriminate and more and more tends to rush into one of the boxes without hesitation or examination, and apparently with the expectation of a shock, but with the intention of getting it over as soon as possible. Now and then under such conditions there is a marked tendency to enter the same box each time. Indiscriminable conditions are likely to render the animals fearful of the experiment; instead of going from *A* to *A* willingly, they fight against making the trip. They refuse to pass from *A* to *B*; and when in *B*, they fight against being driven toward the entrances to the electric- boxes.

In marked contrast with this behavior on the part of the mouse under conditions which do not permit it to choose correctly is that of the animal which has learned what is expected of it. The latter, far from holding back or fighting against the conditions which urge it forward, is so eager to make the trip that it sometimes has to be forced to wait while the experimenter records the results of the tests. There is evidence of delight in the freedom of movement and in the variety of activity which the experiment furnishes. The thoroughly trained dancer runs into *B* almost as soon as it has been placed in *A* by the experimenter; it chooses the right entrance by one of the three methods described above, immediately, or after whirling about a few times in *B*; it runs through *E* and back to *A* as quickly as it can, and almost before the experimenter has had time to record the result of the choice it is again in *B* ready for another choice.

CHAPTER IX

THE SENSE OF SIGHT: COLOR VISION

Is the dancing mouse able to discriminate colors as we do? Does it possess anything which may properly be called color vision? If so, what is the nature of its ability in this sense field? Early in my study of the mice I attempted to answer these and similar questions, for the fact that they are completely deaf during the whole or the greater part of their lives suggested to me the query, are they otherwise defective in sense equipment? In the following account of my study of color vision, I shall describe the evolution of my methods in addition to stating the results which were obtained and the conclusions to which they led me. For in this case the development of a method of research is quite as interesting as the facts which the method in its various stages of evolution revealed.

Observation of the behavior of the dancer under natural conditions caused me to suspect that it is either defective in color vision or possesses a sense which is very different from human vision. I therefore devised the following extremely simple method of testing the animal's ability to distinguish one color from another. In opposite corners of a wooden box 26 cm. long, 23 cm. wide, and 11 cm. deep, two tin boxes 5 cm. in diameter and 1.5 cm. deep were placed, as is shown in part I of Figure 18. One of these boxes was covered on the outside with blue paper (*B* of Figure 18), and the other with orange[1] (*O* of Figure 18). A small quantity of "force" was placed in the orange box. As the purpose of the test was to discover whether the animals could learn to go directly to the box which contained the food, the experiments were made each morning before the mice had been fed. The experimental procedure consisted in placing the individual to be tested in the end of the large wooden box opposite the color boxes, and then permitting it to run about exploring the box until it found the food in the orange box. While it was busily engaged in eating a piece of "force" which it had taken from the box and was holding in its fore paws, squirrel fashion, the color boxes were quickly and without disturbance shifted in the directions indicated by the arrows of Figure 18, I. Consequently, when the animal was ready for another piece of "force," the food-box was in the corresponding corner of the opposite end of the experiment box (position 2, 18, II). After the mouse had again succeeded in finding it, the orange box was shifted in position as is indicated by the arrows in Figure 18, II. Thus the tests were continued, the boxes being shifted after each success on the part of the animal in such a way that for no two successive tests was the position of the food- box the same; it occupied successively the positions 1,

2, 3, and 4 of the figure, and then returned to 1. Each series consisted of 20 tests.

[Footnote 1: These were the Milton Bradley blue and orange papers.]

[Illustration: FIGURE 18.—Food-box apparatus for color discrimination experiments. *O*, orange food-box; *B*, blue food-box; 1, 2, 3, 4, different positions of the food-boxes, *O* and *B*; I, II, III, IV, figures in which the arrows indicate the direction in which the food-boxes were moved.]

[Illustration: FIGURE 19.—Food-box apparatus with movable partitions. *O*, orange food-box; *B*, blue food-box; *X*, starting point for mouse; *A*, point at which both food-boxes become visible to the mouse as it approaches them; 1, 2, two different positions of the food-boxes; *T*, *T*, movable partitions. (After Doctor Waugh.)]

An improvement on this method, which was suggested by Doctor Karl Waugh, has been used by him in a study of the sense of vision in the common mouse. It consisted in the introduction, at the middle of the experiment box, of two wooden partitions which were pivoted on their mid-vertical axes so that they could be placed in either of the positions indicated in Figure 19. Let us suppose that a mouse to be tested for color vision in this apparatus has been placed at *X*. In order to obtain food it must pass through *A* and choose either the orange or the blue box. If it chooses the former, the test is recorded as correct; if it goes to the blue box first, and then to the orange, it is counted an error. While the animal is eating, the experimenter shifts the boxes to position 1 of Figure 19, and at the same time moves the partitions so that they occupy the position indicated by the dotted lines. The chief advantage of this improvement in method is that the animal is forced to approach the color boxes from a point midway between them, instead of following the sides of the experiment box, as it is inclined to do, until it happens to come to the food-box. This renders the test fairer, for presumably the animal has an opportunity to see both boxes from *A* and can make its choice at that point of vantage.

Two males, A and B, of whose age I am ignorant, were each given seventeen series of tests in the apparatus of Figure 18. A single series, consisting of twenty choices, was given daily. Whether the animal chose correctly or not, it was allowed to get food; that is, if it went first to the blue box, thus furnishing the condition for a record of error, it was permitted to pass on to the orange box and take a piece of "force." No attempt was made to increase the animal's desire for food by starving it. Usually it sought the food-box eagerly; when it would not do so, the series was abandoned and work postponed. "Force" proved a very convenient form of food in these tests. The mice are fond of it, and they quickly learned to take a flake out of the box instead of trying to get into the box and sit there eating, for when they attempted the latter they were promptly pushed to one side by the experimenter and the box, as well as the food, was removed to a new position.

The results of the tests appear in Table 15. No record of the choices in the first two of the 17 series was kept. The totals therefore include 15 series, or 300 tests, with each individual. Neither the daily records nor the totals of this table demonstrate choice on the basis of color discrimination. Either the dancers were not able to tell one box from the other, or they did not learn to go directly to the orange box. It might be urged with reason that there is no sufficiently strong motive for the avoidance of an incorrect choice. A mistake simply means a moment's delay in finding food, and this is not so serious a matter as stopping to discriminate. I am inclined, in the light of result of other experiments, to believe that there is a great deal in this objection to the method. Reward for a correct choice should be supplemented by some form of punishment for a mistake. This conclusion was forced upon me by the results of these preliminary experiments on color vision and by my observation of the behavior of the animals in the apparatus. At the time the above tests were made I believed that I had demonstrated the inability of the dancer to distinguish orange from blue, but now, after two years' additional work on the subject, I believe instead that the method was defective.

The next step in the evolution of a method of testing the dancer's color vision was the construction of the apparatus (Figures 14 and 15) which was described in Chapter VII. In connection with this experiment box the basis for a new motive was introduced, namely, the punishment of mistakes by an electric shock. Colored cardboards, instead of the white, black, or grays of the brightness tests, were placed in the electric-boxes.

TABLE 15

ORANGE-BLUE TESTS, WITH FOOD-BOX

SERIES	DATE 1904	MOUSE A RIGHT (ORANGE)	MOUSE A WRONG (BLUE)	MOUSE B RIGHT (ORANGE)	MOUSE B WRONG (BLUE)
1	Dec. 6	—	—	—	—
2	7	—	—	—	—
3	8	12	8	12	8
4	9	10	10	9	11
5	10	15	5	10	10
6	11	10	10	12	8
7	12	9	11	9	11
8	13	10	10	9	11
9	14	12	8	12	8
10	15	13	7	12	8
11	16	13	7	10	10
12	17	12	8	10	10
13	18	11	9	10	10
14	19	13	7	8	12
15	20	13	7	9	11
16	22	14	6	12	8
17	23	10	10	9	11
TOTALS		**177**	**123**	**153**	**147**

In preliminary tests, at the rate of four per day, the colored cardboards were placed only at the entrances to the boxes, not inside, and as was true also in the case of brightness tests under like conditions, no evidence of discrimination was obtained from ten days' training. This seemed to indicate that a considerable area of the colored surface should be exposed to the mouse's view, if discrimination were to be made reasonably easy.

This conclusion was supported by the results of other preliminary experiments in which rectangular pieces of colored papers[1] 6 by 3 cm., were placed on the floor at the entrances to the electric-boxes, instead of on the walls of the boxes. Mouse No. 2 was given five series of ten tests each with a yellow card to indicate the right box and a red card at the entrance to the wrong box. At first he chose the red almost uniformly, and at no time during these fifty tests did he exhibit ability to choose the right box by color discrimination. I present the results of these series in Table 16, because they indicate a fact to which I shall have to refer repeatedly later, namely, that the brightness values of different portions of the spectrum are not the same for the dancer as for us. Previous to this yellow-red training, No. 2, as a result of ten days of white-black training (two tests per day), had partially learned to go to the brighter of the two electric-boxes. It is possible therefore that the choice of the box in the case of these color experiments was in reality the choice of what appeared to the mouse to be the brighter box. If this were not true, how are the results of Table 16 to be accounted for?

[Footnote 1: These were the only Hering papers used in my experiments.]

TABLE 16

YELLOW-RED TESTS

In Color Discrimination Box with 6 by 3 cm. Pieces of Hering Papers at Entrances to Boxes

No. 2

SERIES DATE RIGHT WRONG 1906 (Yellow) (Red) 1 Jan. 16 1 9 2 17 3 7 3 18 4 6 4 19 5 5 5 20 5 5

Without further mention of the many experiments which were necessary for the perfecting of this method of testing color vision, I may at once present the final results of the tests which were made with reflected light. These tests were made with the discrimination apparatus in essentially the same way as were the brightness discrimination tests of Chapter VII.

In all of the color experiments, unless otherwise stated, a series of ten tests each day was given, until satisfactory evidence of discrimination or proof of the lack of the ability to discriminate had been obtained. The difficulties of getting conclusive evidence in either direction will be considered in connection with the results themselves. For all of these tests with reflected light the Milton Bradley colored papers were used. These colored papers were pasted on white cardboard carriers. I shall designate, in the Bradley nomenclature, the papers used in each experiment.

With colored cardboards inside the electric-boxes as well as at their entrances (see Figure 14 for position of cardboards) blue-orange tests were given to Nos. 2 and 3 until they discriminated perfectly. The papers were Bradley's blue tint No. 1 and orange. Number 2 was perfect in the twelfth series (Table 17), No 3 in the fourteenth and again in the sixteenth. They were then tested with a special brightness check series which was intended by the experimenter to reveal any dependence upon a possible brightness difference rather than upon the color difference of the boxes.

TABLE 17

LIGHT BLUE-ORANGE TESTS IN COLOR DISCRIMINATION BOX

SERIES DATE NO. 2 NO. 3 1906 RIGHT WRONG RIGHT WRONG (LIGHT (ORANGE) (LIGHT (ORANGE) BLUE) BLUE)

1 Jan. 26 7 3 1 9
2 27 7 3 5 5
3 28 7 3 6 4
4 29 7 3 7 3
5 30 7 3 4 6
6 31 10 0 7 3
7 Feb. 1 9 1 7 3
8 2 8 2 6 4
9 3 9 1 9 1
10 5 7 3 5 5
11 6 8 2 5 5
12 7 10 0 5 5
Special brightness check series (see Table 18)
13 8 10 0 7 3
Special light blue-dark blue series
14 9 8 2 10 0
15 10 9 1 9 1
Special light blue-dark blue series
16 11 9 1 10 0
Special brightness check series
17 12 10 0 9 1

TABLE 18

LIGHT BLUE-ORANGE

Brightness check series Mouse No. 2, Series 13
Feb. 8, 1906

TEST CONDITION RIGHT WRONG

1 Light blue on right
Orange on left Right ____

2 Light blue on left
Orange on right Right ____

3 Light blue on right
Red substituted for orange Right ____

4 Light blur on left
Red substituted for orange Right ____

5 Dark blue on right
Orange on left Right ____

6 Dark blue on left
Orange on right Right ____

7 Dark blue on left
Orange on right Right ____

8 Dark blue on right
Red substituted for orange Right ____

9 Dark blue on left
Red substituted for orange Right ____

10 Dark blue on left
Red substituted for orange Right ____

Totals 10 0

The nature of this brightness check series, as well as the results which No. 2 gave when tested by it, may be appreciated readily by reference to Table 18. Tint No. 1 of the blue, which is considerably brighter, in my judgment, than the Bradley blue, was replaced at intervals in this series by the latter. For it was thought that in case the mouse were choosing the blue of the series because it seemed brighter than the orange, this substitution might mislead it into choosing the orange. These blues are referred to in the table as light blue (tint No. 1) and dark blue (standard blue). Again a change in the opposite direction was made by substituting Bradley red for orange. As this was for the human eye the substitution of a color whose brightness was considerably less than that of the orange, it seemed possible that the mouse, if it had formed the habit of choosing the box which seemed the darker, might by this change be misled into choosing the red instead of the light blue. In a word, changes in the conditions of the experiments were made in such a way that now one color, now the other, appeared to be the brighter. But I did not attempt to exclude brightness discrimination on the part of the mouse by dependence upon the human judgment of brightness equality, for it is manifestly unsafe to assume that two colors which are of the same brightness for the human eye have a like relation for the eye of the dancer or of any other animal. My tests of color vision have been conducted without other reference to human standards of judgment or comparisons than was necessary for the description of the experimental conditions. In planning the experiments I assumed neither likeness nor difference between the human retinal processes and those of the dancer. It was my purpose to discover the nature of the mouse's visual discriminative ability.

As is indicated in the tables, neither the substitution of dark blue for light blue, nor the replacement of the orange by red or dark blue rendered correct choice impossible, although certain of the combinations did render choice extremely difficult. In other words, despite all of the changes which were made in the brightness of the cardboards in connection with the light blue-orange tests, the mice continued to make almost perfect records. What are we to conclude from this? Either that the ability to discriminate certain colors is possessed by the dancer, or that for some reason the tests are unsatisfactory. If it be granted that the possibility of brightness discrimination was excluded in the check series, the first of these alternatives apparently is forced upon us. That such a possibility was not excluded, later experiments make perfectly clear. The fact was that not even in the check series was the brightness value of the orange as great as that of the blue. Consequently the mice may have chosen the brighter box each time while apparently choosing the blue.

Although conclusive proof of the truth of this statement is furnished only by later experiments, the results of the light blue-orange series, as given in Table 17, strongly suggest such a possibility. Mouse No. 3 had not been experimented with previous to these color discrimination tests. Her preference for the orange, which in the case of the first series was 9 to 1, consequently demands an explanation. If she had been trained previously to choose the white instead of the black, as was true of No. 2, it might be inferred that she went to the orange box because it appeared brighter than the blue. As this explanation is not available, we are driven back upon the results of the white-black preference tests in Chapter VII, which proved that many dancers prefer the black to the white. This may mean that they prefer the lower degree of brightness or illumination, and if so it might be argued, in turn, that the orange was chosen by No. 3 because it appeared darker than the blue. Since, as has already been stated, the orange was far brighter for me than the blue, this would also mean that the brightness values of different colors are not the same for man and mouse.

Practically the same kind of color tests as those described for Nos. 2 and 3 were given to Nos. 1000 and 5. The results appear in Table 19. These tests followed upon the formation of a habit to choose white instead of black (that is, the greater brightness). From the first both No. 1000 and No. 5 chose the light blue in preference to the orange or the red. It therefore seems probable that the former was considerably brighter than the latter. Number 1000, to be sure, was led into three erroneous choices by the brightness check series (series 7), but, on the other hand, No. 5 was not at all disturbed in her choices by similar check tests. It seems natural to conclude from these facts that both of these mice chose the blue at first because of its relatively greater brightness, and that they continued to do so for the same reason. In other words, their behavior indicates that the brightness check tests were valueless because not enough allowance had been made for the possible differences between the vision of mouse and man.

TABLE 19

LIGHT BLUE-ORANGE AND DARK BLUE-RED TESTS

			No. 1000		No. 5	
SERIES	DATE	Condition	Right (Light Blue or Dark Blue)	Wrong (Orange or Red)	Right (Light Blue or Dark Blue)	Wrong (Orange or Red)
1	Jan. 25	Blue-red	8	2	10	0
2	26	Blue-red or Light blue-orange	10	0	10	0
3	27	Light blue-orange	10	0	5	5
4	29	Light blue-orange	9	1	8	2
5	30	Light blue-orange	10	0	8	2
6	31	Light blue-orange	10	0	10	0
7	Feb. 1	Light blue-orange or Dark blue-red	7	3	10	0

If only the final results of my experiments with the dancer and the conclusions to which they lead were of interest, all of this description of experiments which served merely to clear the ground and thus make possible crucial tests might be omitted. It has seemed to me, however, that the history of the investigation is valuable, and I am therefore presenting the evolution of my methods step by step. To be sure, not every detail of this process can be mentioned, and only a few of the individual results can be stated, but my purpose will have been fulfilled if I succeed in showing how one method of experimentation pointed the way to another, and how one set of results made possible the interpretation of others.

As the results of my color vision experiments seemed to indicate that the red end of the spectrum appears much darker to the dancer than to us, tests were now arranged with colors from adjacent regions of the spectrum, green and blue. The papers used were the Bradley green and tint No. 1 of the blue. They were not noticeably different in brightness for the human eye. Green marked the box to be chosen. Three of the individuals which had previously been used in the light blue-orange series, and which therefore had perfect habits of going to the light blue, were used for the green- light blue tests. Of these individuals, No. 1000 became inactive on the fifth day of the experiment, and the tests with him were discontinued. Twenty series were given to each of the other mice, with the results which appear in Table 20. To begin with, both No. 4 and No. 5 exhibited a preference for the light blue, as a result of the previous light blue- orange training. As this preference was gradually destroyed by the electric shock which was received each time the light blue box was entered, they seemed utterly at a loss to know which box to enter. Occasionally a record of six, seven, or even eight right choices would be made in a series, but in no case was this unquestionably due to color discrimination; usually it could be explained in the light of the order of the changes in the positions of the cardboards. For example, series 9, in which No. 5 made a record of 8 right and 2 wrong, had green on the right for the first three tests. The animal happened to choose correctly in the first test, and continued to do so three times in succession simply because there was no change in the position of the cardboards. I have occasionally observed a record of seven right choices result when it was perfectly evident to the observer that the mouse could not discriminate visually. It was to avoid unsafe conclusions and unfair comparisons, as the result of such misleading series, that three perfect series in succession were required as evidence of a perfectly formed habit of discrimination.

TABLE 20

GREEN-LIGHT BLUE TESTS

Date No. 1000 No. 4 No. 5
SERIES 1906 RIGHT WRONG RIGHT WRONG RIGHT WRONG
(GREEN) (BLUE) (GREEN) (BLUE) (GREEN) (BLUE)

1 Feb.3 2 8 3 7 3 7

2 5 7 3 5 5 5 5

3 6 5 5 6 4 5 5

4 7 5 5 5 5 5 5

5 8 2 8 5 5 4 6

6 9 7 3 7 3

7 10 4 6 3 7

8 10 6 4 4 6

9 12 6 4 8 2

10 13 6 4 6 4

11 14 5 5 3 7

12 15 6 4 7 3

13 16 5 5 7 3

14 17 3 7 6 4

15 19 6 4 6 4

16 20 7 3 5 5

17 21 4 6 8 2

18 22 3 7 4 6

19 23 6 4 4 6

20 24 6 4 5 5

Twenty series, 200 tests for each of the individuals in the experiment, yielded no evidence whatever of the dancer's ability to tell green from blue. As it has already been proved that they readily learn to choose the right box under discriminable conditions, it seems reasonable to conclude either that they lack green-blue vision, or that they have it in a relatively undeveloped state.

If it be objected that the number of training tests given was too small, and that the dancer probably would exhibit discrimination if it were given 1000 instead of 200 tests in such an experiment, I must reply that the behavior of the animal in the tests is even more satisfactory evidence of its inability to choose than are the results of Table 20. Had there been the least indication of improvement as the result of 200 tests, I should have continued the experiment; as a matter of fact, the mice each day hesitated more and more before choosing, and fought against being driven toward the entrance to the experiment box. That they were helpless was so evident that it would have been manifestly cruel to continue the experiment.

TABLE 21
VIOLET-RED TESTS
With Odor of All Cardboards the Same

SERIES	DATE	NO. 7 RIGHT (VIOLET)	NO. 7 WRONG (RED)	NO. 998 RIGHT (VIOLET)	NO. 998 WRONG (RED)
A	MAR. 7	8	2	5	5
B	7	3	7	2	8
1	14	3	7	6	4
2	15	4	6	4	6
3	16	5	5	5	5
4	19	4	6	4	6
5	20	5	5	6	4
6	21	4	6	8	2
7	22	8	2	4	6
8	23	4	6	6	4
9	24	6	4	4	6
10	25	4	6	6	4

Further color tests with reflected light were made with violet and red. Two dancers, Nos. 998 and 7, neither of which had been in any experiment previously, were subjected to the ten series of tests whose results are to be found in Table 21. In this experiment the cardboards used had been coated with shellac to obviate discrimination by means of odor. It is therefore impossible to give a precise description of the color or brightness by referring to the Bradley papers.[1] Both the violet and the red were rendered darker, and apparently less saturated, by the coating.

[Footnote 1: The violet was darker than Bradley's shade No. 2, and the red was lighter than Bradley's red.]

These violet-red tests were preceded by two series of preference tests (*A* and *B*), in which no shock was given and escape was possible through either electric-box. Although the results of these preference tests as they appear in

Table 21 seem to indicate a preference for the red on the part of No. 998, examination of the record sheets reveals the fact that neither animal exhibited color preference, but that instead both chose by position. Number 998 chose the box on the right 15 times in 20, and No. 7 chose the box on the left 15 times in 20.

Ten series of tests with the violet-red cardboards failed to furnish the least indication of discrimination. The experiment was discontinued because the mice had ceased to try to discriminate and dashed into one or the other of the boxes on the chance of guessing correctly. When wrong they whirled about, rushed out of the red box and into the violet immediately. They had learned perfectly as much as they were able to learn of what the experiment required of them. Although we are not justified in concluding from this experiment that dancers cannot be taught to distinguish violet from red, there certainly is good ground for the statement that they do not readily discriminate between these colors.

The experiments on color vision which have been described and the records which have been presented will suffice to give the reader an accurate knowledge of the nature of the results, only a few of which could be printed, and of the methods by which they were obtained.

In brief, these results show that the dancer, under the conditions of the experiments, is not able to tell green from blue, or violet from red. The evidence of discrimination furnished by the light blue-orange tests is not satisfactory because the conditions of the experiment did not permit the use of a sufficiently wide range of brightnesses. It is obvious, therefore, that a method of experimentation should be devised in which the experimenter can more fully control the brightness of the colors which he is using. I shall now describe a method in which this was possible.

CHAPTER X

THE SENSE OF SIGHT: COLOR VISION (*Continued*)

There are three well-known ways in which colors may be used as stimuli in experiments on animals: by the use of colored papers (reflected light); by the use of a prism (the spectrum which is obtained may be used as directly transmitted or as reflected light); and by the use of light filters (transmitted light). In the experiments on the color vision of the dancer which have thus far been described only the first of these three methods has been employed. Its advantages are that it enables the experimenter to work in a sunlit room, with relatively simple, cheap, and easily manipulated apparatus. Its chief disadvantages are that the brightness of the light can neither be regulated nor measured with ease and accuracy. The use of the second method, which in many respects is the most desirable of the three, is impracticable for experiments which require as large an illuminated region as do those with the mouse; I was therefore limited to the employment of light filters in my further tests of color discrimination.

The form of filter which is most conveniently handled is the colored glass, but unfortunately few glasses which are monochromatic are manufactured. Almost all of our so-called colored glasses transmit the light of two or more regions of the spectrum. After making spectroscopic examinations of all the colored glasses which were available, I decided that only the ruby glass could be satisfactorily used in my experiments. With this it was possible to get a pure red. Each of the other colors was obtained by means of a filter, which consisted of a glass box filled with a chemical solution which transmitted light of a certain wave length.

For the tests with transmitted light the apparatus of Figures 20 and 21 was constructed. It consisted of a reaction-box essentially the same as that used in the brightness vision tests, except that holes were cut in the ends of the electric-boxes, at the positions *G and* R of Figure 20, to permit the light to enter the boxes. Beyond the reaction-box was a long light-box which was divided lengthwise into two compartments by a partition in the middle. A slit in the cover of each of these compartments carried an incandescent lamp *L* (Figure 20). Between the two lamps, *L*, *L*, and directly over the partition in the light-box was fastened a millimeter scale, *S*, by means of which the experimenter could determine the position of the lights with reference to the reaction-box. The light- box was separated from the reaction-box by a space 6 cm. wide in which moved a narrow wooden carrier for the filter boxes. This carrier, as shown in Figure 20, could be moved readily from side to side through a distance of 20 cm. The filter boxes, which are represented in place in Figures 20 and 21, consisted of three parallel-sided glass boxes 15 cm. long, 5 cm. wide, and 15 cm. deep. Each box contained a substance which acted as a ray filter. Tightly fitted glass covers prevented the entrance of dust and the evaporation of the solutions in the boxes. Figures 20 and 21 represent the two end boxes, *R, R*, as red light filters and the middle one, *G*, as a green light filter. Three filters were used thus side by side in order that the position of a given color with reference to the electric-boxes might be changed readily. As the apparatus was arranged, all the experimenter had to do when he wished to change from green-left, red-right to green-right, red-left was to push the carrier towards the right until the green filter covered the hole on the right at the end of the electric- box. When this had been accomplished the red filter at the left end of the carrier covered the hole on the left at the end of the electric-box. Thus quickly, noiselessly, easily, and without introducing any other change in conditions than that of the interchange of lights, the experimenter was able to shift the positions of his colored lights at will.

[Illustration: FIGURE 20.—Color discrimination apparatus. *A*, nest-box; *B*, entrance chamber; *R, R*, red filters; *G*, green filter; *L, L*, incandescent lamps in light-box; *S*, millimeter scale on light-box; *I*, door between *A* and *B; O, O*, doors between alleys and *A*.]

[Illustration: FIGURE 21—Ground plan of color discrimination apparatus. *E, E*, exits from electric-boxes. *LB*, light-box; *R, G, R*, filter boxes on carrier; *L*, left electric-box; *R*, right electric-box; *IC* induction apparatus; *C*, electric cell; *K*, key; *S*, millimeter scale.]

In the tests which are now to be reported, three portions of the spectrum were used: the red end, the blue-violet end, and a middle region, chiefly green. The red light was obtained by the use of a filter which was made by placing two plates of ruby glass in one of the glass boxes, filling the box with filtered water and then sealing it to prevent evaporation. The blue-violet was obtained by the use of a filter box which contained a 5 per cent solution of copper ammonium sulphate. The green, which, however, was not monochromatic, was obtained by the use of a filter box which contained a saturated solution of nickel nitrate. These three sets of filters were examined spectroscopically both before the experiments had been made and after their completion.[1] The red filters, of which I had two for shifting the lights, transmitted only red light. The blue-violet filters, two also, at first appeared to transmit only portions of the blue and violet of the spectrum, but my later examination revealed a trace of green. It is important to note, however, that the red and the blue-violet filters were mutually exclusive in the portions of the spectrum which they transmitted. Of all the filters used the green finally proved the least satisfactory. I detected some yellow and blue in addition to green in my first examination, and later I discovered a trace of red. Apparently the transmitting power of the solutions changed slightly during the course of the experiments. On this account certain solutions are undesirable for experiments on color vision, for one must be certain of the constancy of the condition of stimulation. It is to be understood, of course, that each of the three filters transmitted, so far as the eye is concerned, only the color named. I consider the red filter perfectly satisfactory, the blue- violet very good, and the green poor. Henceforth, in testing color vision in animals, I shall make use of colored glasses as filters, if it is in any way possible to obtain or have manufactured blue, green, and yellow glasses which are as satisfactory as the ruby.

[Footnote 1: A Janssen-Hoffman spectroscope was used.]

The apparatus needs no further description, as its other important features were identical with those of the reflected light experiment box. The use of artificial light for the illumination of the electric-boxes made it necessary to conduct all of the following tests in a dark-room. The method of experimentation was practically the same as that already described. A mouse which had been placed in *A* by the experimenter was permitted to enter *B* and thence to return to *A* by entering one of the electric-boxes, the red or blue or green one, as the case might be. Mistakes in choice were punished by an electric shock. One further point in the method demands description and discussion before the results of the tests are considered, namely, the manner of regulating and measuring the brightness of the lights.

Regulating brightness with this apparatus was easy enough; measuring it accurately was extremely difficult. The experimenter was able to control the brightness of each of the two colored lights which he was using by changing the position or the power of the incandescent lamps in the light-box. The position of a lamp could be changed easily between tests simply by moving it along toward or away from the electric-box in the slit which served as a lamp carrier. As the distance from the entrances of the electric-boxes to the further end of the light-box was 120 cm., a considerable range or variation in brightness was possible without change of lamps. Ordinarily it was not necessary to change the power of the lamps, by replacing one of a given candle power by a higher or lower, during a series of tests. Both the candle power of the lamps and their distance from the filters were recorded in the case of each test, but for the convenience of the reader I have reduced these measurements to candle meters[1] and report them thus in the descriptions of the experiments.

[Footnote 1: The illuminating power of a standard candle at a distance of one meter.]

But measuring the actual brightness of the red light or the green light which was used for a particular series of tests, and the variations in their brightnesses, was not so simple a matter as might appear from the statements which have just been made. The influence of the light filters themselves upon the brightness must be taken into account. The two red filters were alike in their influence upon the light which entered them, for they were precisely alike in construction, and the same was true of the two blue-violet filters. The same kind of ruby glass was placed in each of the former, and a portion of the same solution of copper ammonium sulphate was put into each of the filter boxes for the latter. But it is difficult to say what relation the diminution in brightness caused by a red filter bore to that caused by a blue-violet or a green filter. My only means of comparison was my eye, and as subjective measurement was unsatisfactory for the purposes of the experiment, no attempt was made to equalize the amounts of brightness reduction caused by the several filters. So far as the value of the tests themselves, as indications of the condition of color vision in the dancer is concerned, I have no apology for this lack of measurement, but I do regret my inability to give that accurate objective statement of brightness values which would enable another experimenter with ease and certainty to repeat my tests. The nearest approach that it is possible for me to make to such an objective measurement is a statement of the composition and thickness of the filters and of the candle-meter value of the light when it entered the filter. The distance from this point to the entrance to the electric-box was 20 cm.

To sum up and state clearly the method of defining the brightness of the light in the following experiments: the candle-meter value of each light by which an electric-box was illuminated, as determined by the use of a Lummer-Brodhun photometer and measurements of the distance of the source of light from the filter, is given in connection with each of the experiments. This brightness value less the diminution caused by the passage of the light through a filter, which has been defined as to composition and thickness of the layer of solution, gives that degree of brightness by which the electric-box was illuminated.

Tests of the dancer's ability to discriminate green and blue[1] in the transmitted light apparatus were made with four animals. An incandescent lamp marked 16-candle-power was set in each of the light-boxes. These lamps were then so placed that the green and the blue seemed to be of equal brightness to three persons who were asked to compare them carefully. Their candle-meter values in the positions selected were respectively 18 and 64, as appears from the statement of conditions at the top of Table 22.

[Footnote 1: Hereafter the light transmitted by the blue-violet filter will be referred to for convenience as blue.]

TABLE 22

GREEN-BLUE TESTS

Brightnesses Equal for Human Eye

Green 18 candle meters Blue 64 candle meters

SERIES	DATE 1906	NO. 10 RIGHT (GREEN)	NO. 10 WRONG (BLUE)	NO. 11 RIGHT (GREEN)	NO. 11 WRONG (BLUE)
A and B[1]	April 2	10	10	12	8
1	3	6	4	5	5
2	4	5	5	6	4
3	5	5	5	5	5
4	6	5	5	5	5
5	7	7	3	5	5
6	8	7	3	3	7
7	9	7	3	5	5
8	10	3	7	7	3
9	11	5	5	4	6
10	12	5	5	6	4

[Footnote: A single preference series of twenty tests.]

Numbers 10 and 11 exhibited no preference for either of these colors in the series of 20 tests which preceded the training tests, and neither of them gave evidence of ability to discriminate as the result of ten series of training tests. In this case, again, the behavior of the animals was as strongly against the inference that they can tell green from blue as are the records of choices which appear in the table. Granted, that they are unable to discriminate green from blue when these colors are of about the same brightness for the human eye, what results when they differ markedly in brightness? Table 23 furnishes a definite answer to this question. Numbers 5 and 12 were given eight series of green-blue tests with each light at 18 candle meters. Little, if any, evidence of discrimination appeared. Then, on the supposition that the difference was not great enough for easy discrimination, the blue light was reduced almost to 0, the green being left at 18. The tests (series 9) immediately indicated discrimination. For series 10 the green was made 64 candle meters, the blue 18, and again there was discrimination. These results were so conclusively indicative of the lack of color vision and the presence of brightness vision, that there appeared to be no need of continuing the experiment further.

Accepting provisionally the conclusion that the dancers cannot tell green from blue except by brightness differences, we may proceed to inquire whether they can discriminate other colors. Are green and red distinguishable?

Green-red discrimination now was tested by a method which it was hoped might from the first prevent dependence upon brightness. The light in the light-box on the left was so placed that it had a value of 18 candle meters, that in the light-box on the right so that it had a value of 1800 candle meters. Neither light was moved during the first four series of the green-red tests which were given to Nos. 151 and 152.

TABLE 23

GREEN-BLUE TESTS

Brightnesses Different for Human Eye

Green 18 candle meters Blue 18 candle meters

No. 5 No. 12
DATE
SERIES 1906 RIGHT WRONG RIGHT WRONG
(GREEN) (BLUE) (GREEN) (BLUE)

1 April 10 6 4 5 5 2 11 5 5 7 3 3 12 6 4 7 3 4 13 4 6 7 3 5 14 7 3 5 5 6 15 4 6 6 4 7 16 6 4 8 2 8 17 5 5 4 6

As it was now evident that the intensity difference was not sufficient to render discrimination easy, the blue was reduced to 0 and the green left at 18.

9 17 7 3 8 2

Now the brightnesses were made, green 64, blue 18, just the reverse of those of series of Table 22.

10 17 8 2 8 2

Each of these series consisted of 20 tests instead of 10. As a result of the arrangement of the lights just mentioned, the green appeared to me very much brighter than the red when it was on the right and very much darker when it was on the left. If this were true for the mouse also, it is difficult to see how it could successfully depend upon brightness for guidance in its choices. Such dependence would cause it to choose now the green, now the red.

The first four series of green-red tests so clearly demonstrated discrimination, of some sort, that it was at once necessary to alter the conditions of the experiment. The only criticism of the above method of excluding brightness discrimination, of which I could think, was that the red at no time had been brighter than the green. In other words, that despite a value of 1800 candle meters for the red and only 18 candle meters for the green, the latter still appeared the brighter to the mouse. To meet this objection, I made the extreme brightness values 1 and 1800 candle meters in some of the later series, of which the results appear in Table 24. From day to day different degrees of brightness were used, as is indicated in the second column of the table. Instead of having first one color and then the other the brighter, after the fourth series I changed the position of the lights each time the position of the filters was changed; hence, the table states a certain brightness value for each color instead of for each electric-box.

Series 5 to 14 so clearly indicated discrimination, that it seemed necessary to devise some other means than that of changing the brightnesses of the colored lights themselves to test the assumption that the animals were choosing the brighter light. I therefore removed the light filters so that the colors which had been present as conditions of discrimination were lacking, and arranged the apparatus so that first one box, then the other, was illuminated the more brightly. The purpose of this was to discover whether as the result of their green-red training the mice had acquired the habit of choosing uniformly either the lighter or the darker box. One series was given under the conditions of illumination specified in Table 24 with the result that the brighter box was chosen eight times in ten by No. 151 and every time by No. 152. Since neither of these individuals had previously been trained by white-black tests to go to the white, and since, furthermore, the dancers usually manifest a slight preference for the lower instead of the higher illumination, this result may be interpreted as indicative of dependence upon brightness in the previous color tests. It looks very much indeed as if the green had been chosen, not because of its greenness, but on account of its relatively greater brightness.

This test of brightness preference was followed by two series, 16 and 17, under conditions similar to those of the first four series of the table. For series 16 the value of the light in the left box was 1 candle meter, that of the light in the right box 1800 candle meters. Discrimination was perfect. For series 17 the value for the left remained at 1 candle meter, but that of the right box was decreased to 0. In this series No. 152 was entirely at a loss to know which box to choose. Of course this was an entirely new set of conditions for choice, namely, a colored box, the green or the red as the case might be, beside a dark box, the one which was not illuminated. If the mice really had been choosing correctly because of a habit of avoiding the red or of seeking the green, this method should bring out the fact, for the red box, since with it the disagreeable electric shock had always been associated, should be a box to be avoided. For No. 151 this seemed to be the case.

Series 23 to 27 of Table 24 were given as final and crucial tests of the relation of brightness discrimination to color discrimination. As it is not possible to express in a simple formula the conditions of the tests, a sample series which indicates the brightness of the colors in each of the twenty tests of a series, and in addition the results given by No. 151 in the first of these final series, is reproduced in Table 25. For an animal which had presumably learned perfectly to choose green in preference to red, the record of 8 mistakes in 20 choices as a result of changes in relative brightness is rather bad, and it renders doubtful the existence of color discrimination in any of these experiments. No. 152 showed no ability whatever to choose the green in the first of the series (series 23 of Table 24) of which that of Table 25 is a sample. His record, 10 mistakes in 20 choices, was even poorer than that of No. 151. That both of these mice learned to choose fairly accurately in these final tests is shown by the results of series 24, 25, 26, and 27. I must admit, however, that these records indicate little ability on the part of the animals to discriminate colors.

TABLE 24

GREEN-RED TESTS

Brightnesses Extremely Different for Human Eye
Intensities are given in candle meters (c.m.)

SERIES	DATE	CONDITIONS	NO. 151 RIGHT (GREEN)	NO. 151 WRONG (RED)	NO. 152 RIGHT (GREEN)	NO. 152 WRONG (RED)
1	April 26	18 c.m. on left 1800 c.m. on right	11	9	7	13
2	27	Same	16	4	16	4
3	28	Same	20	0	17	3
4	29	Same	19	1	19	1
5	30	Green 18 c.m. Red 18 c.m.	9	1	10	0
6	30	Green 64 c.m. Red 18 c.m.	9	1	8	2
7	May 1	Green 6 c.m. Red 1500 c.m.	7	3	9	1
8	1	Green 4 c.m. Red 1500 c.m.	8	2	7	3
9	2	Both varied from 4 to 1500 c.m.	18	2	18	2
10	3	Green 2 c.m. Red 1800 c.m.	6	4	7	3

11 3 Same 10 0 10 0
12 4 Same 7 3 8 2
13 4 Same 8 2 6 4
14 5 Green 1 c.m.
Red 1800 c.m. 19 1 19 1

Filters were now removed. An illumination of 15 c.m. was established on one side and an illumination of 0 on the other side, in order to ascertain whether the mice would choose the brighter box. This was done to test the assumption that the green in the previous tests had always appeared brighter to the mice than did the red, and that in consequence they had chosen the brighter box instead of the green box.

TABLE 24—CONTINUED

No. 151 No. 152

SERIES DATE CONDITIONS RIGHT WRONG RIGHT WRONG (GREEN) (RED) (GREEN) (RED)

15 May 5 Brighter 15 c.m. 8[1] 2[2] 10[1] 0[2]
Darker 0 c.m.
16 5 1 c.m. on left
1800 c.m. on right 10 0 10 0
17 5 1 c.m. on left
0 c.m. on right 9 1 4 6
18 5 Green 18 c.m.
Red 18 c.m. 19 1 17 3
19 9 Same 9 1 9 1
20 9 Same 10 0 10 0
21 10 Same 10 0 10 0
22 11 Same 10 0 10 0
23 June 1 Both varied from
1 to 1800 c.m. 12 8 10 10
24 2 Same 18 2 14 6
25 June 3 Both varied from
2 to 1800 c.m. 19 1 17 3
26 4 Same 17 3 17 3
27 5 Same 18 2 18 2

[Footnote 1: Brighter.]
[Footnote 2: Darker.]

These long-continued and varied tests with Nos. 151 and 152 revealed three facts: that the mice depend chiefly upon brightness differences in visual discrimination; that they probably have something which corresponds to our red-green vision, although their color experience may be totally unlike ours; and that the red end of the spectrum seems much darker to them than to us, or, in other words, that the least refrangible rays are of lower stimulating value for them than for us.

TABLE 25

GREEN-RED TESTS

June 1, 1906 No. 151

TEST	POSITION	BRIGHTNESS VALUE IN CANDLE METERS	RIGHT (GREEN)	WRONG (RED)
1	Green on left	Green 4, Red 448	Right	—
2	Green on right	Green 448, Red 4	Right	—
3	Green on right	Green 4, Red 448	Right	—
4	Green on left	Green 448, Red 4	Right	—
5	Green on left	Green 3, Red 1800	—	Wrong
6	Green on right	Green 1800, Red 3	—	Wrong
7	Green on right	Green 3, Red 1800	—	Wrong
8	Green on left	Green 1800, Red 3	Right	—
9	Green on right	Green 5, Red 34	Right	—
10	Green on left	Green 34, Red 5	Right	—
11	Green on right	Green 6, Red 74	Right	—
12	Green on left	Green 74, Red 6	Right	—
13	Green on left	Green 4, Red 448	—	Wrong
14	Green on right	Green 448, Red 4	Right	—
15	Green on right	Green 4, Red 448	—	Wrong
16	Green on left	Green 448, Red 4	Right	—
17	Green on right	Green 3, Red 1800	—	Wrong
18	Green on left	Green 1800, Red 3	—	Wrong
19	Green on right	Green 1800, Red 3	—	Wrong
20	Green on left	Green 3, Red 1800	Right	—

Totals 12 8

So many of the results of my color experiments have indicated the all-important role of brightness vision that I have hesitated to interpret any of them as indicative of true color discrimination. But after I had made all the variations in brightness by which it seemed reasonable to suppose that the mouse would be influenced under ordinary conditions, and after I had introduced all the check tests which seemed worth while, there still remained so large a proportion of correct choices that I was forced to admit the influence of the quality as well as of the intensity of the visual stimulus.

The first of the facts mentioned above, that brightness discrimination is more important in the life of the mouse than color discrimination, is attested by almost all of the experiments whose results have been reported. The second fact, namely, that the dancer possesses something which for the present we may call red-green vision, also has been proved in a fairly satisfactory manner by both the reflected and the transmitted light experiments. I wish now to present, in Table 26, results which strikingly prove the truth of the statement that red appears darker to the dancer than to us.

The brightness conditions which appeared to make the discrimination between green and red most difficult were, so far as my experiments permit the measurement thereof, green from 1 to 4 candle meters with red from 1200 to 1600. Under these conditions the red appeared extremely bright, the green very dark, to the human subject.

According to the description of conditions in Table 26, Nos. 2 and 5 were required to distinguish green from red with the former about 3 candle meters in brightness and the latter about 1800 candle meters. In the eighth series of 20 tests, each of these animals made a perfect record. As it seemed possible that they had learned to go to the darker of the two boxes instead of to the green box, I arranged the following check test. The filters were removed, the illumination of one electric-box was made 74 candle meters, that of the other 3, and the changes of the lighter box from left to right were made at irregular intervals. In February, No. 2 had been trained to go to the black in black-white tests, and at the same time No. 5 had been trained to go to the white in white-black tests. The results of these brightness check tests, as they appear in the table, series 8 *a*, are indeed striking. Number 2 chose the darker box each time; No. 5 chose it eight times out of ten. Were it not for the fact that memory tests four weeks after his black-white training had proved that No. 2 had entirely lost the influence of his previous experience (he chose white nine times out of ten in the memory series), it might reasonably be urged that this individual chose the darker box because of his experience in the black-white experiment. And what can be said in explanation of the choices of No. 5? I can think of no more reasonable way of accounting for this most unexpected result of the brightness tests than the assumption that both of these animals had learned to discriminate by brightness difference instead of by color.

TABLE 26

GREEN-RED TESTS

Brightnesses Different for Human Eye

No. 2 No. 5

SERIES DATE BRIGHTNESS RIGHT WRONG RIGHT WRONG VALUES (GREEN) (RED) (GREEN) (RED)

1 May 7 Green
Red 1800 c.m. 10 10 12 8
2 8 Same 12 8 11 9
3 9 Same 15 5 14 6
4 10 Same 18 2 12 8
5 11 Same 18 2 14 6
6 12 Same 19 1 16 4
7 13 Same 19 1 18 2
8 14 Same 20 0 20 0

Brightness tests without colors were now given to determine whether the mice had been choosing the brighter or the darker instead of the green.

TABLE 26—CONTINUED

NO. 2 NO. 5

SERIES DATE BRIGHTNESS VALUES RIGHT WRONG RIGHT WRONG (GREEN) (RED) (GREEN) (RED)

8a 14 Brighter 74 c.m. 0[1] 10[2] 2[1] 8[2]
Darker 3 c.m.
9 15 3 c.m. on left
1800 c.m. on right 8 12 16 4
10 16 4 c.m. on left
36 c.m. on right 5 5 7 3
11 16 Green 4 c.m.
Red 36 c.m. 9 1 8 2
12 17 11 c.m. on left
1800 c.m. on right 7 3 6 4
13 17 Green 11 c.m.
Red 1800 c.m. 9 1 8 2
14 18 Mixed values
3 to 1800 c.m. 7 3 8 2
15 19 Same 7 3 7 3

16 20 Same 7 3 7 3
17 21 Same 7 3 9 1
18 22 Same 9 1 8 2
19 23 Same 7 3 9 1
20 24 Same 10 0 8 2
21 25 Same 10 0 9 1
22 26 Same 9 1 10 0

[Footnote 1: Brighter]
[Footnote 2: Darker]

Immediately after the brightness series, the influence of making first one color, then the other, the brighter was studied. Throughout series 9 the brightness value of the left box remained 3 candle meters, that of the right side 1800 candle meters. Number 2 was so badly confused by this change that his mistakes in this series numbered 12; No. 5 made only 4 incorrect choices. Then series after series was given under widely differing conditions of illumination. The expression "mixed values," which occurs in Table 26 in connection with series 14 to 22 inclusive, means that the brightnesses of the green and the red boxes were changed from test to test in much the way indicated by the sample series of Table 25. In view of the results of these 22 series, 320 tests for each of two mice, it is evident that the dancer is able to discriminate visually by some other factor than brightness. What this factor is I am not prepared to say. It may be something akin to our color experience, it may be distance effect. No other possibilities occur to me.

Table 26 shows that discrimination was relatively easy for Nos. 2 and 5 with green at 3 candle meters and red at 1800. That their discrimination was made on the basis of the greater brightness of the red, instead of on the basis of color, is indicated by the results of the brightness check series 8a. Increase in the brightness of the green rendered discrimination difficult for a time, but it soon improved, and by no changes in the relative brightness of the two colors was it possible to prevent correct choice.

In addition to giving point to the statement that red appears darker to the dancer than to us, the above experiment shows that the animals depend upon brightness when they can, and that their ability to discriminate color differences is extremely poor, so poor indeed that it is doubtful whether their records are better than those of a totally color blind person would be under similar conditions. Surely in view of such results it is unsafe to claim that the dancer possesses color vision similar to ours.

Perfectly trained as they were, by their prolonged green-red tests, to choose the green, or what in mouse experience corresponds to our green, Nos. 2 and 5 offered an excellent opportunity for further tests of blue- green discrimination. For in view of their previous training there should be no question of preference for the blue or of a tendency to depend upon brightness in the series whose results constitute Table 27.

TABLE 27 BLUE-GREEN TESTS

NO. 2 NO. 5

SERIES DATE BRIGHTNESS VALUES RIGHT WRONG RIGHT WRONG (BLUE) (GREEN) (BLUE) (GREEN)

1 June 1 Blue 74 c.m.
Green 36 c.m. 3 7 3 7
2 2 Same 5 5 4 6
3 3 Same 5 5 6 4
4 4 Same 6 4 3 7
5 5 Same 6 4 5 5
6 6 Blue 21 c.m.
Green 21 c.m. 6 4 7 3
7 7 Same 2 8 3 7
8 8 Same 5 5 4 6
9 9 Same 3 7 6 4
10 10 Same 2 8 4 6
11 12 Same 6 4 3 7
12 13 Blue 36 c.m.
Green 21 c.m. 3 7 4 6
13 14 Same 5 5
14 15 Blue 62 c.m.
Green 21 c.m. 4 6
15 16 Same 5 5
16 17 Same 5 5
17 18 Same 6 4

Now, as a final test, blue and green glasses were placed over the electric-boxes, the brightness of the two was equalized for the human eye, and the tests of series 18 and 19 were given to No. 2:—

TABLE 27—CONTINUED

NO. 2

SERIES	DATE	BRIGHTNESS VALUES	RIGHT (Blue)	WRONG (Green)
18	18	Blue 62 c.m. Green 21 c.m	4	6
19	19	Same	6	4
20	20	Blue 21 c.m. Green 88 c.m.	2	8

The green was now made much the brighter.

SERIES	DATE	BRIGHTNESS VALUES	RIGHT (Blue)	WRONG (Green)
21	21	Blue 21 c.m. Green 18 c.m.	7	3
22	23	Same	8	2

To begin with, the blue and the green were made quite bright for the human subject, blue 74 candle meters, green 36. Later the brightness of both was first decreased, then increased, in order to ascertain whether discrimination was conditioned by the absolute strength of illumination. No evidence of discrimination was obtained with any of the several conditions of illumination in seventeen series of ten tests each.

On the supposition that the animals were blinded by the brightness of the light which had been used in some of the tests, similar tests were made with weaker light. The results were the same. I am therefore convinced that the animals did justice to their visual ability in these experiments.

Finally, it seemed possible that looking directly at the source of light might be an unfavorable condition for color discrimination, and that a chamber flooded with colored light from above and from one end would prove more satisfactory. To test this conjecture two thicknesses of blue glass were placed over one electric-box, two plates of green glass over the other; the incandescent lamps were then fixed in such positions that the blue and the green within the two boxes appeared to the experimenter, as he viewed them from the position at which the mouse made its choice, of the same brightness.

Mouse No. 2 was given two series of tests, series 18 and 19, under these conditions, with the result that he showed absolutely no ability to tell the blue box from the green box. The opportunity was now taken to determine how quickly No. 2 would avail himself of any possibility of discriminating by means of brightness. With the blue at 21 candle meters, the green was increased to about 1800. Immediately discrimination appeared, and in the second series (22 of Table 27) there were only two mistakes.

The results of the blue-green experiments with light transmitted from in front of the animal and from above it are in entire agreement with those of the experiments in which reflected light was used. Since the range of intensities of illumination was sufficiently great to exclude the possibility of blinding and of under illumination, it is necessary to conclude that the dancer does not possess blue-green vision.

Again I must call attention to the fact that the behavior of the mice in these experiments is even more significant of their lack of discriminating ability than are the numerical results of the tables. After almost every series of tests, whether or not it came out numerically in favor of discrimination, I was forced to add the comment, "No satisfactory evidence of discrimination."

We have now examined the results of green-red, green-blue, and blue-green tests. One other important combination of the colors which were used in these experiments is possible, namely, blue-red. This is the most important of all the combinations in view of the results already described, for these colors represent the extremes of the visible spectrum, and might therefore be discriminable, even though those which are nearer together in the spectral series were not.

TABLE 28 BLUE-RED TESTS

SERIES	DATE	BRIGHTNESS VALUES	No. 2 RIGHT (BLUE)	No. 2 WRONG (RED)	No. 205 RIGHT (BLUE)	No. 205 WRONG (RED)
1	July 31	1800 c.m. on left 24 c.m. on right	5	5	6	4
2	Aug. 1	21 c.m. on left 1800 c.m. on right	6	4	6	4
3	2	1800 c.m. on left 21 c.m. on right	8	2	6	4
4	3	19 c.m. on left 1800 c.m. on right	9	1	6	4
5	4	1800 c.m. on left 7 c.m. on right	7	3	5	5
6	5	6 c.m. on left 1800 c.m. on right	10	0	7	3
7	6	18 c.m. on left				

74 c.m. on right 10 0 9 1
8 7 1800 c.m. on left
7 c.m. on right 8 2 8 2
9 8 7 c.m. on left
1800 c.m. on right 7 3 8 2
10 9 Mixed values
6 to 1800 c.m. 8 2 9 1
11 10 Blue 3 c.m.
Red 1800 c.m. 7 3 6 4

Brightness tests were now made, without the use of colors.

11a 10 4 6 5 5

12 10 Blue 3 c.m. Red 8 c.m. 4 6 6 4 13 11 Blue 3 c.m. Red 7200 c.m. 8 2 5 5 14 13 Mixed values 3 to 7200 c.m. 7 3 7 3 15 13 Same 7 3 9 1 16 14 Blue 3 to 6 c.m. Red 112 to 3650 c.m. 10 0 10 0

Series were now given to test the assumption that red appears dark to the dancer.

17 14 Darkness on one side
Red 3 c.m. 5 5 7 3
18 14 Blue 3 to 3650 c.m.
Red 3 to 3650 c.m. 10 0 10 0
19 15 Darkness on one side
Red 3 c.m. 5 5 4 6
20 15 Blue 3 to 3650 c.m.
Red 3 to 3650 c.m. 10 0 9 1
21 16 Darkess on one side
Red 72 c.m. 5 5 7 3
22 16 Darkness on one side
Red 1800 c.m. 6 4 10 0

As is shown by the results in Table 28, no combination of brightnesses rendered correct choice impossible in the case of the blue-red tests which are now to be described. Choice was extremely difficult at times, even more so perhaps than the table would lead one to suppose, and it is quite possible that color played no part in the discrimination. But that brightness difference in the colors was not responsible for whatever success these mice attained in selecting the right box is proved by the brightness-without-color series which follows series II of the table. Neither No. 2 nor No. 205 showed preference for the lighter or the darker box. At the end of the sixteenth blue-red series, I was convinced that one of two conclusions must be drawn from the experiment: either the dancers possess a kind of blue-red vision, or red is of such a value for them that no brightness of visible green or blue precisely matches it.

The latter possibility was further tested by an experiment whose results appear in series 17 to 22 inclusive, of Table 28. The conditions of series 17 were a brightness value of 0 in one box (darkness) and in the other red of a brightness of 3 candle meters. Despite the fact that they had been perfectly trained in *blue-red tests* to avoid the red, neither of the mice seemed able to discriminate the red from the darkness and to avoid it. This was followed by a series in which the brightness of both the blue and the red was varied between 3 and 3650 candle meters, with the striking result that neither mouse made any mistakes. In series 19 red was used with darkness as in series 17, and again there was a total lack of discrimination. Series 20 was a repetition of series 18, with practically the same result. I then attempted to find out, by increasing the brightness of the red, how great must be its value in order that the dancers should distinguish it readily from darkness. For the tests of series 21 it was made 72 candle meters, but discrimination did not clearly appear. At 1800 candle meters, as is shown in series 22, the red was sufficiently different in appearance from total darkness to enable No. 205 to discriminate perfectly between the two electric-boxes. For No. 2 discrimination was more difficult, but there was no doubt about his ability. It would appear from these tests that the dancers had not learned to avoid red. Therefore we are still confronted with the question, can they see colors?

TABLE 29

VISUAL CHECK TESTS
With the Electric-boxes Precisely Alike Visually

No. 151 No. 152
SERIES DATE
RIGHT WRONG RIGHT WRONG

1 Sept. 29 6 4 4 6 2 30 5 5 6 6 3 Oct. 1 3 7 4 6 4 2 5 5 3 7 5 3 3 7 5 5 6 4 6 4 5 5 7 5 5 5 5 5 8 6 —— 3 7 9 7 —— 6 4 10 8 —— 4 6

Averages 4.7 5.3 4.5 5.5

The account of my color vision experiments is finished. If it be objected that other than visual conditions may account for whatever measure of discriminating ability, apart from brightness discrimination, appears in some of the series, the results of the series of Table 29, in which all conceivable visual means of discrimination were purposely excluded, and those of the several check tests which have been described from time to time in the foregoing account, should furnish a satisfactory and definite answer. I am satisfied that whatever discrimination occurred was due to vision; whether we are justified in calling it color vision is quite another question.

I conclude from my experimental study of vision that although the dancer does not possess a color sense like ours, it probably discriminates the colors of the red end of the spectrum from those of other regions by difference in the stimulating value of light of different wave lengths, that such specific stimulating value is radically different in nature from the value of different wave lengths for the human eye, and that the red of the spectrum has a very low stimulating value for the dancer. In the light of these experiments we may safely conclude that many, if not most, of the tests of color vision in animals which have been made heretofore by other investigators have failed to touch the real problem because the possibility of brightness discrimination was not excluded.

Under the direction of Professor G. H. Parker, Doctor Karl Waugh has examined the structure of the retina of the dancing mouse for me, with the result that only a single type of retinal element was discovered. Apparently the animals possess rod-like cells, but nothing closely similar to the cones of the typical mammalian retina. This is of peculiar interest and importance in connection with the results which I have reported in the foregoing pages, because the rods are supposed to have to do with brightness or luminosity vision and the cones with color vision. In fact, it is usually supposed that the absence of cones in the mammalian retina indicates the lack of color vision. That this inference of functional facts from structural conditions is correct I am by no means certain, but at any rate all of the experiments which I have made to determine the visual ability of the dancer go to show that color vision, if it exists at all, is extremely poor. It is gratifying indeed to learn, after such a study of behavior as has just been described, that the structural conditions, so far as we are able to judge at present, justify the conclusions which have been drawn.

CHAPTER XI

THE ROLE OF SIGHT IN THE DAILY LIFE OF THE DANCER

Darting hither and thither in its cage, whirling rapidly, now to the left, now to the right, running in circles, passing through holes in the nest box quickly and neatly, the dancer, it would seem, must have excellent sight. But careful observation of its behavior modifies this inference. For it appears that a pair of mice dancing together, or near one another, sometimes collide, and that it is only those holes with which the animal is familiar that are entered skillfully. In fact, the longer one observes the behavior of the dancer under natural conditions, the more he comes to believe in the importance of touch, and motor tendencies. Sight, which at first appears to be the chief guiding sense, comes to take a secondary place. In this chapter it is my purpose to show by means of simple experiments what part sight plays in the dancer's life of habit formation.

The evidence on this subject has been obtained from four sources: (1) observation of the behavior of dancers in their cages; (2) observation of their behavior when blinded; (3) observation of their behavior in a great variety of discrimination experiments, many of which have already been described; and (4) observation of their behavior in labyrinth experiments which were especially planned to exhibit the importance of the several kinds of vision which the dancer might be supposed to possess. The evidence from the first three of these sources may be presented summarily, for much of it has already appeared in earlier chapters. That from the fourth source will constitute the bulk of the material of this chapter.

My observation of the behavior of the mice has furnished conclusive evidence of their ability to see moving objects. But that they do not see very distinctly, and that they do not have accurate perception of the form of objects, are conclusions which are supported by observations that I have made under both natural and experimental conditions. In Chapters VII, VIII, IX, and X, I have presented an abundance of evidence of brightness vision and, in addition, indications of a specific sensitiveness to wave length which may be said to correspond to our color vision. It is noteworthy, however, that all of the experimental proofs of visual ability were obtained as the result of long periods of training. Seldom, indeed, in my experience with them, have the dancers under natural conditions exhibited forms of activity which were unquestionably guided by vision.

It is claimed by those who have experimented with blinded dancers that the loss of sight decreases the amount and rapidity of movement, and the ability of the animals to avoid obstacles.

By means of the discrimination method previously used in the preliminary experiments on color vision, a full description of which may be found in Chapter IX, p. 133, the dancers' ability to perceive form was tested. Immediately after the two males *A* and *B* had been given the "food-box" tests, whose results appear in Table 15, they were tested in the same apparatus and by the same method for their ability to discriminate a rectangular food-box from a round one. In the case of the color discrimination tests, it will be remembered that the circular tin boxes 5 cm. in diameter by 1.5 cm. in depth, one of which was covered with blue paper, the other with orange, were used. For the form discrimination tests I used instead one of the circular boxes of the dimensions given above and a rectangular box 8.5 cm. long, 5.5 cm. wide and 2.5 cm. deep. "Force" was placed in the circular box. The tests were given, in series of 20, daily.

TABLE 30

VISUAL FORM TESTS

SERIES	DATE	MOUSE A		MOUSE B	
		RIGHT (CIRCULAR BOX)	WRONG (RECTANGULAR BOX)	RIGHT (CIRCULAR BOX)	WRONG (RECTANGULAR BOX)
1	Jan. 5	10	10	9	11
2	7	12	8	13	7
3	10	6	14	10	10
4	11	7	13	10	10
5	12	9	11	10	10
6	13	11	9	11	9
7	14	13	7	9	11
8	15	10	10	11	9
9	16	10	10	11	9
10	17	11	9	9	11
11	18	11	9	12	8
12	19	12	8	10	10
13	20	10	10	12	8
14	21	10	10	8	12
15	22	10	10	10	10
Totals		152	148	155	145

The results of 15 series of these tests, as may be seen by the examination of Table 30, are about as definitely negative, so far as form discrimination is in question, as they possibly could be. From the first series to the last there is not one which justifies the inference that either of the dancers depended upon the form of the boxes in making its choice. In view of the general criticisms I have made concerning the use of hunger as a motive in experiments on animal behavior, and in view of the particular criticisms of this very method of testing the discriminating powers of the mouse, it may seem strange that space should be given to a report of these tests. I sympathize with the feeling, if any one has it, but, at the same time, I wish to call attention to the fact that almost any mammal which is capable of profiting by experience, and which, under the same conditions, could distinguish the rectangular box from the circular one, would have chosen the right box with increasing accuracy as the result of such experience. The results are important in my opinion, not because they either prove or disprove the ability of the dancer to discriminate these particular forms, the discrimination of which might fairly be expected of any animal with an image-forming eye, but because they demonstrate an important characteristic of the dancing mouse, namely, its indifference to the straightforward or direct way of doing things.

Most mammals which have been experimentally studied have proved their eagerness and ability to learn the shortest, quickest, and simplest route to food without the additional spur of punishment for wandering. With the dancer it is different. It is content to be moving; whether the movement carries it directly towards the food is of secondary importance. On its way to the food-box, no matter whether the box be slightly or strikingly different from its companion box, the dancer may go by way of the wrong box, may take a few turns, cut some figure-eights, or even spin like a top for seconds almost within vibrissa-reach of the food-box, and all this even though it be very hungry. Activity is pre-eminently important in the dancer's life.

In passing I may emphasize the importance of the fact that at no time did the brightness or color discrimination tests furnish evidence of attempts on the part of the dancers to choose by means of slight differences in the form of the cardboards or the cardboard carriers. Several times form differences, which were easily perceivable by the human subject, were introduced in order to discover whether the mice would detect them and learn to discriminate thereby instead of by the visual conditions of brightness or color. As these experiments failed to furnish evidences of form discrimination, the following special test in the discrimination box was devised.

[Illustration: FIGURE 22.—Cards used for tests of form discrimination.]

The color discrimination box of Chapter X was arranged so that the light at the entrance to each electric-box had a value of 20 candle meters, less the diminution caused by a piece of ground glass which was placed over the end of the electric-boxes to diffuse the light. The windows through which the light entered the electric-boxes were covered with pieces of black cardboard; in one of these cardboards I had cut a circular opening 4 cm. in diameter, and in the other an opening of the same area but markedly different shape. These openings are shown in Figure 22. As the mouse approached the entrance to the electric-boxes, it was confronted by these two equally illuminated areas, whose chief difference was one of form. Difference in the amount of light within the boxes was excluded so far as possible. The question which I asked was, can the dancer discriminate by means of this difference in visual form?

For the purpose of settling this point and of gaining additional knowledge of the role of vision, two individuals were tested in the discrimination box under the conditions which have just been described. During the first ten days of the experiment each of these mice, Nos. 420 and 425, was given a series of ten tests daily. At the end of this period experimentation with No. 425 had to be discontinued, and the number of daily tests given to No. 420 was increased to twenty.

Instead of taking space for the presentation of the daily records, I may state the general results of the tests. Neither of the mice learned to choose the right box by means of form discrimination. In fact, there was absolutely no sign of discrimination at any time during the tests. This result is as surprising as it is interesting. I could not at first believe that the mice were unable to perceive the difference in the lighted areas, but assumed that they were prevented from getting the outlines of the areas by the blinding effect of the light. However, decreasing the intensity of the illumination did not alter the result. According to the indications of this experiment, the dancer's ability to perceive visual form is extremely poor.

Thus far the purpose of our experiments has been to ascertain what the dancer is enabled to do by sight. Suppose we now approach the problem of the role of this sense by trying to find out what it can do without sight.

[Illustration: FIGURE 23.—Labyrinth B. *I*, entrance; *O*, exit; 1, 2, 3, doorways between alleys.]

For the investigation of this matter the labyrinth method seemed eminently suitable. The first form of labyrinth which was used in these visual tests appears in ground plan in Figure 23. It was made of 1-1/2 cm. boards. The length was 52 cm., the width 17 cm., the depth 10 cm. Each of the doorways, *I* (the entrance), 1, 2, 3, and *O* (the exit), was 5 by 5 cm. The alleys were 2-1/2 cm. wide. For this width the necessity is obvious from what has already been said of the animal's propensity to whirl on all occasions. As the mice almost never tried to climb up the walls, no cover for the labyrinth was needed. The direct route is indicated by the symbols *I*-1-2-3-*O*. If an error be defined as a choice of the wrong path as the animal progressed toward the exit, five mistakes were possible in the forward course: the first by turning to the left at the entrance; the second by failing to pass through doorway 1; the third by turning to the right after passing through doorway 1; the fourth by failing to pass through doorway 3, and the fifth by turning to the left after passing through 3. In case the mouse retraced its course, any mistakes made as it again progressed towards *O* were counted, as at first, no matter how many times it went over the same ground. Thus an individual might make the same mistake several times in the course of a single test in the labyrinth.

With this labyrinth Nos. 7, 998, 15, 16, 151, and 152 were tested. At first a record was kept of the time which elapsed from the instant the animal entered *I* to the instant it emerged at *O*, of the path which it followed, and of the number of errors which it made; but later only the number of errors was recorded.

TABLE 31

THE ROLE OF SIGHT

Labyrinth-B Experiments

		NO. 7		NO. 998	
TEST	DATE	TIME	ERRORS	TIME	ERRORS
1	June 16	66"	8	127"	19
2	16	11	0	94	12
3	16	15	2	18	3
4	16	7	0	13	2
5	16	5	0	10	1
6	18	61	15	12	3
7	18	13	3	14	4
8	18	14	5	8	1
9	18	24	9	16	2
10	18	10	1	9	1
11	19	36	13	80	17
12	19	8	3	10	1
13	19	6	1	7	1
14	19	9	1	8	0
15	19	12	2	7	0
16	20	14	1	25	0
17	20	28	3		
18	20	No efforts to escape		No efforts to escape	

TABLE 32

LABYRINTH-B EXPERIMENTS

with

Electric Shock given as Punishment for Mistakes

No. 7 No. 998
TEST DATE CONDITION ERRORS CONDITION ERRORS

1 June 29 Light 4 Light 9 2 29 Light 1 Light 3 3 29 Light 1 Light 2 4 29 Light 0 Light 0 5 29 Light 0 Light 0 6 29 Light 0 Light 0 7 29 Light 1 Light 0 8 29 Light 0 Light 0 9 29 Light 1 Darkness 0 10 29 Light 1 Light 0 11 29 Light 1 Darkness 0 12 29 Light 0 Light 0 13 29 Light 0 Light 0 14 29 Light 0 Light 0 15 29 Light 0 Light 0 16 29 Light 0 Light 0 17 29 Darkness 2 Darkness 0 18 29 Light 2 Light 0 with paper 19 29 Light 0 Light 0 20 29 Darkness 0 Light 0 with paper 21 29 Light 0 Light 0 22 29 Light 0 Darkness 0 23 29 Light 0 Odorless 0 24 June 29 Light 0 Darkness 0 25 29 Light 0 26 29 Darkness 4 27 29 Light with paper 1 28 29 Light 0 29 29 Light with paper 1 30 29 Darkness 0 31 29 Odorless 2 32 29 Darkness 4

As the results in Table 31 show, the time and number of errors rapidly diminished. Number 7, for example, made no errors in the second test. The chiefly significant fact which appeared in these preliminary experiments, however, was that the mice soon ceased to care whether they got out of the labyrinth or not. After they knew the path perfectly, they would enter the wrong passages repeatedly and wander about indefinitely. It was obvious, therefore, that the labyrinth could not be used to reveal the role of sight unless some sufficiently strong motive for continuous effort to escape from it could be discovered. Naturally I looked to the electric shock for aid.

The labyrinth of Figure 23, which for convenience in distinguishing it from several other forms to be described later I have designated as labyrinth B, was placed upon a board 90 cm. long and 30 cm. wide about which had been wound two pieces of phosphor bronze wire after the manner described on p. 94. At *O*, Figure 24, there was an opening closed by a swinging door which led into a box 40 by 24 cm. In one corner of this box was a small nest-box. The significance of this rearrangement of the labyrinth is apparent. As in the preliminary tests, the dancer was started at I, but instead of being allowed to wander about without any other result than delay in escape, it was given a shock each time it made an error. The satisfaction of escaping from the narrow bounds of the labyrinth's passages, which alone was not strong enough to impel a dancer constantly to do its best to escape, was thus supplemented by the powerful and all-controlling tendency to avoid the disagreeable stimulus which resulted from entering certain of the passages. The result of this modification of method is strikingly exhibited by the data of Table 32.

[Illustration: Figure 24.—Labyrinth B on an interrupted circuit board. *I*-1-2-3-*O*, labyrinth path; *B*, nest-box; *N*, nest; *EW*, board wound with phosphor bronze wire; *IC*, induction apparatus; *C* electric cell; *K*, key.]

This table was constructed for the purpose of exhibiting the principal features of the results obtained with labyrinth *B* in certain preliminary experiments in which the conditions were changed in various ways. Chief among the important facts which appear in the illustrative data (for Nos. 7 and 998) which are presented, are the following. The dancers readily learn the path of labyrinth B so that they can follow it quickly and with perfect accuracy. After familiarity with the direct path from entrance to exit has been gained, they become indifferent about escaping and tend to wander aimlessly. The introduction of the electric shock as punishment for the choice of the wrong passage impels them to do their best to avoid errors. The path once learned can be followed in total darkness with few or no errors. Table 32 indicates marked differences in the behavior of No. 7 and No. 998. The latter learned the path readily and was little disturbed by any of the changes in conditions. In total darkness he followed the path rapidly and accurately, as was indicated by the time of the trip and the path that he left on a sheet of smoked paper that had been placed on the floor of the labyrinth as a means of obtaining a record of the errors made. The presence of the smoked paper did not seem to interfere at all with his behavior, nor did the thorough washing of the labyrinth and the resultant removal of its odors. In the case of No. 7 the opposite was true. She did not learn the path readily, was confused by any change in conditions, had great difficulty in finding her way in darkness, made errors when the smoked paper was placed on the floor and after the odors of the labyrinth had been removed by washing. Of the six dancers which were observed in these preliminary tests, No. 7 alone gave convincing evidence of the importance of sight.

I think we may say in the light of the results of the table that such errors as appear in the darkness tests are due rather to the disturbing influence of a change in the conditions of the experiment than to the exclusion of visual data, for as many or more errors were sometimes caused simply by changing the position of the labyrinth, placing smoked paper on the floor, or by introducing a new odor at some point. The exclusion of the possibility of guidance by smell and touch did not seriously interfere with the animal's ability to follow the path.

The results which have just been considered seemed to be of sufficient interest and importance to justify the further use of the labyrinth method in the investigation of the role of vision. A series of experiments with labyrinth B was therefore planned so that the importance of sight, touch, and smell in connection with this form of habit should be more satisfactorily exhibited. Does the dancer follow the path by sight, touch, smell, by all, or by no one of them?

This series of tests with labyrinth B, whose several purposes may best be explained in connection with the various kinds of tests enumerated below, consisted of:

I. A preliminary test in which the dancer was permitted to wander about in the labyrinth, without being shocked, until it finally escaped to the nest-box by way of the exit. Thus the animal was given an opportunity to discover that escape from the maze was possible.

II. This was immediately followed by a series of tests at the rate of about one per minute, with an electric shock as punishment for every mistake. This was continued without interruption until the path had been followed without error five times in succession.

III. The labyrinth was now moved about 3 cm. to one side so that it covered a new floor area, and a test was given for the purpose of ascertaining whether the mouse had been following a trail on the floor.

IV. Tests with smoked paper on the floor were now alternated with tests in which the floor was plain. The alternation was rendered necessary by the fact that the paper was laid over the electric wires and therefore prevented the punishment of mistakes. The purpose of these tests was to discover whether the smoked paper, which was an essential condition for the next test, was itself a disturbing condition. These tests were continued until the animal had followed the path correctly, despite the smoked paper, twice in succession.

V. The electric lights were now turned out and tests were given in total darkness, with smoked paper on the floor as a means of obtaining a record of the number of errors. These tests were continued until the path had been followed once correctly.

VI. The labyrinth was now thoroughly washed with warm water, to which a little kerosene had been added, and quickly dried over a steam radiator. This usually necessitated a delay of about five minutes. As soon as the labyrinth was dry, tests were given to discover whether the odors of the various passages had been serving as important guiding conditions. These tests were continued until the path had been followed once without error.

VII. A final test in darkness completed the series.

As it was not possible for the observer to watch the animal and thus to count the number of mistakes which it made in total darkness, the simple method of placing a piece of smoked paper on the floor of the labyrinth was used. The mouse left a graphic record of its path on the paper and from this the number of errors could be ascertained. In the tests now to be described the smoked paper was placed upon the electric wires, but later a form of electric labyrinth was devised in which it was underneath and therefore did not interfere with the electric shock.

The above series of tests was given under the same external conditions in a dark-room to six pairs of dancers. In all cases, two individuals, a male and a female, which had been kept in the same cage, were experimented with at the same time, *i.e.* one was permitted to rest in the nest-box while the other was being put through a test. This was done in order that the comparison of the results for males and females should be perfectly fair.

The detailed results of this long series of tests may be presented for only two individuals, Nos. 210 and 215, Table 33. In this table lines separate the results of the seven different kinds of tests.

TABLE 33

THE ROLE OF SIGHT, TOUCH, AND SMELL IN LABYRINTH EXPERIMENTS

No. 210 No. 215

TEST CONDITION ERRORS CONDITION ERRORS

I. 1 No shock 9 I. No shock 2

II. 2 Shock 5 II. Shock 3 3 Shock 4 Shock 1 4 Shock 2 Shock 0 5 Shock 3 Shock 0 6 Shock 0 Shock 0 7 Shock 0 Shock 0 8 Shock 0 Shock 0

9 Shock 0 III. Labyrinth 0 moved

10 Shock 0 IV. Paper on floor 4

III. 11 Labyrinth 0 No paper (shock) 0
moved

IV. 12 Paper on 0 0
floor
13 No paper 0 No paper 0
(shock)
14 Paper 1 Paper 1

15 No paper 0 No paper 0
16 Paper 7 Paper 4
17 No paper 0 No paper 0
18 Paper 0 Paper 0
19 No paper 0 No paper 0
20 Paper 4 Paper 0
21 No paper 0 No paper 0
22 Paper 2 V. Darkness 0
23 No paper 2 VI. Labyrinth 2
24 Paper 1 washed 0
25 No paper 0 VII. Darkness 2
26 Paper 0
27 No paper 0
28 Paper 0
29 No paper 0
V. 30 Darkness 0
VI. 31 Labyrinth 2
washed
32 0
VII. 33 Darkness 0

The average results for the twelve individuals (six of each sex) which were subjected to the tests, I have arranged in Table 34. The Roman numerals at the top of the table designate the seven groups of tests, and the figures under each, the numerical results of the tests. I may explain and comment upon the averages of the several columns of this table in turn.

Column I gives the number of errors made in the preliminary test. Curiously enough, the males made many more errors than the females.

For the second group of tests (II) two results have been tabulated: the number of the first correct test, and the total number of tests before the path was followed correctly five times in succession. The first correct trip came usually after not more than five or six tests, but five successive correct trips demanded on the average at least fourteen training tests.

Destruction of the floor path by movement of the labyrinth to one side, without changing its relations to the points of the compass, disturbed the mice very little. Only four of the twelve individuals made any mistakes as a result of the change in the tactual conditions, and the average error as it appears in Column III is only .3.

TABLE 34

ROLE OF SIGHT, TOUCH, AND SMELL IN LABYRINTH EXPERIMENTS

II. IV. TRAINING TESTS SMOKED I. NO OF TESTS BEFORE III. PAPER ON MALES PRELIMINARY CORRECT LABYRINTH FLOOR TEST. ______________________ MOVED. NO OF TIMES ERRORS FIRST TIME FIVE TIMES ERRORS BEFORE COR- RECT TWICE

210 9 5 9 0 9 212 2 3 8 1 3 214 6 10 28 0 22 220 25 4 8 0 14 410 11 6 20 0 10 420 14 6 14 1 7

AVERAGES 11.2 5.7 14.5 .3 10.8

FEMALES

211 16 6 10 1 5 213 7 5 14 1 21 215 2 3 7 0 6 225 14 6 18 0 14 415 6 6 13 0 3 425 10 7 13 0 8

AVERAGES 9.2 5.5 12.5 .3 9.5

V. DARKNESS VI. MALES LABYRINTH VII. ERRORS IN NO. OF TESTS WASHED. DARKNESS. FIRST TEST BEFORE COR'CT ERRORS ERRORS

210 0 1 2 0 212 2 2 0 0 214 0 1 — 0 220 2 4 2 0 410 1 3 2 1 420 2 4 1 4

Averages 1.2 2.5 1.2 0.8

FEMALES

211 2 2 0 0 213 2 2 — 3 215 0 1 2 2 225 3 2 0 0 415 1 3 2 1 425 1 7 0 0

Averages 1.5 2.8 0.7 1.0

That covering the floor with smoked paper forced the mice to relearn the path, in large measure, is evident from the results of Column IV. An average of ten tests was necessary to enable the mice to follow the path correctly. It is almost certain, however, that the interference with the perfectly formed labyrinth habit which this change in the condition of the floor caused was not due to the removal of important tactual sense data.

As Column V shows, the number of errors in total darkness is very small. Some individuals gave no sign of being disturbed by the absence of visual guidance, others at first seemed confused. I have given in the table the number of errors in the first darkness test and the number of the first test in which no mistakes occurred.

No more disturbance of the dancer's ability to follow the path which it had learned resulted from washing the labyrinth thoroughly than from darkening the room. Indeed it is clear from Column VI that the path was not followed by the use of smell. However, the test in darkness, after the odor of the box had been removed, proved conclusively that in most cases the mice could follow the path correctly without visual or olfactory guidance.

The behavior of 18 individuals as it was observed in labyrinth B makes perfectly evident three important facts, (1) In following the path which it has learned, the dancer in most instances is not guided to any considerable extent by a trail (odor or touch) which has been formed by its previous journeys over the route; (2) sight is quite unnecessary for the easy and perfect execution of the labyrinth habit, for even those individuals which are at first confused by the darkening of the experiment room are able after a few tests to follow the path correctly; (3) and, finally, smell, which according to current opinion is the chiefly important sense of mice and rats, is not needful for the performance of this habitual act.

At this point we may very fittingly ask, what sense data are necessary for the guidance of the series of acts which constitutes the labyrinth habit? I answer, probably none. A habit once formed, the senses have done their part; henceforth it is a motor process, whose initiation is conditioned by the activity of a receptive organ (at times a sense receptor), but whose form is not necessarily dependent upon immediate impressions from eye, nose, vibrissae, or even from internal receptors. These are statements of my opinion; whether they express the truth, either wholly or in part, only further experimentation can decide.

In considering the results of these labyrinth tests it is important that we distinguish clearly those which have to do with the conditions of habit formation from those which instead have to do with the conditions of habit performance. Sense data which are absolutely necessary for the learning of a labyrinth path may be of little or no importance for the execution of the act of following the path after the learning process has been completed. Thus far in connection with the labyrinth tests we have discussed only the relations of sight, touch, and smell to what I have called habit performance. We may now ask what part these senses play in the formation of a labyrinth habit.

A very definite answer to this question is furnished by observation of the behavior of the dancers in the tests. Most of them continuously made use of their eyes, their noses, and their vibrissae. Some individuals used one form of receptive organ almost exclusively. I frequently noticed that those individuals which touched and smelled of the labyrinth passages most carefully gave least evidence of the use of sight. It is safe to say, then, that under ordinary conditions habit formation in the dancer is conditioned by the use of sight, touch, and smell, but that these senses are of extremely different degrees of importance in different individuals. And further, that, although in the case of some individuals the loss of sight would not noticeably delay habit formation, in the case of others it would seriously interfere with the process. When deprived of one sense, the dancer depends upon its remaining channels of communication with environment. Indeed there are many reasons for inferring that if deprived of sight, touch, and smell it would still be able to learn a labyrinth path; and there are reasonable grounds for the belief that a habit once formed can be executed in the absence of all special sense data. Apparently the various receptive organs of the body furnish the dancer with impressions which serve as guides to action and facilitate habit formation, although they are not necessary for habit performance.

The reader may wonder why I have not carried out systematic experiments to determine accurately and quantitatively the part which each sense plays in the formation of a labyrinth habit instead of basing my inferences upon incidental observation of the behavior of the dancers. The reason is simply this: the number and variety of experiments which were suggested by the several directions in which this investigation developed rendered the performance of all of them impossible. I have chosen to devote my time to other lines of experimentation because a very thorough study of the conditions of habit formation has recently been made by Doctor Watson.[1]

[Footnote 1: Watson, J. B., *Psychological Review*, Monograph Supplement, Vol. 8, No. 2, 1907.]

What is the role of sight in the dancing mouse? How shall we answer the question? The evidence which has been obtained in the course of my study of the animal indicates that brightness vision is fairly acute, that color vision is poor, that although form is not clearly perceived, movement is readily perceived. My observations under natural conditions justify the conclusion that sight is not of very great importance in the daily life of the dancer, and my observations under experimental conditions strongly suggest the further conclusion that movement and changes in brightness are the only visual conditions which to any considerable extent control the activity of the animal.

CHAPTER XII

EDUCABILITY: METHODS OF LEARNING

Nearly all of the experiments described in earlier chapters have revealed facts concerning the educability of the dancer. In order to supplement the knowledge of this subject thus incidentally gained and to discover the principles of educability, the specially devised experiments whose results appear in this and succeeding chapters were arranged and carried out with a large number of mice. In the work on the modifiability of behavior I have attempted to determine (1) by what methods the dancer is capable of profiting by experience, (2) the degree of rapidity of learning, (3) the permanency of changes wrought in behavior, (4) the effect of one kind of training upon others, (5) the relation of re-training to training, and (6) the relation of all these matters to age, sex, and individuality.

As it is obvious that knowledge of these subjects is a necessary condition for the intelligent appreciation of the capacities of an animal, as well as of the choice of methods by which it may be trained advantageously, perhaps it is not too much to expect that this investigation of the nature and conditions of educability in the dancing mouse may give us some new insight into the significance of certain aspects of human education and may serve to suggest ways in which we may measure and increase the efficiency of our educational methods.

Merely for the sake of convenience of description I shall classify the methods which have been employed as problem methods, labyrinth methods, and discrimination methods. That these names are not wholly appropriate is suggested by the fact that discrimination necessarily occurs in connection with each of them. As problem methods we may designate those tests of initiative and modifiability which involve the opening of doors by pushing or pulling them, and the climbing of an inclined ladder. An example of the labyrinth method has been presented in Chapter XI. The name discrimination method I have applied to those tests which involve the choice of one of two visual, tactual, or olfactory conditions. The white-black discrimination tests, for example, served to reveal the rapidity and permanency of learning as well as the presence of brightness vision.

In the case of most mammals whose educability has been studied experimentally, problem methods have proved to be excellent tests of docility and initiative. The cat, the raccoon, the monkey, in their attempts to obtain food, learn to pull strings, turn buttons, press latches, slide bolts, pull plugs, step on levers. The dancer does none of these things readily. Are we therefore to infer that it is less intelligent, that it is less docile, than the cat, the raccoon, or the monkey? Not necessarily, for it is possible that these methods do not suit the capacity of the animal. As a matter of fact, all of the tests which are now to be described in their relation to the educability of the dancer bear witness to the importance of the selection of methods in the light of the motor equipment and the habits of the animal which is to be tested. Judged by ordinary standards, on the basis of results which it yields in problem and labyrinth tests, the dancer is extremely stupid. But that this conclusion is not justified is apparent when it is judged in the light of tests which are especially adapted to its peculiarities.

Problems which are easy for other mammals because of their energetic and persistent efforts to secure food in any way which their motor capacity makes possible are useless as tests of the dancer's abilities, because it is not accustomed to obtain its food as the result of strenuous and varied activities. There are problems and problems; a condition or situation which presents a problem to one organism may utterly lack interest for an organism of different structure and behavior. What is a problem test in the case of the cat or even of the common mouse, is not necessarily a problem for the dancer. Similarly, in connection with the labyrinth method, it is clear that the value of the test depends upon the desire of the organism to escape from the maze. The cat, the rat, the tortoise do their best to escape; the dancer is indifferent. Clearly, then, methods of training should be chosen on the basis of a knowledge of the characteristics of the animal whose educability is to be investigated.

The simplest possible test of the intelligence of the dancer which I could devise was the following. Beside the cage in which the mice were kept I placed a wooden box 26 cm. long, 23 cm. wide, and 12 cm. deep. Neither this box nor the cage was covered, for the animals did not attempt to climb out. As a way of passing from one of these boxes to the other I arranged a ladder made of wire fly-screen netting. This ladder was about 8 cm. broad and it extended from the middle of one side of the wooden box upward at an angle of about 30° to the edge of the box and then descended at the same angle into the cage.

A dancer when taken from the nest-box and placed in the wooden box could return to its cage and thus find warmth, food, and company by climbing the ladder. It was my aim to determine, by means of this apparatus, whether the dancers can learn such a simple way of escape and whether they learn by watching one another. As it turned out, a third value belonged to the tests, in that they were used also to test the influence of putting the mice through the act.

In the first experiment three dancers, Nos. 1000, 2, and 6, were together placed in the wooden box. At the end of 15 minutes not one of them had succeeded in returning to the cage. They were then driven to the bottom of the ladder and started upward by the experimenter; with this assistance all escaped to the nest-box. At the expiration of 5 minutes they were again placed in the wooden box, whence the chilly temperature (about 60° F.) and the lack of food made them eager to return to their cage. No attempt to climb up the ladder was made by any of them within 15 minutes, so the experimenter directed them to the ladder and started them upward as in the first test. This completed the experiment for the day. The following day two tests were given in the same way. In the second of these tests, that is, on its fourth trial, No. 1000 climbed over of his own initiative in 5 minutes. The others had to be assisted as formerly. On the third day No. 1000 found his way back to the nest-box quickly and fairly directly, but neither No. 2 or No. 6 climbed of its own initiative in the first test. When their movements were restricted to the region of the box about the base of the ladder, both of them returned to the cage quickly. And on the second test of the third day all the mice climbed the ladder directly.

In Table 35 I have given the time required for escape in the case of 40 tests which were given to these 3 individuals at the rate of 2 tests per day.

When the time exceeded 15 minutes the mice were helped out by the experimenter; a record of 15 minutes, therefore, indicates failure. Naturally enough the motives for escape were not sufficiently strong or constant to bring about the most rapid learning of which the dancer is capable. Sometimes they would remain in the wooden box washing themselves for several minutes before attempting to find a way of escape. On this account I made it a rule to begin the time record with the appearance of active running about. The daily average time of escape as indicated in the table does not decrease regularly and rapidly. On the fourth day, which was the first on which all three of the dancers returned to the cage by way of the ladder of their own initiative in both tests, the average is 214 seconds. In contrast with this, on the twentieth day the time was only 5 seconds. It is quite evident that the dancers had learned to climb the ladder.

At the end of the twentieth day the experiment was discontinued with Nos. 2 and 6, and after two weeks they were given memory tests, which showed that they remembered perfectly the ladder-climbing act, for when placed in the wooden box, with Nos. 4 and 5 as controls, they returned to the cage by way of the ladder immediately and directly.

TABLE 35

LADDER CLIMBING TEST

Time in Minutes and Seconds

No. of Date No. 1000 No. 2 No. 6 Average Daily Av.
Exp. 1905 For All For All

1 Nov. 14 15' 15' 15' — —
2 15' 15' 15' — —

3 15 15' 15' 15' — —
4 300" 15' 15' — —

5 16 480" 15' 15' — —
6 180" 300" 420" 300" 300"

7 17 450" 240" 540" 410"
8 20" 15" 18" 18" 214"

9 18 90" 180" 135" 135"
10 135" 105" 165" 135" 135"

11 19 480" 240" 330" 350"
12 30" 120" 90" 80" 143"

13 20 360" 75" 120" 185"
14 5" 6" 8" 6" 95"

15 21 105" 450" 120" 192"
16 8" 80" 20" 54" 123"

17 22 255" 300" 180" 245"
18 10" 30" 270" 103" 174"

19 23 300" 660" 450" 470"
20 90" 120" 150" 120" 295"

21 24 240" 125" 225" 197"
22 4" 6" 168" 59" 128"

23 Nov. 25 305" 85" 130" 173"
24 5" 6" 118" 43" 108"

25 26 3" 8" 44" 18"
26 19" 1" 176" 98" 58"

27 27 150" 79" 269" 166"
28 26" 3" 31" 20" 93"

29 28 214" 18" 267" 166"
30 40" 3" 4" 16" 91"

31 29 130" 45" 250" 142"
32 12" 3" 25" 13" 77"

33 Dec. 2 61" 35" 44" 47"
34 50" 5" 24" 26" 36"

35 3 66" 18" 2" 29"
36 8" 5" 10" 8" 19"

37 4 9" 4" 3" 5"
38 10" 5" 6" 7" 6"

39 5 5" 3" 5" 4"
40 10" 4" 3" 6" 5"

One of the most interesting and important features of the behavior of the dancer in the ladder experiment was a halt at a certain point on the ladder. It occurred just at the edge of the wooden box at the point where the ladder took a horizontal position, and led over into the cage. Every individual from the first test to the last made this halt. Although from the point of view of the experimenter the act was valueless, it may have originated as an attempt to find a way to escape from the uncomfortable position in which the animal found itself on reaching the top of the ladder. Its persistence after a way of escape had been found is an indication of the nature of habit. Day after day the halt became shorter until finally it was little more than a pause and a turn of the head toward one side of the ladder. I think we may say that in this act we have evidence of the persistence of a particular resolution of physiological states which is neither advantageous nor disadvantageous to the organism. Had the act resulted in any gain, it would have become more marked and elaborate; had it resulted in injury or discomfort, it would have disappeared entirely. I have observed the same kind of behavior in the frog and in other animals. What the animal begins to do it persists in unless the act is positively harmful or conflicts with some beneficial activity. The only explanation of certain features of behavior is to be found in the conditions of their original occurrence. They persist by sheer force of conservatism. They have value only in the light of the circumstances under which they first appeared. Although this is merely a fact of habit formation, it suggests that many of the problems which have puzzled students of behavior for ages may be solved by a study of the history of activity.

That there are marked individual differences in intelligence in the dancing mice is apparent from the results of the ladder-climbing experiment. No. 1000 learned to climb quickly, and largely by his own initiative; Nos. 2 and

6, on the contrary, learned only by reason of tuition (being put through the required act by the experimenter). It occurred to me that this experiment, since it was difficult for some individuals and easy for others, might be used to advantage as a test of imitation. If a dancer which knows how to escape to the cage by way of the ladder be placed in the wooden box with one which, despite abundant opportunity, has proved unable to form the habit on his own initiative, will the latter profit by the activity of the former and thus learn the method of escape?

On November 20, Nos. 4 and 5 were placed in the wooden box and left there for half an hour. As they had failed to escape at the end of this interval, they were taken out of the box by the experimenter and returned to the nest-box. November 21 and 22 this test of their ability to learn to climb the ladder was repeated with the same result. On November 23 they were placed in the box with the three mice which had previously been trained to climb the ladder. The latter escaped at once. Apparently the attention of Nos. 4 and 5 was drawn to the ladder by the disappearance of their companions, for they approached its foot and No. 5 climbed up a short distance. Neither succeeded in escaping, however, and they made no further efforts that day. On the 24th, and daily thereafter until the 29th, these two dancers were placed in the box for half an hour, with negative results. At the end of the half hour on the 29th, Nos. 2 and 6 were placed in the box and permitted to go back and forth from one box to the other repeatedly within sight of Nos. 4 and 5. The latter made no attempts to follow them, although at times they seemed to be watching their movements as they ascended the ladder.

To render the results of this test of imitation still more conclusive No. 5 was given further opportunity to learn from No. 1000. Beginning December 2, the following method of experimentation was employed with these two individuals. They were placed in the wooden box together. No. 1000 usually climbed out almost immediately. Sometimes No. 5 apparently saw him disappear up the ladder; sometimes she paid no attention whatever either to the presence or absence of her companion. After he had been in the nest-box for a few seconds, No. 1000 was returned to the wooden box by the experimenter and again permitted to climb out for the benefit of No. 5. This mode of procedure was kept up until No. 1000 had made from three to ten trips. No. 5 was left in the box for half an hour each day. This test was repeated on 18 days within a period of 3 weeks. No. 5 showed no signs of an imitative tendency, and she did not learn to climb the ladder.

To this evidence of a lack of an imitative tendency in the dancer I may here add the results of my observations in other experiments. In the discrimination tests and in the labyrinth tests I purposely so arranged conditions, in certain instances, that one individual should have an opportunity to imitate another. In no case did this occur. Seldom indeed did the animals so much as follow one another with any considerable degree of persistence. They did not profit by one another's acts.

Excellent evidence in support of this conclusion was furnished by the behavior of the mice in the discrimination experiments. Some individuals learned to pull as well as to push the swinging wire doors of the apparatus and were thus enabled to pass through the doorways in either direction; other individuals learned only to pass through in the direction in which the doors could be pushed open. Naturally I was interested to discover whether those which knew only the trick of opening the doors by pushing would learn to pull the doors or would be stimulated to try by seeing other individuals do so. At first I arranged special tests of imitation in the discrimination box; later I observed the influence of the behavior of one mouse upon that of its companion in connection with visual discrimination experiments. This was made possible by the fact that usually a pair of individuals was placed in the discrimination box and the tests given alternately to the male and to the female. Both individuals had the freedom of the nest-box and each frequently saw the other pass through the doorway between the nest-box, *A*, and the entrance chamber, *B* (Figure 14), either from *A* to *B* by pushing the swing door or from *B* to *A* by pulling the door.

Although abundant opportunity for imitation in connection with the opening of the doors in the discrimination box was given to twenty-five individuals, I obtained no evidence of ability to learn by imitation. The dancers did not watch the acts which were performed by their companions, and in most instances they did not attempt to follow a mate from nest-box to entrance chamber.

These problem tests, simple as they are, have revealed two important facts concerning the educability of the dancer. First, that it does not learn by imitation to any considerable extent, and, second, that it is aided by being put through an act. Our general conclusion from the results of the experiments which have been described in this chapter, if any general conclusion is to be drawn thus prematurely, must be that the dancing mouse in its methods of learning differs markedly from other mice and from rats.

CHAPTER XIII

HABIT FORMATION: THE LABYRINTH HABIT

The problem method, of which the ladder and door-opening tests of the preceding chapter are examples, has yielded interesting results concerning the individual initiative, ingenuity, motor ability, and ways of learning of the dancer; but it has not furnished us with accurate measurements of the rapidity of learning or of the permanency of the effects of training. In this chapter I shall therefore present the results of labyrinth experiments which were planned as means of measuring the intelligence of the dancer.

The four labyrinths which have been used in the investigation may be designated as *A, B, C,* and *D*. They differ from one another in the character of their errors, as well as in the number of wrong choices of a path which the animal might make on its way from entrance to exit. In the use of the labyrinth method, as in the case of the discrimination method of earlier chapters, the steps by which a satisfactory form of labyrinth for testing the dancer was discovered are quite as interesting and important for those who have an intelligent appreciation of the problems and methods of animal psychology as are the particular results which were obtained. For this reason, I shall describe the various forms of labyrinth in the order in which they were used, whether they proved satisfactory or not. At the outset of this part of my investigation, it was my purpose to compare directly the capacity for habit formation in the dancer with that of the common mouse. This proved impracticable because the same labyrinth is not suited to the motor tendencies of both kinds of mice.

[Illustration: FIGURE 25.—Labyrinth A. *I*. entrance; *O*, exit; 1, 2, 3, 4, blind alleys.]

The first of the four labyrinths, A, appears in ground plan in Figure 25. It was constructed of wood, as were the other labyrinths also, and measured 60 cm. in length and width, and 10 cm. in depth. The outside alleys were 5 cm. wide. In the figure, *I* marks the starting point or entrance to the maze, and *O* the exit through which the mouse was permitted to pass into its nest-box. Any turn in the wrong direction which the animal made in its progress from entrance to exit was recorded as an error. The four errors, exclusive of the mistake of turning back, which were possible in this labyrinth, are indicated in the figure by the numerals 1, 2, 3, and 4. By retracing its steps a mouse might repeat any one or all of these errors, and add to them the error of turning back.

In the experiments a mouse was permitted to enter the maze from a small box which had been placed by the experimenter at *I*, and an accurate record was kept of the number of errors which it made in finding its way from entrance to exit, and of the time occupied. Each of five dancers was given 31 tests in this labyrinth. The number of tests per day varied, as is indicated in Table 36, from 1 to 4. The results of the tests, so far as errors and times are in question, appear in the table. *T* at the head of a column is an abbreviation for time, *E* for errors.

The dancers did not learn to escape from this labyrinth easily and quickly. In fact, the average time of the thirty-first test (198") is considerably longer than that of the first (130"). The number of errors decreased, it is true, but even for the last test it was 6.6 as compared with only a little more than twice that number for the first test. The last column of the table furnishes convincing proof of the truth of the statement that the animals did not acquire a perfect labyrinth-A habit. Was this due to inability to learn so complex a path, or to the fact that the method is not adapted to their nature? Observation of the behavior of the mice in the experiments enables me to say with certainty that there was no motive for escape sufficiently strong to establish a habit of following the direct path. Often, especially after a few experiences in the maze, a dancer would wander back and forth in the alleys and central courts, dancing much of the time and apparently exploring its surroundings instead of persistently trying to escape. This behavior, and the time and error results of the accompanying table, lead me to conclude that the labyrinth method, as it has been employed in the study of the intelligence of several other mammals, is not a satisfactory test of the ability of the dancer to profit by experience. That the fault is not in the labyrinth itself is proved by the results which I obtained with common mice.

TABLE 36

RESULTS OF LABYRINTH A TESTS WITH DANCERS

TEST	DATE 1905	No. 1000		No. 2		No. 6		No. 4		No. 5		AVERAGE FOR ALL	
		T	E	T	E	T	E	T	E	T	E	T	E
1	Nov 23	130"	14	100"	8	170"	13	60"	6	190"	26	130"	13.4
2	24	140	19	78	7	60	8	149	6	211	25	128	13.0
3	25	392	31	87	1	98	5	185	13	120	9	176	11.8
4	26	448	38	38	3	47	2	50	3	121	12	141	11.3
5	27	142	8	21	2	27	3	27	2	17	1	47	3.2
6	28	45	2	61	7	63	5	102	8	33	4	61	5.2
7	29	303	17	64	7	36	3	42	2	57	4	100	6.6

8 30 222 15 26 2 37 5 42 3 7 0 67 5.0
9 Dec 1 185 9 36 5 48 3 63 3 94 8 85 5.6
10 2 52 2 71 4 19 0 196 5 95 11 87 4.4
11 3 180 8 32 2 107 4 52 3 38 4 82 4.2
12 4 310 10 133 11 65 3 242 6 125 6 175 7.2
13 4 153 9 335 55 130 10 195 15 154 18 193 21.4
14 5 330 7 69 2 42 2 201 6 130 10 154 5.4
15 5 287 7 34 4 61 4 136 7 25 2 109 4.8
16 5 455 15 65 4 25 0 110 8 160 15 183 8.4
17 6 120 15 280 9 33 0 168 4 39 2 128 6.0
18 6 120 4 164 10 81 4 101 5 85 4 110 5.4
19 6 132 12 78 7 110 6 40 2 151 12 102 7.8
20 7 258 10 223 16 33 1 92 5 37 1 129 6.6
21 7 110 7 23 3 44 4 20 4 305 23 100 8.2
22 7 100 4 60 8 167 15 44 7 58 4 86 7.6
23 8 43 1 179 7 356 6 34 3 65 3 135 4.0
24 8 92 5 56 5 42 3 17 1 23 1 46 3.0
25 9 85 5 114 3 62 3 129 8 31 0 84 3.8
26 9 30 2 36 4 109 15 12 1 34 2 44 4.8
27 9 69 5 40 4 85 6 36 3 16 1 49 3.8
28 10 169 7 80 3 28 0 142 5 35 2 89 3.4
29 10 155 5 266 8 91 5 27 0 37 2 115 4.0
30 10 29 1 25 2 124 14 83 6 111 12 74 7.0
31 10 465 6 208 8 95 3 65 3 159 13 198 6.6

On the basis of two tests per day, two common mice, a white one and a gray one, quickly learned to escape from labyrinth *A* by the shortest path. The time of escape for the gray individual (Table 37) decreased from 180" in the first test to 21" in the tenth, and the number of errors from 6 to 1. Similarly in the case of the white individual, the time decreased from 122" to 8", and the errors from 5 to 1. A fraction of the number of tests to which the dancer had been subjected sufficed to establish a habit of escape in the common mouse. It is evident, therefore, that the dancer differs radically from the common mouse in its behavior in a maze, and it is also clear that the labyrinth method, if it is to be used to advantage, must be adapted to the motor tendencies of the animal which is to be tested.

TABLE 37

RESULTS OF LABYRINTH A TESTS WITH COMMON MICE

TEST	GREY MOUSE T	GREY MOUSE E	WHITE MOUSE T	WHITE MOUSE E
1	180"	6	122"	5
2	26	2	80	6
3	37	1	56	4
4	18	0	27	1
5	68	2	33	2
6	10	1	19	1
7	11	1	17	1
8	13	1	17	1
9	10	0	8	1
10	21	1	8	1

The behavior of the dancer made obvious two defects in labyrinth A. Its passages are so large that the mouse is constantly tempted to dance, and it lacks the basis for a strong and constant motive of escape by the direct path. To obviate these shortcomings labyrinth B was constructed, as is shown in Figures 23 and 24, with very narrow passages, and a floor which was covered with the wires of an interrupted electric circuit so that errors might be punished. The length of this labyrinth was 52 cm. and the passages were 2.5 cm. wide and 10 cm. deep. Dancing in these narrow alleys was practically impossible, for the mice could barely turn around in them. In the case of all except the common mice and two dancers, a depth of 10 cm. was sufficient to keep the animals in the maze without the use of a cover.

As an account of the behavior of the dancer in labyrinth B has already been given in Chapter XI, I may now state the general results of the experiments. In all, thirty individuals were trained in this labyrinth. Each individual was given tests at the rate of one per minute until it had succeeded in following the correct path five times in succession. The weak electric shock, which was given as a punishment for mistakes, provided an activity-impelling motive for escape to the nest-box.

An idea of the extreme individual difference in the rapidity with which the labyrinth-B path was learned by these dancers may be obtained by an examination of Table 38, from which it appears that the smallest number of training tests necessary for a successful or errorless trip through the maze was one and the largest number fourteen. It is to be remembered that each mouse was given an opportunity to pass through the labyrinth once without punishment for errors, and thus to discover, before the training tests were begun, that a way of escape existed. This first test we may designate as the preliminary trial. Table 38 further indicates that the females acquired the labyrinth habit more quickly than did the males.

TABLE 38

RESULTS OF LABYRINTH-B EXPERIMENTS, WITH TWENTY DANCERS

MALES			FEMALES		
NO. OF MOUSE	**NO. OF FIRST CORRECT TEST**	**NO. OF LAST OF FIVE CORRECT TESTS**	**NO. OF MOUSE**	**NO. OF FIRST CORRECT TEST**	**NO. OF LAST OF FIVE CORRECT TESTS**
76	8	14	75	4	15
78	5	20	77	7	11
86	13	22	87	12	22
58	2	14	49	1	5
50	6	23	57	3	20
60	13	37	59	14	28
410	6	20	415	4	13
220	4	8	225	6	18
212	3	7	211	6	10
214	10	28	213	5	14
AV.	7.0	19.3	AV.	6.2	15.6

A graphic representation of certain of the important features of the process of formation of the labyrinth-B habit is furnished by Figure 26 in which the solid line is the curve of learning for the ten males of Table 38, and the broken line for the ten females. These two curves were plotted from the number of errors made in the preliminary trial (P in the figure) and in each of the subsequent tests up to the sixteenth. In the case of both the males and the females, for example, the average number of errors in the preliminary trial was 11.3, as is indicated by the fact that the curves start at a point whose value is given in the left margin as 11.3. In the second training test the number of errors fell to 3.3 for the males and 2.7 for the females. The number of the test is to be found on the base line; the number of errors in the left margin. If these two curves of learning were carried to their completion, that for the males would end with the thirty-seventh test, and that for the females with the twenty- eighth.

[Illustration: FIGURE 26.—Curves of habit formation, plotted from the data of labyrinth-B tests with ten males and ten females. The figures in the left margin indicate the number of errors; those below the base line the number of the test. *P* designates the preliminary test. Males ____[solid line]; Females ——[broken line].]

Time records are not reported for these and subsequent labyrinth tests because they proved to be almost valueless as measures of the rapidity of habit formation. At any point in its progress through a labyrinth, the dancer may suddenly stop to wash its face, look about or otherwise examine its surroundings; if a shock be given to hurry it along it may be surprised into an error. It is my experience, and this is true of other animals as well as of the dancing mouse, that a long trip, as measured in time units, does not necessarily indicate the lack of ability to follow the labyrinth path correctly and rapidly. Hence, whenever it is possible (and the experimenter can always plan his tests so that it shall be possible), the number of errors should be given first importance and the time of the test second place. I have presented in Table 38 the number of the first correct test, and the number of the last of five successive correct tests. Space cannot be spared for records of the errors made in the several tests by each individual.

In general, labyrinth B proved very satisfactory as a means of testing the ability of the dancer to learn a simple path. The narrow passages effectively prevented dancing, and the introduction of the electric shock as a punishment for mistakes developed a motive for escape which was uniform, constant, and so strong that the animals clearly did their best to escape from the labyrinth quickly and without errors. This maze was so simple that it did not tend to discourage them as did the one which is next to be described. It must be admitted, however, that, though labyrinth B is perfectly satisfactory as a test of the dancer's ability to learn to follow a simple path, it is not an ideal means of measuring the rapidity of habit formation. This is due to the fact that the preliminary trial and the first training test play extremely different roles in the case of different individuals. A dancer which happens to follow the correct path from entrance to exit in the preliminary trial may continue to do so, with only an occasional error, during several of the early training tests, and it may therefore fail for a considerable time to discover that there are errors which should be avoided. The learning process is delayed by its accidental success. On the other hand, an individual which happens to make many mistakes to begin with immediately attempts to avoid the points in the maze at which it receives the electric shock. I was led to conclude, as a result of the labyrinth-B experiments, that the path was too easy, and that a more complex labyrinth would, in all probability, furnish a more satisfactory means of measuring the rapidity of habit formation.

[Illustration: FIGURE 27—A record sheet, showing the plan of labyrinth C (as made on the sheet by means of a rubber stamp) on which the experimenter recorded the path followed by the mouse. This sample sheet presents the path records for the first, fifth, tenth, and eleventh tests of No. 2 in labyrinth C. 1, 2, 3, 4, 5 designate the several errors of the labyrinth.]

On the basis of the supposition that a maze whose path was so complex that the animal would not be likely to follow it correctly in the early trials would be more to the purpose than either A or B, labyrinth C was devised. As is shown in the plan of this maze, Figure 27, five mistakes in choice of path were possible on the forward trip. These errors, as a rule, were more difficult for the dancers to avoid than those of labyrinths A and B. Those which are designated by the numerals 2, 3, and 4 were especially difficult. Error 4 was much more troublesome for left whirlers than for right whirlers because, after turning around abruptly at the entrance to the blind alley, the former type of dancer almost always followed the side wall of the maze so far that it missed the correct path. Undoubtedly the various errors are not of the same value for different individuals; but it would be extremely difficult, if not impossible, to devise a maze which should be equally difficult for several normal individuals.

In order that records of the path followed by a mouse in test after test might be kept with ease and accuracy by the experimenter, the plan of this labyrinth, and also that of labyrinth D, were cast in rubber. The outlines of labyrinths C and D which appear in Figures 27 and 28 respectively were made with the rubber stamps which were thus obtained. Figure 27 is the reproduction of a record sheet which presents the results of the first, the fifth, the tenth, and the eleventh tests of No. 2 in labyrinth C. The path followed by this individual in the first test was far too complex to be traced accurately on the record sheet. The record therefore represents merely the number of errors which was made in each region of the maze. For the fifth test, and again for the tenth and the eleventh, the path was recorded accurately. This simple device for making record blanks which can readily be filled in at the time of the experiment should recommend itself to all students of animal behavior.

In labyrinth C ten pairs of dancers were given continuous training tests at the rate of one test per minute until they were able to follow the direct path correctly. Because of the difficulty in learning this maze perfectly, it was not demanded of the mice that they should follow the path correctly several times in succession, but instead the training was terminated after the first successful trip.

TABLE 39

RESULTS OF LABYRINTH-C EXPERIMENTS, WITH TWENTY DANCERS

MALES FEMALES

NO. OF NO. OF FIRST NO. OF NO. OF FIRST MOUSE CORRECT TEST MOUSE CORRECT TEST

2 11 29 15 30 33 49 34 50 49 57 15 52 22 59 15 58 16 215 10 60 17 415 10 76 3 75 8 78 6 77 11 86 5 87 9 88 25 85 11

AV. 18.7 AV. 13.8

The results of the experiments with this labyrinth as they are presented in Table 39 indicate that its path is considerably more difficult for the dancer to learn than that of labyrinth B, that the females learn more quickly than the males, and finally, that individual differences are just as marked as they were in the case of the simpler forms of labyrinth. It therefore appears that increasing the complexity of a labyrinth does not, as I had supposed it might, diminish the variability of the results. Certain of the individual differences which appear in Table 39 are due, however, to the fact that in some cases training in labyrinth B had preceded training in labyrinth C, whereas in the other cases C was the first labyrinth in which the animals were tested. But even this does not serve to account for the wide divergence of the results given by No. 2 and No. 50, for the latter had been trained in B previous to his training in C, and the former had not been so trained. Yet, despite the advantage which previous labyrinth experience gave No. 50, he did not learn the path of C as well in fifty tests as No. 2 did in eleven. The facts concerning the value of training in one form of labyrinth for the learning of another, as they were revealed by these experiments, may more fittingly be discussed in a later chapter in connection with the facts of memory and re-learning.

[Illustration: FIGURE 28.—Plan of Labyrinth *D*, as reproduced from a print made with a rubber stamp. *I*, entrance; *O*, exit; numerals 1 to 13, errors.]

Labyrinth C is a type of maze which might properly be described as irregular, since the several possible errors are extremely different in nature. In view of the results which this labyrinth yielded, it seemed important that the dancer be tested in a perfectly regular maze of the labyrinth-D type. The plan which I designed as a regular labyrinth has been reproduced, from a rubber stamp print, in Figure 28. As is true also of the mazes previously described, it provides four kinds of possible mistakes: namely, by turning to the left (errors 1, 5, 9, and 13), by turning to the right (errors 3, 7, and 11), by moving straight ahead (errors 2, 4, 6, 8, 10, and 12), and by turning back and retracing the path just followed. The formula for the correct path of *D* is simple in the extreme, in spite of the large number of mistakes which are possible, for it is merely "a turn to the right at the entrance, to the left at the first doorway, and thereafter alternately to the right and to the left until the exit is reached." This concise description would enable a man to find his way out of such a maze with ease. Labyrinth D had been constructed with an exit at 10 so that it might be used as a nine-error maze if the experimenter saw fit, or as a thirteen-error maze by the closing of the opening at 10. In the experiments which are now to be described only the latter form was used.

Can the dancer learn a regular labyrinth path more quickly than an irregular one? Again, I may give only a brief statement of results. Each of the twenty dancers, of Table 40, which were trained in labyrinth D had previously been given opportunity to learn the path of C, and most of them had been trained also in labyrinth B. All of them learned this regular path with surprising rapidity. The numerical results of the tests with labyrinths B, C, and D, as well as the behavior of the mice in these several mazes, prove conclusively that the nature of the errors is far more important than their number. Labyrinth D with its thirteen chances of error on the forward trip was not nearly as difficult for the dancer to learn to escape from as labyrinth C with its five errors. That the facility with which the twenty individuals whose records are given in Table 40 learned the path of D was not due to their previous labyrinth experience rather than to the regularity of the maze is proved by the results which I obtained by testing in D individuals which were new to labyrinth experiments. Even in this case, the number of tests necessary for a successful trip was seldom greater than ten. If further evidence of the ease with which a regular labyrinth path may be followed by the dancer were desired, it might be obtained by observation of the behavior of an individual in labyrinths C and D. In the former, even after it has learned the path perfectly, the mouse hesitates at the doorways from time to time as if uncertain whether to turn to one side or go forward; in the latter there is seldom any hesitation at the turning points. The irregular labyrinth is followed carefully, as by choice of the path from point to point; the regular labyrinth is followed in machine fashion,—once started, the animal dashes through it.

TABLE 40

RESULTS OF LABYRINTH-D EXPERIMENTS, WITH TWENTY DANCERS

MALES FEMALES

NO. OF NO. OF FIRST NO. OF LAST OF NO. OF NO. OF FIRST NO. OF LAST OF MOUSE CORRECT TWO CORRECT MOUSE CORRECT TWO CORRECT TEST TESTS TEST TESTS

2	3	7	29	10	11
58	7	10	49	7	8
30	9	10	57	3	6
60	10	14	215	6	10
402	10	11	415	7	8
76	4	7	75	4	13
78	4	5	77	11	12
86	3	9	87	4	9
88	4	8	85	3	4
90	7	8	83	4	7

Av. 6.1 8.9 Av. 5.9 8.8

From the results of these labyrinth experiments with dancers I am led to conclude that a standard maze for testing the modifiability of behavior of different kinds of animals should be constructed in conformity with the following suggestions. Errors by turning to the right, to the left, and by moving forward should occur with equal frequency, and in such order that no particular kind of error occurs repeatedly in succession. If we should designate these three types of mistake by the letters *r*, *l*, and *s* respectively, the error series of labyrinth C would read *l-l-r-s-l*. It therefore violates the rule of construction which I have just formulated. In the case of labyrinth D the series would read *l-s-r-s-l-s-r-s-l-s-r-s- l*. This also fails to conform with the requirement, for there are three errors of the first type, four of the second, and six of the third. Again, in a standard maze, the blind alleys should all be of the same length, and care should be taken to provide a sufficiently strong and uniform motive for escape. In the case of one animal the desire to escape from confinement may prove a satisfactory motive; in the case of another, the desire for food may conveniently supplement the dislike of confinement; and in still other cases it may appear that some form of punishment for errors is the only satisfactory basis of a motive for escape. Readers of this account of the behavior of the dancing mouse must not infer from my experimental results that the electric shock as a means of forcing discrimination will prove satisfactory in work with other animals or even with all other mammals. As a matter of fact it has already been proved by Doctor G. van T. Hamilton that the use of an electric shock may so intimidate a dog that experimentation is rendered difficult and of little value. And finally, in connection with this discussion of a standard Labyrinth, I wish to emphasize the importance of so recording the results of experiments that they may be interpreted in terms of an animal's tendency to turn to the right or to the left. My work with the dancer has clearly shown that the avoidance of a particular error may be extremely difficult for left whirlers and very easy for right whirlers.

I hope I have succeeded in making clear by the foregoing account of my experiments that the labyrinth method is more satisfactory in general than the problem method as a means of measuring the rapidity of habit formation in the dancer, and I hope that I have made equally clear the fact that it is very valuable as a means of discovering the roles of the various senses in the acquirement of a habit (Chapter XI). From my own experience in the use of the labyrinth with the dancer and with other animals, I am forced to conclude that its chief value lies in the fact that it enables the experimenter so to control the factors of a complex situation that he may readily determine the importance of a given kind of sense data for the formation or the execution of a particular habit. As a means of measuring the intelligence of an animal, of determining the facility with which it is capable of adjusting itself to new environmental conditions, and of measuring the permanency of modifications which are wrought in its behavior by experimental conditions, I value the labyrinth method much less highly now than I did previous to my study of the dancer. It is necessarily too complex for the convenient and reasonably certain interpretation of results. Precisely what is meant by this statement will be evident in the light of the results of the application of the discrimination method to the dancer, which are to be presented in the next chapter. The labyrinth method is an admirable means of getting certain kinds of qualitative results; it is almost ideal as a revealer of the role of the senses, and it may be used to advantage in certain instances for the quantitative study of habit formation and memory. Nevertheless, I think it may safely be said that the problem method and the discrimination method are likely to do more to advance our knowledge of animal behavior than the labyrinth method.

CHAPTER XIV

HABIT FORMATION: THE DISCRIMINATION METHOD

Discrimination is demanded of an animal in almost all forms of the problem and labyrinth methods, as well as in what I have chosen to call the discrimination method. In the latter, however, discrimination as the basis of a correct choice of an electric-box is so obviously important that it has seemed appropriate to distinguish this particular method of measuring the intelligence of the dancer from the others which have been used, by naming it the discrimination method.

It has been shown that neither the problem nor the labyrinth method proves wholly satisfactory as a means of measuring the rapidity of learning, or the duration of the effects of training, in the case of the dancer. The former type of test serves to reveal to the experimenter the general nature of the animal's capacity for profiting by experience; the latter serves equally well to indicate the parts which various receptors (some of which are sense organs) play in the formation and execution of habits. But neither of them is sufficiently simple, easy of control, uniform as to conditions which constitute bases for activity, and productive of interpretable quantitative results to render it satisfactory. The problem method is distinctly a qualitative method, and, in the case of the dancing mouse, my experiments have proved that the labyrinth method also yields results which are more valuable qualitatively than quantitatively. I had anticipated that various forms of the labyrinth method would enable me to measure the modifiability of behavior in the dancer with great accuracy, but, as will now be made apparent, the discrimination method proved to be a far more accurate method for this purpose.

Once more I should emphasize the fact that my statements concerning the value of methods apply especially to the dancing mouse. Certain of the tests which have proved to be almost ideal in my study of this peculiar little rodent would be useless in the study of many other mammals. An experimenter must work out his methods step by step in the light of the daily results of patient and intelligent observation of the motor capacity, habits, instincts, temperament, imitative tendency, intelligence, hardihood, and life-span of the animal which he is studying. The fact that punishment has proved to be more satisfactory than reward in experiments with the dancer does not justify the inference that it is more satisfactory in the case of the rat, cat, dog, or monkey. Methods which yielded me only qualitative results, if applied to other mammals might give accurate quantitative results; and, on the other hand, the discrimination method, which has proved invaluable for my quantitative work, might yield only qualitative results when applied to another kind of animal.

The form of the discrimination method whose results are to be presented in this chapter has already been described as white-black discrimination. In the discrimination box (Figures 14 and 15, p. 92) the two electric-boxes which were otherwise exactly alike in appearance were rendered discriminable for the mouse by the presence of white cardboards in one and black cardboards in the other. In order to escape from the narrow space before the entrances to the two electric-boxes, the dancer was required to enter the white box. If it entered the black box a weak electric shock was experienced. After two series of ten tests each, during which the animal was permitted to choose either the white or the black box without shock or hindrance, the training was begun. These two preliminary series serve to indicate the natural preference of the animal for white or black previous to the training. An individual which very strongly preferred the white might enter, from the first, the box thus distinguished, whereas another individual whose preference was for the black might persistently enter the black box in spite of the disagreeable shocks. First of all, therefore, the preliminary tests furnish a basis for the evaluation of the results of the subsequent training tests. On the day succeeding the last series of preliminary tests, and daily thereafter until the animal had acquired a perfect habit of choosing the white box, a series of training tests was given. These experiments were usually made in the morning between nine and twelve o'clock, in a room with south-east windows. The entrances to the electric-boxes faced the windows, consequently the mouse did not have to look toward the light when it was trying to discriminate white from black. All the conditions of the experiment, including the strength of the current for the shock, were kept as constant as possible.

Choice by position was effectively prevented, as a rule, by shifting the cardboards so that now the left now the right box was white. The order of these shifts for the white-black series whose results are quantitatively valuable appear in Table 12 (p. III). That the order of these changes in position may be criticised in the light of the results which the tests gave, I propose to show hereafter in connection with certain other facts. The significant point is that the defects which are indicated by the averages of thousands of tests could not have been predicted with certainty even by the most experienced investigator in this field.

In Table 41 are to be found the average number of errors in each series of ten white-black discrimination tests for five males and for five females which were trained by being given ten tests per day, and similarly for the same number of individuals of each sex, trained by being given twenty tests per day. Since the results for these two conditions of training are very similar, the averages for the twenty individuals are presented in the last column of the table. For the present we may neglect the interesting individual, sex, and age differences which these experiments revealed and examine the significant features of the general averages, and of the white-black discrimination curve (Figure 29).

TABLE 41

WHITE BLACK DISCRIMINATION TESTS. NUMBER OF ERRORS IN THE VARIOUS SERIES

MALES FEMALES

AVERAGES AVERAGES GENERAL AVERAGES AVERAGES GENERAL AVERAGES SERIES FOR 5, FOR 5, AVERAGES FOR 5, FOR 5, AVERAGES FOR ALL 10 TESTS 20 TESTS FOR 10 10 TESTS 20 TESTS FOR 10 (20) MALES PER DAY PER DAY PER DAY PER DAY AND FEMALES

A	5.8	6.0	5.9	5.8	5.8	5.8	5.85
B	5.6	6.2	5.9	5.8	5.6	5.7	5.8
1	5.0	5.0	5.0	5.6	4.6	5.1	5.05
2	2.6	4.6	3.6	4.4	5.0	4.7	4.15
3	3.0	3.4	3.2	3.4	3.4	3.4	3.3
4	2.6	3.8	3.2	2.4	2.2	2.3	2.75
5	2.4	2.0	2.2	2.6	1.8	2.2	2.2
6	1.6	1.6	1.6	1.0	2.2	1.6	1.6
7	1.0	1.4	1.2	2.0	0.4	1.2	1.2
8	0.2	0.6	.4	1.4	1.6	1.5	.95
9	0.2	1.0	.6	0.6	0.8	.7	.65
10	0	.8	.4	1.0	0.8	.9	.65
11	0	.8	.4	0.8	0	.4	.40
12	0	.6	.3	0.4	0	.2	.25
13	0	0	0	0	0	0	0
14	0	0	0	0	0	0	
15	0	0	0	0	0	0	

[Illustration: FIGURE 29.—Error curve plotted from the data given by twenty dancers in white-black discrimination tests. The figures in the left margin indicate the number of errors; those below the base line, the number of the series. *A* and *B* designate the preference series.]

The preference series, *A* and *B*, reveal a constant tendency to choose the black box, whose strength as compared with the tendency to choose the white box is as 5.8 is to 4.2. In other words, the dancer on the average chooses the black box almost six times in ten. The first series of training tests reduced this preference for black to zero, and succeeding series brought about a rapid and fairly regular decrease in the number of errors, until, in the thirteenth series, the white was chosen every time. Since I arbitrarily define a perfect habit of discrimination as the ability to choose the right box in three successive series of ten tests each, the tests ended with the fifteenth series.

The discrimination curve, Figure 29, is a graphic representation of the general averages of Table 41.—It is an error curve, therefore. Starting at 5.85 for the first preliminary series, it descends to 5.8 for the second series, and thence abruptly to 5.05 for the first training series. This series of ten tests therefore served to reduce the black preference very considerably. The curve continues to descend constantly until the tenth series, for which the number of errors was the same as for the preceding series, .65. This irregularity in the curve, indicative, as it would appear, of a sudden cessation in the learning process, demands an explanation. My first thought was that an error in computation on my part might account for the shape of the curve. The error did not exist, but in my search for it I discovered what I now believe to be the cause of the interruption in the fall of the error curve. In all of the training series up to the tenth the white cardboard had been on the right and the left alternately or on one side two or three times in succession, whereas in the tenth series, as may be seen by referring to Table 12 (p.111), it was on the left for the first four tests, then on the right four times, and, finally, on the left for the ninth test and on the right for the tenth. This series was therefore a decidedly more severe test of the animal's ability to discriminate white from black and to choose the white box without error than were any that had preceded it. If my interpretation of the results is correct, it was so much more severe than the ninth series that the process of habit formation was obscured. It would not be fair to say that the mouse temporarily ceased to profit by its experience; instead it profited even more than usually, in all probability, but the unavoidably abrupt increase in the difficultness of the tests was just sufficient to hide the improvement.

As I have suggested, the plan of experimentation may be criticised adversely in the light of this irregularity in the error curve. Had the conditions been perfectly satisfactory the curve would not have taken this form. I admit this, but at the same time I am glad that I chose that series of shifts in the position of the cardboards which, as it happens, served to exhibit an important aspect of quantitative measures of the modifiability of behavior that otherwise would not have been revealed. Our mistakes in method often teach us more than our successes. I have taken pains, therefore, to describe the unsatisfactory as well as the satisfactory steps in my study of the dancer.

[Illustration: FIGURE 30.—Error curve plotted from the data given by thirty dancers, of different ages and under different conditions of training, in white-black discrimination tests.]

The form of the white-black discrimination curve of Figure 29 is more surprising than disappointing to me, for I had anticipated many more irregularities than appear. What I had expected, as the result of training five or even ten pairs of mice, was the kind of curve which is presented, for contrast with the one already discussed, in Figure 30. This also is an error curve, but, unlike the previous one, it is based upon results which were got from individuals of different ages which were trained according to the following different methods. Ten of these individuals were given two or five tests daily, ten were given ten tests daily, and ten were given twenty tests daily. The form of the curve serves to call attention to the importance of uniform conditions of training, in case the results are to be used as accurate measures of the rapidity of learning.

Examination of the detailed results of the white-black discrimination tests as they appear in the tables of Chapter VII will reveal the fact that some individuals succeeded in choosing correctly in a series of ten tests after not more than five series, whereas others required at least twice as many tests as the basis of a perfect series. In very few instances, however, was a perfect habit of discrimination established by fewer than one hundred tests. As the averages just presented in Table 41 indicate, fifteen series, or one hundred and fifty tests, were required for the completion of the experiment. One might search a long time, possibly, for another mammal whose curve of error in a simple discrimination test would fall as gradually as that of the dancer. It is fair to say that this animal learns very slowly as compared with most mammals which have been carefully studied. It is to be remembered, however, that quantitative results such as are here presented for the dancer are available for few if any other animals except the white rat. Neither in the form of the curve of learning nor in the behavior of the animal as it makes its choice of an electric-box is there evidence of anything which might be described as a sudden understanding of the situation. The dancer apparently learns by rote. It exhibits neither intelligent insight into an experimental situation nor ability to profit by the experience of its companions. That the selection of the white box occurs in various ways in different individuals, and even in the same individual at different periods in the training process, is the only indication of anything suggestive of implicit reasoning. Naturally enough comparison of the two boxes is the first method of selection. It takes the dancers a surprisingly long time to reach the point of making this comparison as soon as they are confronted by the entrances to the two electric-boxes. The habit of running from entrance to entrance repeatedly before either is entered, once having been acquired, is retained often throughout the training experiments. But in other cases, an individual finally comes to the point of choosing by what appears to be the immediate recognition of the right or the wrong box. In the former case the mouse enters the white box immediately; in the latter, it rushes from the black box into the white one without hesitation. So much evidence the discrimination tests furnish of forms of behavior which in our fellow-men we should interpret as rational.

[Illustration: FIGURE 31.—Curve of habit formation, plotted from the data of labyrinth-D tests with ten males and ten females.]

Comparison of the error curves for the labyrinth tests (Figures 26 and 31) with those for the discrimination tests (Figures 29 and 30) reveals several interesting points of difference. The former fall very abruptly at first, then with decreasing rapidity, to the base line; the latter, on the contrary, fall gradually throughout their course. Evidently the labyrinth habit is more readily acquired by the dancer than is the visual discrimination habit. Certain motor tendencies can be established quickly, it would seem, whereas others, and especially those which depend for their guidance upon visual stimuli, are acquired with extreme slowness. From this it might be inferred that the labyrinth method is naturally far better suited to the nature of the dancer than is any form of the discrimination method. I believe that this inference is correct, but at the same time I am of the opinion that the discrimination method is of even greater value than the labyrinth method as a means of discovering the capacity of the animal for modification of behavior.

Inasmuch as my first purpose in the repetition of white-black discrimination tests with a number of individuals was to obtain quantitative results which should accurately indicate individual, age, and sex differences in the rapidity of learning, it is important to consider the reliability of the averages with which we have been dealing. Possibly two groups of five male dancers each, chosen at random, would yield very different results in discrimination tests. This would almost certainly be true if the animals were selected from different lots, or were kept before and during the tests under different environmental conditions. But from my experiments it has become apparent that the average of the results given by five individuals of the same sex, age, and condition of health, when kept in the same environment and subjected to the same experimental tests, is sufficiently constant from group to group to warrant its use as an index of modifiability for the race. This expression, index of modifiability, is a convenient mode of designating the average number of tests necessary for the establishment of a perfect habit of white-black discrimination. Hereafter I shall use it instead of a more lengthy descriptive phrase.

As an indication of the degree of accuracy of measurements of the rapidity of learning which are obtained by the use of 5 individuals I may offer the following figures. For one of two directly comparable groups of 5 male dancers which were chosen from 16 individuals which had been trained, the number of tests which resulted in a perfect habit of white-black discrimination was 92; for the other group it was 96. These indices for strictly comparable groups of 5 individuals each differ from one another by less than 5 per cent. Similarly, in the case of two groups of females, the indices of modifiability were 94 and 104. These figures designate the number of tests up to the point at which errors ceased for at least three successive series (30 tests).

The determination of the probable error of the index of modifiability further aids us in judging of the reliability of the measure of the rapidity of learning which is obtained by averaging the results for 5 individuals. For a group of 5 males (Table 43, p. 243) the index was 72 ± 3.5; and for a group of 5 females of the same age as the males and strictly comparable with respect to conditions of white-black training, it was 104 ± 2.9. A probable error of ± 3.5 indicates the reliability of the first of these indices of modifiability; one of ± 2.9, that of the second.

I do not doubt that 10 individuals would furnish a more reliable average than 5, but I do doubt whether the purposes of my experiments would have justified the great increase in work which the use of averages based upon so large a group would have necessitated.

Further discussion of the index of modifiability may be postponed until the several indices which serve as measures of the efficiency of different methods of training have been presented in the next chapter.

From the data which constitute the materials of the present chapter it is apparent that the results of the discrimination method are amenable to much more accurate quantitative treatment than are those of the problem method or the labyrinth method. But I have done little more as yet than describe the method by which it is possible to measure certain dimensions of the intelligence of the dancer, and to state some general results of its application. In the remaining chapters it will be our task to discover the value of this method and of the results which it has yielded.

CHAPTER XV

THE EFFICIENCY OF TRAINING METHODS

The nature of the modifications which are wrought in the behavior of an organism varies with the method of training. This fact is recognized by human educators, as well as by students of animal behavior (makers of the science of comparative pedagogy), but unfortunately accurate measurements of the efficiency of our educational methods are rare.

Whatever the subject of investigation, there are two preeminently important aspects of the educative process which may be taken as indications of the value of the method of training by which it was initiated and stimulated. I refer to the rapidity of the learning process and its degree of permanency, or, in terms of habit formation, to the rapidity with which a habit is acquired, and to its duration. Of these two easily measurable aspects of the modifications in which training results, I have chosen the first as a means to the special study of the efficiency of the training to which the dancing mouse has been subjected in my experiments.

The reader who has followed my account of the behavior of the dancer up to this point will recall that in practically all of the discrimination experiments the number of tests in a series was ten. Some readers doubtless have wondered why ten rather than five or twenty tests was selected as the number in each continuous series. I shall now attempt to answer the question. It was simply because the efficiency of that number of tests, given daily, when taken in connection with the amount of time which the conduct of the experiments required, rendered it the most satisfactory number. But this statement demands elaboration and explanation.

Very early in my study of the dancer, I learned that a single experience in a given experiment day after day had so little effect upon the animal that a perfect habit could not be established short of several weeks or months. Similarly, experiments in which two tests per day were given proved that even a simple discrimination habit cannot be acquired by the animal under this condition of training with sufficient rapidity to enable the experimenter to study the formation of the habit advantageously. Next, ten tests in succession each day were given. The results proved satisfactory, consequently I proceeded to carry out my investigation on the basis of a ten-test series. After this method had been thoroughly tried, I decided to investigate the efficiency of other methods for the purpose of instituting comparisons of efficiency and discovering the number of tests per day whose efficiency, as measured by the rapidity of the formation of a white-black discrimination habit, is highest.

For this purpose I carefully selected five pairs of dancers of the same age, descent, and previous experience, and gave them white-black tests in series of two tests per day (after the twentieth day the number was increased to five) until they had acquired a perfect habit of discriminating. Similarly other dancers were trained by means of series of ten tests, twenty tests, or one hundred tests per day. Since it was my aim to make the results of these various tests strictly comparable, I spared no pains in selecting the individuals, and in maintaining constancy of experimental conditions. The order of the changes in the position of the cardboards which was adhered to in these efficiency tests was that given in Table 12.

At the beginning of the two-test training I thought it possible that the animals might acquire a perfect habit with only a few more days' training than is required by the ten-test method. This did not prove to be the case, for at the end of the twentieth day (after forty tests in all) the average number of mistakes, as Table 42 shows, was 3.2 for the males and 3.0 for the females. Up to this time there had been clear evidence of the formation of a habit of discriminating white from black, but, on the other hand, the method had proved very unsatisfactory because the first test each day usually appeared to be of very different value from the second. On account of the imminent danger of the interruption of the experiment by the rapid spread of an epidemic among my mice, I decided to increase the number of tests in each series to five in order to complete the experiment if possible before the disease could destroy the animals. On the twenty- first day and thereafter, five-test series were given instead of two-test. Unfortunately I was able to complete the experiment up to the point of thirty successive correct tests with only six of the ten individuals whose numbers appear at the top of Table 42. That the results of this table are reliable, despite the fact that some of the individuals had to be taken out of the experiment on account of bad condition, is indicated by the fact that all the mice continued to do their best to discriminate so long as they were used. Possibly the habit would have been acquired a little more quickly by some of the individuals had they been stronger and more active.

It should be explained at this point that the results in all the efficiency-of-training tables of this chapter are arranged, as in the previous white-black discrimination tables, in tens, that is, each figure in the tables indicates the number of errors in a series of ten tests. In all cases *A* and *B* mark preliminary series of tests which were given at the rate of ten tests per series. The numbers in the first column of these tables designate groups of ten tests each, and not necessarily daily series. In Table 42, for example, 1 includes the results of the first five days of training, 2, of the next five days, and so on. The table shows that No. 80 made seven wrong choices in the first five series of two tests each. This method of grouping results serves to make the data for the different methods directly comparable, and at the same time it saves space at the sacrifice of very little valuable information concerning the nature of the daily results. It is to be noted, with emphasis, that the two-five tests per day training established a perfect habit after four weeks of training. This method is therefore costly of the experimenter's time.

TABLE 42

EFFICIENCY OF TRAINING. WHITE-BLACK TESTS AT THE RATE OF 2 OR 5 PER DAY

MALES FEMALES SETS 80 82 84 86 88 AV. 73 79 83 85 89 AV. OF 10

A 5 5 4 8 5 5.4 5 6 7 7 6 6.2 B 5 3 6 5 6 5.0 7 5 7 6 7 6.4

1 7 7 6 6 6 6.4 7 6 9 4 6 6.4
2 2 1 0 6 6 3.0 6 5 6 5 5 5.4
3 4 5 5 1 2 3.2 6 5 2 4 1 3.6
4 3 4 7 2 0 3.2 4 3 1 4 3 3.0
5 2 3 3 2 4 2.8 - 3 4 3 1 2.7
6 2 2 - 2 2 2.0 - 0 2 2 0 1.0
7 - 1 - 0 1 0.7 - 1 0 2 1 1.0
8 - - - 1 1 1.0 - 1 1 0 0 0.5
9 - - - 0 1 0.5 0 1 1 0 0 0.5
10 - - - 0 0 0 - 0 0 0 0 0
11 - - - 0 0 0 - 0 0 0
12 - - - 0 0 - 0 0 0

TABLE 43

EFFICIENCY OF TRAINING. WHITE-BLACK TESTS AT THE RATE OF 10 PER DAY

MALES FEMALES SETS 210 220 230 410 420 AV. 215 225 235 415 425 AV. OF 10

A 6 5 6 6 6 5.8 8 4 4 8 5 5.8 B 6 8 8 5 1 5.6 8 7 6 6 2 5.8

1 6 7 6 2 4 5.0 7 6 5 6 4 5.6

2 4 3 1 2 3 2.6 5 6 4 2 5 4.4

3 3 1 4 3 4 3.0 3 3 4 2 5 4.4

4 5 0 3 3 2 3.2 2 1 3 3 3 2.4

5 3 0 4 1 4 2.4 1 3 3 3 3 2.6

6 2 1 4 0 1 1.6 2 1 1 1 0 1.0

7 1 0 3 1 0 1.0 1 1 2 3 3 2.0

8 0 0 1 0 0 0.2 0 0 2 2 3 2.0

9 0 0 0 1 0 0.2 1 0 0 1 1 0.6

10 0 0 0 0 0 2 1 0 2 1.0

11 0 0 0 0 3 0 1 0 0.8

12 0 0 0 0 0 2 0 0.4

13 0 0 0 0 0

14 0 0 0

15 0 0

TABLE 44

EFFICIENCY OF TRAINING. WHITE-BLACK TESTS AT THE RATE OF 20 PER DAY

MALES FEMALES SETS 72 74 208 240 402 AV. 217 230 245 403 407 AV. OF 10

A 4 6 7 7 6 6.0 5 4 7 7 6 5.8 B 6 4 6 8 7 6.2 7 3 5 8 5 5.6

1 3 5 7 5 5 5.0 3 6 4 4 6 4.6
2 4 3 7 5 4 4.6 7 3 5 4 6 5.0
3 3 3 3 5 3 3.4 4 3 3 2 5 3.4
4 6 3 1 4 5 3.8 5 0 1 2 3 2.2
5 4 1 0 2 3 2.0 6 0 0 1 2 1.8
6 3 1 0 2 2 1.6 4 1 1 0 6 2.2
7 3 2 0 1 1 1.4 1 0 0 0 1 0.4
8 2 0 1 1 0.6 0 3 3 0 2 1.6
9 2 1 1 1 1.0 1 0 0 3 0.8
10 1 2 1 0 0.8 0 1 1 2 0.8
11 3 1 0 0 0.8 0 0 0 0 0
12 1 2 0 0 0.6 0 0 0 0 0
13 0 0 0 0 0 0 0 0
14 0 0 0
15 0 0 0

The results of the ten-test training as they appear in Table 43 need no special comment, for quite similar data have already been examined in other connections. In the case of this table it is to be remembered that each figure represents the number of errors for a single day as well as for a series of ten successive tests. The results of Table 44, on the other hand, appear as subdivided series, since each daily series was constituted by two series of ten tests, or in all twenty tests.

Finally, in Table 45 I have arranged the results of what may fairly be called the continuous training method. In connection with several of the labyrinth experiments of Chapter XIII continuous training proved very satisfactory. It therefore seemed worth while to ascertain whether the same method would not be more efficient than any other for the establishment of a white-black discrimination habit. That this method was not applied to ten individuals as were the two-five-test, the ten-test, and the twenty-test methods is due to the fact that it proved practically inadvisable to continue the tests long enough to complete the experiment. I have usually designated the method as one hundred or more tests daily. I applied this training method first to individuals Nos. 51 and 60. At the end of one hundred and twenty tests with each of these individuals I was forced to discontinue the experiment for the day because of the approach of darkness. In the table the end of a series for the day is indicated by a heavy line. The following day Nos. 51 and 60 succeeded in acquiring a perfect habit after a few more tests.

TABLE 45

EFFICIENCY OF TRAINING. WHITE-BLACK TESTS AT THE RATE OF 100 OR MORE PER DAY

SETS OF 10	51[1]	60	87	Av.

A 5 5 6 5.3 B 5 3 7 5.0

1 6 6 5 5.7 2 3 2 5 3.3 3 5 4 7 5.3 4 7 4 5 5.3 5 6 2 3 3.7 6 1 1 3 1.7 7 4 2 3 3.0 8 3 3 0 2.0 9 2 2 3 2.3 10 5 0 2 2.3 11 1 2 2 1.7 12 2 1 1 1.3

13 4 1 2 2.3 14 1 2 1 1.3 15 3 1 5 3.0 16 3 3 2 2.7 17 1 0 1 0.7 18 2 0 1 1.0 19 0 0 2 0.7 20 0 0 0 21 0 1 0.3 22 - 23 - 24 -

[Footnote 1: Age of No. 51, 22 weeks. Age of No. 60, 17 weeks. Age of No. 87, 8 weeks.]

The results of the continuous training method for these two mice were so strikingly different from those yielded by the other methods that I at once suspected the influence of some factor other than that of the number of tests per day. The ages of Nos. 51 and 60 at the time of their tests were twenty-two and seventeen weeks, respectively, whereas all the individuals used in connection with the other efficiency tests were four weeks of age. It seemed possible that the slow habit formation exhibited in the continuous training experiments might be due to the greater age of the mice. I therefore selected a healthy active female which was only eight weeks old, and tried to train her by the continuous training method. With this individual, No. 87, the results were even more discouraging than those previously obtained, for she was still imperfect in her discrimination at the end of two hundred and ten tests. At that point the experiment was interrupted, and it seemed scarcely worth while to continue it further at a later date. The evidence of the extremely low efficiency of the continuous method in comparison with the other methods which we have been considering is so conclusive that further comment seems superfluous.

We are now in a position to compare the results of the several methods of training which have been applied to the dancer, and to attempt to get satisfactory quantitative expressions of the efficiency of each method. I have arranged in Table 46 the general averages yielded by the four methods. Although these general results hide certain important facts which will be exhibited later, they clearly indicate that an increase in the number of tests per day does not necessarily result in an increase in the rapidity of habit formation. Should we attempt, on superficial examination, to interpret the figures of this table, we would doubtless say that in efficiency the two-five-test method stands first, the continuous-test method last, while the ten-test and twenty-test methods occupy intermediate positions.

TABLE 46

EFFICIENCY OF TRAINING

Number of Errors in White-Black Series for Different Methods of Training

SETS OF 10 2 OR 5 TESTS 10 TESTS 20 TESTS 100 OR MORE PER DAY PER DAY PER DAY TESTS PER DAY

A 5.8 5.8 5.9 5.3 B 5.7 5.7 5.9 5.0

1 6.4 5.3 4.8 5.7 2 4.2 3.5 4.8 3.3 3 3.4 3.2 3.4 5.3 4 3.1 2.5 3.0 5.3 5 2.7 2.5 1.9 3.7 6 1.5 1.3 1.9 1.7 7 0.9 1.5 0.9 3.0 8 0.7 0.8 1.1 2.0 9 0.5 0.4 0.9 2.3 10 0 0.5 0.8 2.3 11 0 0.4 0.4 1.7 12 0 0.2 0.3 1.3 13 0 0 2.3 14 0 0 1.3 15 0 0 3.0 16 2.7 17 0.7 18 1.0 19 0.7 20 0

We may now apply to the results of our efficiency-of-training tables the method of measuring efficiency which was mentioned at the end of the preceding chapter as the *index of modifiability (that number of tests after which no errors occur for at least thirty tests)*. By taking the average number of tests for the several individuals in each of the Tables 42, 43, 44, and 45 we obtain the following expressions of efficiency:—

METHOD INDEX OF MODIFIABILITY (EFFICIENCY)

Two-five-test 81.7 ± 2.7
Ten-test 88.0 ± 4.1
Twenty-test 91.0 ± 5.3
Continuous-test 170.0 ± 4.8

Since the difference between the indices for the ten-test and the twenty- test methods lies within the limits of their probable errors (±4.1 and ±5.3) it is evident that it is not significant. Except for this, I think these indices may be accepted as indications of real differences in the value of the several methods of training.

A somewhat different interpretation of our results is suggested by the grouping of individuals according to sex. In Table 47 appear the general averages for the males and the females which were tested by the several methods. The most striking fact exhibited by this table is that of the high efficiency of the twenty-test method for the females. Apparently they profited much more quickly by this method than by the ten-test method, whereas just the reverse is true of the males. I present the data of this table merely to show that general averages may hide important facts.

TABLE 47

EFFICIENCY OF TRAINING

CONDITION	MALES INDEX OF MODIFIABILITY	FEMALES INDEX OF MODIFIABILITY
2 or 5 tests per day	85.0	80.0
10 tests per day	72.0	104.0
20 tests per day	94.0	88.0
100 or more tests per day	160.0	180.0

From all considerations that have been mentioned thus far the reader would be justified in concluding that I made a mistake in selecting the ten-test method for my study of the modifiability of the behavior of the dancer. That this conclusion is not correct is due to the time factor in the experiments. If the dancer could acquire a perfect habit as a result of twelve days' training, no matter whether two, five, ten, or twenty tests were given daily, it would, of course, be economical of time for the experimenter to employ the two-test method. But if, on the contrary, the two-test method required twice as many days' training as the five-test method, it would be economical for him to use the five-test method despite the fact that he would have to give a larger number of tests than the two- test method would have demanded. In a word, the time which the work requires depends upon the number of series which have to be given, as well as upon the number of tests in each series. As it happens, the ten-test method demands less of the experimenter's time than do methods with fewer tests per day. The twenty-test method is even more economical of time, but it has a fatal defect. It is at times too tiresome for both mouse and man. These facts indicate that a balance should be struck between number of tests and number of series. The fewer the tests per day, within the limits of two and one hundred, the higher the efficiency of the method of training, as measured in terms of the total number of tests necessary for the establishment of a perfect habit, and the lower its efficiency as measured in terms of the number of series given. The greater the number of tests per day, on the other hand, the higher the efficiency of the method in terms of the number of series, and the lower its efficiency in terms of the total number of tests. By taking into account these facts, together with the fact of fatigue, we are led to the conclusion that ten tests per day is the most satisfactory number.

If my time and attention had not been fully occupied with other problems, I should have determined the efficiency of various methods of training in terms of the duration of habit, as well as in terms of the rapidity of its formation. As these two measures of efficiency might give contradictory results, it is obvious that a training method cannot be fairly evaluated without consideration of both the rapidity of habit formation and the permanency of the habit. A *priori* it seems not improbable that slowness of learning should be directly correlated with a high degree of permanency. By the further application of the method which I have used in this study of the efficiency of training we may hope to get a definite answer to this and many other questions concerning the nature of the educative process and the conditions which influence it.

CHAPTER XVI

THE DURATION OF HABITS: MEMORY AND RE-LEARNING

The effects of training gradually disappear. Habits wane with disuse. In the dancer, it is not possible to establish with certainty the existence of memory in the introspective psychological sense; but it is possible to measure the efficiency of the training to which the animal is subjected, and the degree of permanency of habits. The materials which constitute this chapter concern the persistence of unused habits, and the influence of previous training on the re-acquisition of a habit which has been lost or on the acquisition of a new habit. For convenience of description, I shall refer to certain of the facts which are to be discussed as facts of memory, with the clear understanding that consciousness is not necessarily implied. By memory, wherever it occurs in this book, I mean the ability of the dancer to retain the power of adaptive action which it has acquired through training.

I first discovered memory in the dancer, although there was previously no reason for doubting its existence, in connection with the ladder-climbing tests of Chapter XII. In this experiment two individuals which had perfectly learned to escape from the experiment box to the nest-box by way of the wire ladder, when tested after an interval of two weeks, during which they had remained in the nest-box without opportunity to exercise their newly acquired habit, demonstrated their memory of the method of escape by returning to the nest-box by way of the ladder as soon as they were given opportunity to do so. As it did not lend itself readily to quantitative study, no attempts were made to measure the duration of this particular habit. At best the climbing of a wire ladder is of very uncertain value as an indication of the influence of training.

Similarly, the persistence of habits has been forced upon my attention day after day in my various experiments with the mice. It is obvious, then, that the simple fact of memory is well established, and that we may turn at once to an examination of the facts revealed by special memory and re- learning experiments.

The visual discrimination method, which proved invaluable as a means of measuring the rapidity of habit formation, proved equally serviceable in the measurement of the permanency or duration of habits. Memory tests for discrimination habits were made as follows. After a dancer had been trained in the discrimination box so that it could choose the correct electric-box, white, red, blue, or green as it might be, in three successive daily series of ten tests each, it was permitted to remain for a certain length of time without training and without opportunity to exercise its habit of visual discrimination and choice. At the expiration of the rest interval, as we may designate the period during which the habit was not in use, the mouse was placed in the discrimination box under precisely the same conditions in which it had been trained and was given a series of ten memory tests with the box to be chosen alternately on the right and on the left. In order that the entire series of ten tests, and sometimes two such series given on consecutive days, might be available as indications of the duration of a habit, the mouse was permitted to enter and pass through either of the electric-boxes without receiving a shock. Had the shock been given as punishment for a wrong choice, it is obvious that only the first test of the memory series would be of value as an indication of the existence of a previously acquired habit. Even under the conditions of no shock and no stop or hindrance the first test of each memory series is of preeminent importance, for the mouse tends to persist in choosing either the side or the visual condition (sometimes one, sometimes the other) which it chooses in the first test. If the wrong box is chosen to begin with, mistakes are likely to continue because of the lack of punishment; in this case the animal discriminates, but there is no evidence that it remembers the right box. Likewise, if the right electric- box is chosen in the first test, correct choices may continue simply because the animal has discovered that it can safely enter that particular box; again, the animal discriminates without depending necessarily upon its earlier experience. I have occasionally observed a series of ten correct choices, made on the basis of an accidental right start, followed by another series in which almost every choice was wrong, because the animal happened to start wrong.

As the results of my tests of memory are of such a nature that they cannot advantageously be averaged, I have arranged in Table 48 a number of typical measurements of the duration of visual discrimination habits. In this table I have indicated the number and age of the individual tested, the habit of discrimination which had been acquired, the length of the rest interval, the result of the first test (right or wrong), and the number of errors made in each series of ten memory tests.

TABLE 48

MEASUREMENTS OF THE DURATION OF A HABIT

Memory

ERRORS NO. AGE NAME OF TEST REST FIRST FIRST SECOND INTERVAL CHOICE SERIES SERIES

1000 25 weeks White-black 4 weeks Right 0
5 27 White-black 4 Right 5 7
210 15 White-black 8 Right 5
220 15 White-black 8 Right 4
230 15 White-black 8 Wrong 5
215 15 White-black 8 Right 5
225 15 White-black 8 Right 2
235 15 White-black 8 Right 7
410 15 White-black 8 Wrong 4
415 15 White-black 8 Wrong 6
420 15 White-black 8 Wrong 3
425 15 White-black 8 Right 3
2 28 Black-white 4 Wrong 9
7 17 Black-white 2 Wrong 1
7 21 Black-white 6 Right 1
7 27 Black-white 10 Right 1 6
998 18 Black-white 2 Wrong 3
998 22 Black-white 4 Right 0
998 28 Black-white 10 Right 5 5
13 10 Black-white 4 Right 3
14 10 Black-white 4 Right 3
15 10 Black-white 4 Right 2
16 10 Black-white 4 Right 4
1000 25 Light blue-orange 4 Right 4
2 28 Light blue-orange 2 Wrong 5
5 28 Light blue-orange 6 Wrong 4 6
3 25 Light blue-orange 4 Wrong 8
10 24 Light blue-orange 2 Right 8
10 26 Light blue-orange 2 Right 5
11 25 Light blue-orange 2 Right 6
11 27 Light blue-orange 2 Wrong 5

151 13 Green-red 2 Right 1 0
152 13 Green-red 2 Right 5 1

This quantitative study of the duration of simple habits of choice showed that in the majority of cases a perfectly acquired habit persists for at least two weeks. To be perfectly fair to the animal I must restrict this statement to visual conditions other than colors, for the dancer exhibited little ability either to acquire or to retain a habit of distinguishing spectral colors. Altogether, I made a large number of white-black and black-white memory tests after rest intervals of four, six, eight, or ten weeks. The results for the four-week interval show extreme individual differences in memory. Number 1000, for example, was able to choose correctly every time in a series of white-black tests after a rest interval of four weeks, whereas No. 5 was wrong as often as she was right after the same interval. I have placed the results for these two individuals at the head of the table because they suggest the variations which render averages undesirable. Number 1000 had a perfect habit at the end of four weeks of disuse; No. 5 had no habit whatever. I shall reserve further discussion of age, sex, and individual differences in the permanency of habits for the next chapter.

With Nos. 7 and 998 memory tests were made after three different rest intervals. At the end of two weeks the black-white habit was present in both individuals, although it was not perfect. After six and four weeks, respectively (see Table 48), it still persisted; in fact, it apparently had improved as the result of additional training after the earlier memory tests. At the expiration of ten weeks it had wholly disappeared. In her first series of memory tests after the ten-week interval No. 7 made only one error, but a chance choice of the black (right) in the first test and the subsequent choice of the box in which no shock had been received serve to account for results which at first appear to be indicative of memory. That this explanation is correct is proved by the fact that a second memory series, in which the first choice happened to be wrong, resulted in six mistakes. Evidently she had lost the habit.

In no instance have memory tests definitely indicated the presence of a habit after a rest interval of more than eight weeks. It is safe, therefore, to conclude from the results which have been obtained that a white-black or black-white discrimination habit may persist during an interval of from two to eight weeks of disuse, but that such a habit is seldom perfect after more than four weeks.

The measurements of memory which were made in connection with color discrimination experiments are markedly different from those which were obtained in the brightness tests. As might have been anticipated (?), in view of the extreme difficulty with which the dancer learns to discriminate colors, the habit of discriminating between qualitatively different visual conditions does not persist very long. I have never obtained evidence of a perfect habit after an interval of more than two weeks, and usually, as is apparent from Table 48, the tests indicated very imperfect memory at the end of that interval. It seems probable that even in these so-called color tests discrimination is partly by brightness difference, and that the imperfection of the habit and its short duration are due to the fact that the basis of discrimination is inadequate. This is the only explanation which I have to offer for the difference which has been demonstrated to exist between the duration of brightness discrimination habits and color discrimination habits.

The duration of a discrimination habit having been measured with a fair degree of accuracy, I undertook the task of ascertaining whether training whose results have wholly disappeared, so far as memory tests are in question, influences the re-acquisition of the same habit. Can a habit be re-acquired with greater facility than it was originally acquired? Is re- learning easier than learning? To obtain an answer to the question which may be asked in these different forms, ten individuals were experimented with in accordance with a method whose chief features are now to be stated. In each of these ten individuals a perfect white-black habit was established by the use of the standard series of tests the order of which is given in Table 12. At the expiration of a rest interval of eight weeks precisely the same series of tests were repeated as memory and re-training tests. In this repetition, the preliminary series, *A* and *B*, served as memory tests, and the subsequent training series, as re-training series.

[Illustration: FIGURE 32.—Error curves plotted from the data given by ten dancers in white-black discrimination tests. The solid line ([Symbol: solid line]) is the error curve of the original learning process; the broken line (—
——) is that of the re-learning process, after an interval of eight weeks.]

The striking results of this investigation of re-learning are exhibited in the curves of learning and re-learning of Figure 32. These curves make it appear that the mice re-acquired the white-black discrimination habit much more readily than they had originally acquired it. But in addition to furnishing the basis for some such statement as the foregoing, the curves suggest a serious criticism of the experiment.

In the original tests, the preliminary series indicated a strong preference for black. In series *A* it was chosen on the average 5.8 times in 10, and in series *B*, 5.7 times. This preference was rapidly overcome by the training series, and at the end of 130 tests discrimination was perfect. All this appears in the curve of learning (solid line of figure). On the other hand, these preliminary series when repeated as memory tests, after a rest-interval of eight weeks, gave markedly different results. Series *A* indicated preference for white (5.6 times in 10) instead of black, and series *B* indicated only a slight preference for black. In brief, series *A* and *B* show that the preference for black was considerably stronger at the beginning of the training than at the beginning of the re-training.

In the light of these facts it is fair to claim that the effects of the white-black training had not wholly disappeared as the result of eight weeks of rest, and that the experiment therefore fails to furnish satisfactory grounds for the statement that re-learning occurs more rapidly than learning. I accept this criticism as pertinent, although not necessarily valid, and at the same time I freely admit that the results have a significance which I had not anticipated. But they are not less interesting or valuable on that account. Granting, then, that at least some of the ten individuals which took part in the experiment had not completely lost the memory of their white-black training at the end of eight weeks, it is still possible that an examination of the individual results may justify some conclusion concerning the question which was proposed at the outset of the investigation. Such an examination is made possible by Tables 49 and 50, in which I have arranged separately the results for the males and the females.

TABLE 49

WHITE-BLACK TRAINING. TEN TESTS PER DAY

Males

	TRAINING						RETRAINING					
	210	220	230	410	420	AV.	210	220	230	410	420	AV.
A	6	5	6	6	6	5.8	5	4	5	4	3	4.2
B	6	8	8	5	1	5.6	8	4	5	4	6	5.4
1	6	7	6	2	4	5.0	3	3	4	7	3	4.0
2	4	3	1	2	3	2.6	2	4	2	5	3	3.2
3	3	1	4	3	4	3.0	1	4	1	4	1	2.2
4	5	0	3	3	2	2.6	0	1	0	1	2	0.8
5	3	0	4	1	4	2.4	0	2	0	2	0	0.8
6	2	1	4	0	1	1.6	0	1	0	0	2	0.6
7	1	0	3	1	0	1.0	0	0	0	0	0	
8	0	0	1	0	0	0.2	0	0	1	0.2		
9	0	0	0	1	0	0.2	0	0	0			
10	0	0	0	0	1	0.2						
11	0	0	0	0	0							
12	0	0	0	0								
13	0	0										
14												
15												

Only three of the ten individuals failed to re-acquire the habit of white-black discrimination more quickly than it had originally been acquired, and, in the case of these exceptions, No. 220 required exactly the same number of tests in each case, and No. 420 was placed at a slight disadvantage in the re-learning series by an interruption of the training between the seventh and the eighth series. Had his training been completed by the sixth series he too would have had the same number of tests in training and re-training. Moreover, and this is of preëminent importance for a fair interpretation of the results, in several instances even those individuals which exhibited as strong a preference for the black in the memory series as in the preliminary series re-learned more quickly than they had learned. Number 210, for example, although he gave no evidence of memory, and, in fact, chose the black more frequently in the memory series than he did in the preliminary series, re-acquired the discrimination habit in less than half the number of tests which had been necessary for the establishment of the habit originally.

TABLE 50

WHITE-BLACK TRAINING. TEN TESTS PER DAY

Females

TRAINING RE-TRAINING
215 225 235 415 425 Av. 215 225 235 415 425 Av.
A 8 4 4 8 5 5.8 5 2 7 6 3 4.6
B 8 7 6 6 2 5.8 8 5 6 4 3 5.2
1 7 6 5 6 4 5.6 4 1 5 4 3 3.4
2 5 6 4 2 5 4.4 1 1 1 2 3 1.6
3 3 3 4 3 4 3.4 1 0 3 6 0 2.0
4 2 1 3 3 3 2.4 0 0 3 3 1 1.4
5 1 3 3 3 3 2.6 0 0 died 2 0 0.5
6 2 1 1 1 0 1.0 0 1 0 0.2
7 1 1 2 3 3 2.0 0 0 0
8 0 0 2 2 3 1.4 1 0.2
9 1 0 0 1 1 0.6 0 0
10 0 2 1 0 2 1.0 0 0
11 0 3 0 1 0 0.8 0 0
12 0 0 0 2 0 0.4
13 0 0 0 0 0
14 0 0 0
15 0 0

The facts which have been presented thus far become more significant when the indices of modifiability for the learning and the re-learning processes are compared.

INDICES OF MODIFIABILITY

LEARNING RE-LEARNING

Females 104 42.5
Males 72 54

The behavior of the mice in the experiments, the detailed results of Tables 49 and 50, and the indices of modifiability together justify the following conclusions. Most of the ten dancers, at the end of a rest interval of eight weeks, had so far lost the habit of white-black discrimination that memory tests furnished no conclusive evidence of the influence of previous training; a few individuals seemed to possess traces of the habit after such an interval. In the case of each group of individuals re-training brought about the establishment of a perfect habit far more quickly than did the original training. This suggests the existence of two kinds or aspects of organic modification in connection with training; those which constitute the basis of a definite form of motor activity, and those which constitute the bases or dispositions for the acquirement of certain types of behavior. There are several indications that further study of the modifiability of behavior will furnish the facts which are necessary to render this suggestion meaningful.

Closely related to the facts which have been revealed by the re-training experiments are certain results of the labyrinth experiments. For the student of animal behavior, as for the human educator, it is of importance to learn whether one kind of training increases the efficiency of similar forms of training. Can a dancer learn a given labyrinth path the more readily because it has previously had experience in another form of labyrinth?

The answer to this question, which my experimental results furnish, is given in Table 51. In the upper half of the table have been arranged the results for six individuals which were trained first in labyrinth B, then in labyrinth C, and finally in labyrinth D. Below, in similar fashion, are given the results for six individuals which were trained in the same three labyrinths in the order C, B, D, instead of B, C, D. My purpose in giving the training in these two orders was to ascertain whether labyrinth C, which had proved to be rather difficult for most individuals, would be more easily learned if the training in it were preceded by training in labyrinth C.

TABLE 51

THE INFLUENCE OF ONE LABYRINTH HABIT UPON THE FORMATION OF ANOTHER LABYRINTH B LABYRINTH C LABYRINTH D NO. OF NO. OF NO. OF NO. OF NO. OF NO. OF NO. FIRST COR- LAST OF FIRST COR- LAST OF FIRST COR- LAST OF RECT TEST FIVE COR- RECT TEST FIVE COR-RECT TEST FIVE COR- RECT TESTS RECT TESTS RECT TESTS

76 8 14 3 19 4 7 78 5 20 6 14 4 5 86 13 22 5 12 3 9 75 4 15 8 19 4 13 77 7 11 11 29 11 12 87 12 22 9 20 4 9

AV. 8.2 17.3 7.0 18.8 5.0 9.2

LABYRINTH C LABYRINTH B LABYRINTH D

58 16 — 2 14 7 10 60 17 — 13 37 10 14 88 25 35 9 22 4 8 49 34 — 1 5 7 8 57 15 — 3 20 3 6 85 11 18 2 11 3 4

AV. 19.7 26.5 5.0 18.2 5.7 8.3

The results are sufficiently definite to warrant the conclusion that experience in B rendered the learning of C easier than it would have been had there been no previous labyrinth training. Those individuals whose first labyrinth training was in C made their first correct trip as the result of 19.7 trials, whereas those which had previously been trained in labyrinth B were able to make a correct trip as the result of only 7.0 trials. Similarly the table shows that training in C rendered the subsequent learning of B easier. To master B when it was the first labyrinth required 8.2 trials; to master it after C had been learned required only 5 trials. In addition to proving that the acquisition of one form of labyrinth habit may facilitate the acquisition of others, comparison of the averages of Table 51 furnishes evidence of the truth of the statement that no results of training can be properly interpreted in the absence of knowledge of the previous experience of the organism.

CHAPTER XVII

INDIVIDUAL, AGE, AND SEX DIFFERENCES IN BEHAVIOR

All dancers are alike in certain important respects, but to the trained observer of animal behavior their individual peculiarities are quite as evident, and even more interesting than their points of resemblance. Omitting consideration of the structural marks of individuality, we shall examine the individual, age, and sex differences in general behavior, rapidity of learning, memory, and discrimination, which have been revealed by my experiments. Observations which bear on the subject of differences are scattered through the preceding chapters, but in no case have they been given sufficient prominence to force them upon the attention of those who are not especially interested in individual peculiarities. It has seemed worth while, therefore, to assemble all the available material in this chapter for systematic examination and interpretation.

In the pages which follow, individual, age, and sex peculiarities are discussed in turn. Within each of these three groups of differences I have arranged in order what Royce has appropriately named the facts of discriminating sensitiveness, docility, and initiative. Individuals of the same age and sex no less than those which differ in sex or age exhibit important differences in ability to discriminate among sense impressions ("discriminative sensitiveness"), in ability to profit by experience ("docility"), and in ability to try new kinds of behavior ("initiative").

Individual differences in sensitiveness to visual, auditory, tactual, and olfactory stimuli have been revealed by many of my experiments. The brightness discrimination tests conclusively proved that a degree of difference in illumination which is easily detectable by one dancer may be beyond the discriminating sensitiveness of another. Both the tests with gray papers and those with the Weber's law apparatus furnished striking evidence of individual differences in the kind of visual sensitiveness which throughout this book has been called brightness vision. I suspect that certain of the differences which were observed should be referred to the experience of the individuals rather than to the capacity of the visual organs, for training improves visual discrimination to a much greater extent than would ordinarily be thought possible. To the truth of this statement the results of the Weber's law experiments with No. 51 bear witness. Likewise in color discrimination there are individual differences, examples of which may be discovered by the examination of the results given in Chapters IX and X.

No differences in auditory sensitiveness appeared in my adult dancers, for in none of them was there definite response to sounds, but among the young individuals differences were prominent. I may call attention to the data on this subject which Table 5, p. 89, contains. The mice in four out of twelve litters gave no indications of hearing any sounds that I was able to produce; the remaining individuals responded with varying degrees of sensitiveness. I made no attempt to measure this sensitiveness, but it obviously differed from mouse to mouse. I feel justified, therefore, in stating that the young dancers exhibit extreme individual difference in sensitiveness to sounds.

My observations of differences in sensitiveness to other forms of stimulation were made in connection with training tests, and although they are not quantitative, I venture to call attention to them. Indeed, I am led by the results of my study of various aspects of the dancer's behavior to conclude that the race exhibits individual differences in discriminating sensitiveness to a far greater extent than do most mammals, not excepting man. The importance of this fact (for I am confident that any one who carefully examines the detailed results of the various experiments which are described in this book will agree that it is an established fact) cannot be overlooked. It alters our interpretation of the results of training, memory, heredity, and discrimination experiments, and it leads us to suspect that the dancing race is exceedingly unstable. I do not venture to make comparison of my own observations of the dancer's sense equipment with those of Cyon, Rawitz, Zoth, and Kishi, for the differences are too great in many instances to be thought of as other than species or variety peculiarities. It has seemed fairer to compare only individuals of the same breed, or, as I have done and shall continue to do throughout this chapter, of two lines of descent.

With respect to docility individual differences are prominent. We need only turn to the various tables of results to discover that in modifiability of behavior, in memory, in re-learning, not to mention other aspects of docility, dancers of the same sex and age differed strikingly. Let me by way of illustration cite a few cases of difference in docility. Number 1000 learned to discriminate white from black more quickly and retained his habit longer than any other dancer with which I have experimented. I should characterize him as an exceptionally docile individual. Table 44 offers several examples. Numbers 403 and 407, though they were born in the same litter and were alike in appearance and in conditions of life, acquired the white-black habit with a difference in rapidity which is expressed by the indices of modifiability 50 and 100. In other words, it took

No. 407 twice as long to acquire this habit as it took No. 403. Similarly the ladder-climbing tests revealed important individual differences in ability to profit by experience. In the tables of labyrinth tests (38, 39, 40) individual differences are too numerous to mention. It required forty-nine tests to establish in No. 50 a labyrinth-C habit which was approximately equal in degree of perfection to that which resulted from twenty-two tests in the case of No. 52. The figures in this and other instances do not exaggerate the facts, for repeatedly I have tested individuals of the same litter, the same sex, and, so far as I could judge, of the same stage of development, and obtained results which differ as markedly as do those just cited. If space limits permitted, I could present scores of similar differences in docility which the problem, labyrinth, and discrimination methods have revealed.

In examining the detailed individual results of the various tables for differences of this sort, it is important to bear in mind that sex, age, and descent should be taken into account, for with each of them, as will be shown clearly later in this chapter, sensitiveness, docility, and initiative vary. I have therefore based my statements concerning individual differences in docility upon the results of comparison of mice of the same litter, sex, and age. It is safe to say that human beings similarly selected for comparison do not exhibit greater differences in ability to profit by experience than did these dancing mice.

The facts concerning individual differences in initiative which I have discovered are not less definite than those of the preceding paragraphs. From the beginning of my study of the dancer I observed that what one individual would readily learn of his own initiative another never learned. For example, in the ladder-climbing experiment No. 1000 distinguished himself for his initiative, whereas Nos. 4 and 5 never acquired the habit of escaping from confinement by using the ladder. I noticed, in this test of the animal's ability to learn, that while one individual would be scurrying about trying all ways of escape, investigating its surroundings, looking, sniffing, and dancing by turns, another would devote all its time to whirling, circling, or washing itself. One in the course of its activity would happen upon the way of escape, the other by reason of the limited scope of its activity, not the lack of it, would fail hour after hour to discover even the simplest way of getting back to its nest, to food, and to its companions. Hundreds of times during the past three years I have noticed important individual differences in initiative in connection with the discrimination experiments. The swinging wire doors which one dancer learned to push open before he had been in the box five minutes, another might not become familiar with through his own initiative for hours or days. In fact, it was not seldom that I had to teach an individual to pass from one compartment to the other by gently pushing him against the door until it opened sufficiently to allow him to squeeze through. Occasionally a mouse learned to pull the doors open so that he could pass through the openings in either direction with facility. This was a form of individual initiative which I had not anticipated and did not especially desire, so I did not encourage its development, but, nevertheless, at least one fourth of the mice which I experimented with in the discrimination box learned the trick. The other three fourths, although they were used in the box day after day sometimes for weeks, never discovered that they might return to the nest-box by pulling the swing-door through which they had just passed as well as by entering one of the electric-boxes.

Another indication of individual initiative in action appeared in the tendency of certain mice to climb out of the experiment boxes or labyrinths. It would have been extremely easy for any of the mice to escape from the labyrinths by scaling the walls of the alleys, for they were only 10 cm. in height, and when a dancer stood on its hind legs it could easily reach the top with its nose. But, strange though it will seem to any one who has not worked with the dancer, not more than one in ten of the animals which I observed made any attempt to escape in this manner. They lacked initiative. That it was not due to a lack of the power to climb, I abundantly demonstrated by teaching a few individuals that a scramble in one corner meant easy escape from the maze of paths. I do not think any one of the mice was physically incapable of climbing, but I am confident that they differed markedly, not only in the willingness to try new modes of action, but in the readiness with which they could climb. I have already said that individuals differ noticeably in the scope of their activity. By this statement I mean that they try a varying number of kinds of activity. As in the case of men, so in mice, one individual will do a greater number of things in a few hours than another will in weeks or months. The dancers differ in versatility, in individual initiative, as do we, albeit not so markedly.

Important differences which may with certainty be described as age differences are not so obvious as are such marks of individuality as have been set forth in the preceding pages. I have noted few changes in discriminative sensitiveness, other than those with regard to auditory sensitiveness, which could be correlated with age. In certain instances adults appeared to be able to discriminate more accurately and more easily than young mice, but it is difficult to say whether this change belongs under sensitiveness or docility. I have not made an ontogenetic study of the senses, and I am therefore unable to describe in detail the course of their development and decline. Of one important fact I am certain, that discriminative sensitiveness increases up to a certain point with age and with training.

Differences in docility which are obviously to be correlated with age abound. In the prime of its life (from the second to the tenth month) the dancer is active, full of energy, quick to learn; in its senility (during the second year) it is inactive, but at times even more docile than during the period of greatest physical development. Frequently I have noticed in connection with labyrinth tests that individuals of the age of a year or more learn much more quickly than do individuals of the age of two or three months. But, on the other hand, I have contradictory observations, for now and then I obtained just the opposite result in experiments to test docility. Evidently this is a matter which demands systematic, quantitative investigation. Casual observation may suggest conclusions, but it will not justify them.

Early in my investigation of the behavior of the dancer I conceived the idea of determining the relation of modifiability of behavior (docility) to age. The question which was foremost in my mind and for which I first sought an answer may be stated thus: can the dancer acquire a given habit with the same facility at different ages? Since the visual discrimination experiment seemed to be well suited for the investigation of this problem I planned to train, in the white-black discrimination experiment, five pairs of dancers at the age of one month, and the same number for each of the ages four, seven, ten, thirteen, sixteen, and nineteen months.[1]

[Footnote 1: I have not been able thus far to determine the average length of the dancer's life. The greatest age to which any of my individuals has attained is nineteen months.]

To test the same individuals month after month would be the ideal way of obtaining an answer to our question, but I could devise no satisfactory way of doing this. The effects of training last so long, as the results of the previous chapter proved, and the uncertainty of their entire disappearance is so serious, that the same training process cannot be used at successive ages. The use of different methods of training is even more unsatisfactory because it is extremely difficult to make accurate quantitative comparison of their results. It was these considerations that forced me to attempt to discover the relation of docility to age by carrying out the same experiments with groups of individuals of different ages.

As my plan involved the execution of precisely the same set of tests with at least seventy individuals whose age, history, and past experience were accurately known, and of which some had to be kept for nineteen months before they could be trained, the amount of labor and the risk of mishap which it entailed were great. To make possible the completion of the investigation within two years, I accumulated healthy individuals for several months without training any of them. In March, 1907, I had succeeded in completing the tests for the age of one month, and I had on hand for the remaining tests almost a hundred individuals, whose ages ranged from a few days to eighteen months. Had everything gone well, the work would have been finished within six months. Suddenly, and without discoverable external cause, my mice began to die of an intestinal trouble, and despite all my efforts to check the disease by changing food supply and environment, all except a single pair died within a few weeks. Thus ended a number of experiments whose final results I had expected to be able to present in this volume. However, the work which I have done is still of value, for the single pair of survivors have made possible the continuance of my tests with other individuals of the same line of descent as those which perished, and I have to regret only the loss of time and labor.

As I have on hand results for ten individuals of the age of one month, and for four individuals of the age of four months, it has seemed desirable to state the problem, method, and incomplete results of this study of the relation of modifiability to age. The indices of modifiability for these two groups of dancers differ so strikingly that I feel justified in persisting in my efforts to obtain comparable data for the seven ages which have been mentioned.

TABLE 52

PLASTICITY (RELATION or MODIFIABILITY TO AGE)

Number of Errors in Successive Daily Series of Ten White-Black Tests, with Dancers Four Months Old

SERIES	MALES NO. 76	NO. 78	AV.	FEMALES NO. 75	NO. 77	AV.	GENERAL AV.
A	7	7	7.0	4	8	6.0	6.50
B	8	6	7.0	6	5	5.5	6.25
1	5	5	5.0	5	5	5.0	5.00
2	5	4	4.5	2	2	2.0	3.25
3	4	5	4.5	2	5	3.5	4.00
4	3	4	3.5	1	1	1.0	2.25
5	5	2	3.5	0	1	0.5	2.00
6	3	2	2.5	1	0	0.5	1.50
7	2	1	1.5	1	2	1.5	1.50
8	5	1	3.0	0	0	0	1.50
9	1	3	2.0	0	0	0	1.00
10	1	2	1.5	1	0	0.5	1.00
11	1	1	1.0	0	0		0.50

12	1	1	1.0	0	0	0.50	
13	0	0	0	0	0	0	0
14	0	0	0	0			
15	0	0	0	0			

[Illustration: FIGURE 33.—Plasticity curves. In the left margin are given the indices of modifiability (the number of tests necessary for the establishment of a perfect habit). Below the base line the age of the individuals is given in months. Curve for males, ————; curve for females, - - - -; curve for both males and females,——. When these three plasticity curves are completed, they will represent the indices of modifiability as determined for ten individuals at the age of 1 month, and similarly for the same number of individuals at each of the ages, 4, 7, 10, 13, 16, and 19 months.]

The detailed results for the one-month old individuals appear in Table 43; those for the four-month individuals in Table 52. The general averages for the former are to be found in the third column of Table 46, under the heading "10 tests per day"; those for the latter in the last column of Table 52. Mere inspection of these tables reveals the curious sex difference which goes far towards justifying the presentation of this uncompleted work. The index of modifiability for the ten one-month individuals is 88 (that is, 88 tests were necessary for the establishment of a habit); for the four-month individuals it is 102.5. The heavy solid line of Figure 33 joins the points on the ordinates at which these values are located. Apparently, then, the dancer acquires the white-black discrimination habit less readily at the age of four months than at the age of one month.

Further analysis of the results proves that this statement is not true. When the averages for the two sexes are compared, it appears that the males learned much less quickly at four months than at one month, whereas just the reverse is true of the females. The dash and dot line of the figure extends from the index of modifiability of the one-month males (72) to that of the four-month males (120); and the regularly interrupted line similarly joins the indices of the one-month (104) and the four-month (85) females. In seeking to discover age differences in docility or ability to profit by experience we have stumbled upon what appears to be an important sex difference. Perhaps I should add to this presentation of partial results the following statement. Since there are only four individuals in the four-month group, two of each sex, the indices are not very reliable, and consequently too much stress should not be laid upon the age and sex differences which are indicated.

In view of this impressive instance of the way in which averages may conceal facts and lead the observer to false inferences, I wish to remark that my study of the dancer has convinced me of the profound truth of the statement that the biologist, whether he be psychologist, anthropologist, physiologist, or morphologist, should work with the organic individual and should first of all deal with his results as individual results. Averages have their place and value, but to mass data before their individual significance has been carefully sought out is to conceal or distort their meaning. Too many of us, in our eagerness for quantitative results and in our desire to obtain averages which shall justify general statements, get the cart before the horse.

Figure 33 presents the beginning of what I propose to call plasticity curves. When these three curves are completed on the basis of experiments with five dancers of each sex for each of the ages indicated on the base line of the figure, they will indicate what general changes in plasticity, modifiability of behavior, or ability to learn (for all of these expressions have been used to designate much the same capacity of the organism) occur from the first month to the nineteenth in the male and the female dancer, and in the race without respect to sex. So far as I know, data for the construction of plasticity curves such as I hope in the near future to be able to present for the dancing mouse have not been obtained for any mammal.

At present it would be hazardous for me to attempt to state any general conclusion concerning the relation of docility to age.

The initiative of the dancer certainly varies with its age. In scope the action system rapidly increases during the first few months of life, and if the animal be subjected to training tests, this increase may continue well into old age. The appearance of noticeable quiescence does not necessarily indicate diminished initiative. Frequently my oldest mice have shown themselves preëminent in their ability to adjust their behavior to new conditions. However, I have not studied individuals of more than eighteen months in age. One would naturally expect initiative to decrease in senility. All that I can say is that I have seen no indications of it.

We may now briefly consider the principal sex differences which have been revealed by the experiments. In sensitiveness I have discovered no difference, but it should be stated that no special attention has been given to the matter. In docility the males usually appeared to be superior to the females. This was especially noticeable early in my visual discrimination tests. The males almost invariably acquired a perfect habit quicker than the females. I may cite the following typical instances. Number 14 acquired the black-white habit with 40 tests; No. 13, with 60 (Table 10, p. 109). Of the five pairs of individuals whose records in white-black training appear in

Table 43, not one contradicts the statement which has just been made. It is to be noted, however, that under certain conditions of training, for example, 20 tests per day, the female is at an advantage. Recently I have with increasing frequency obtained measures of docility which apparently favor the female. That this difference in the results is due to a difference in age is probable.

In labyrinth tests the female is as much superior to the male as the male is to the female in discrimination tests. From the tables of Chapter XIII I may take a few averages to indicate the quantitative nature of this difference. A degree of proficiency in labyrinth B attained by the males after 7.0 trials was equaled by the females after 6.2 trials. In labyrinth C the males acquired a habit as a result of 18.7 trials; the females, as a result of 13.8. And similarly in labyrinth D, 6.1 trials did no more for the males than 5.9 did for the females.

That at the age of about one month the male dancer should be able to acquire a visual discrimination habit more rapidly than the female, whereas the female can acquire a labyrinth habit more readily than the male, suggests an important difference in the nature of their equipment for habit formation. One might hazard the suggestion that the male depends more largely upon discrimination of external conditions, whereas the female depends to a greater extent than does the male upon the internal, organic changes which are wrought by acts. At any rate the female seems to follow a labyrinth path more mechanically, more accurately, more easily, and with less evidence of sense discrimination than does the male.

Finally, in concluding this chapter, I may add that in those aspects of behavior which received attention in the early chapters of this volume the dancers differ very markedly. Some climb readily on vertical or inclined surfaces to which they can cling; others seldom venture from their horizontally placed dance floor. Some balance themselves skillfully on narrow bridges; others fall off almost immediately. My own observations, as well as a comparison of the accounts of the behavior of the dancer which have been given by Cyon, Zoth, and other investigators, lead me to conclude that there are different kinds of dancing mice. This may be the result of crosses with other species of mice, or it may be merely an expression of the variability of an exceptionally unstable race.

I can see no satisfactory grounds for considering the dancer either abnormal or pathological. It is a well-established race, with certain peculiarities to which it breeds true; and no pathological structural conditions, so far as I have been able to learn, have been discovered.

I have presented in this chapter on differences a program rather than a completed study. To carry out fully the lines of work which have been suggested by my observations and by the presentation of results would occupy a skilled observer many months. I have not as yet succeeded in accomplishing this, but my failure is not due to lack of interest or of effort.

CHAPTER XVIII

THE INHERITANCE OF FORMS OF BEHAVIOR

In a general way those peculiarities of behavior which suggested the name dancing mouse are inherited. Generation after generation of the mice run in circles, whirl, and move the head restlessly and jerkily from side to side. But these forms of behavior vary greatly. Some individuals whirl infrequently and sporadically; others whirl frequently and persistently, at certain hours of the day. Some are unable to climb a vertical surface; others do so readily. Some respond to sounds; others give no indications of ability to hear. I propose in this chapter to present certain facts concerning the inheritance of individual peculiarities of behavior, and to state the results of a series of experiments by which I had hoped to test the inheritance of individually acquired forms of behavior.

My study of the nature of the whirling tendency of the dancer has revealed the fact that certain individuals whirl to the right almost uniformly, others just as regularly to the left, and still others now in one direction, now in the other. On the basis of this observation, the animals have been classified as right, left, or mixed whirlers. Does the dancer transmit to its offspring the tendency to whirl in a definite manner?

Records of the direction of whirling of one hundred individuals have been obtained. For twenty of these mice the determination was made by counting the number of complete turns in five-minute intervals at six different hours of the day. For the remaining eighty individuals the direction was discovered by observation of the activity of the animals for a brief interval at five different times. Naturally, the former results are the more exact; in fact, they alone have any considerable quantitative value. But for the problem under consideration all of the determinations are sufficiently accurate to be satisfactory.

The distribution of the individuals which were examined as to direction of whirling is as follows.

RIGHT WHIRLERS LEFT WHIRLERS MIXED WHIRLERS TOTAL

Males 19 19 12 50
Females 12 23 15 50

The frequency of occurrence of left whirlers among the females is unexpectedly high. Is this to be accounted for in terms of inheritance? In my search for an answer to this question I followed the whirling tendency from generation to generation in two lines of descent. These two groups of mice have already been referred to as the 200 line and the 400 line. The former were descended from Nos. 200 and 205, and the latter from Nos. 152 and 151. Individuals which resulted from the crossing of these lines will be referred to hereafter as of mixed descent. There were some striking differences in the behavior of the mice of the two lines of descent. As a rule the individuals of the 200 line climbed more readily, were more active, danced less vigorously, whirled less rapidly and less persistently, and were in several other respects much more like common mice than were the individuals of the 400 line. It is also to be noted (see Table 5) that few of the litters of the 200 line exhibited auditory reactions, whereas almost all of the litters of the 400 line which were tested gave unmistakable evidence of sensitiveness to certain sounds. These differences at once suggest the importance of an examination of the whirling tendency of each line of descent.

The results for the several generations of each line which I had opportunity to examine are unexpectedly decisive so far as the question in point is concerned.

INDIVIDUALS OF THE 200 LINE

MALES FEMALES

First generation No. 200, ? No. 205, ?
Second generation No. 210, Mixed whirler No. 215, Left whirler
Third generation No. 220, Mixed whirler No. 225, Mixed whirler
Fourth generation No. 230, Right whirler No. 235, Mixed whirler
Fifth generation No. 240, Right whirler No. 245, Left whirler

INDIVIDUALS OF THE 400 LINE

MALES FEMALES

First generation No. 152, Left whirler No. 151, Left whirler
Second generation No. 410, Left whirler No. 415, Right whirler
Third generation No. 420, Left whirler No. 425, Left whirler

One line of descent exhibited no pronounced whirling tendency; the other exhibited a strong tendency to whirl to the left. Are these statements true for the group of one hundred individuals whose distribution among the three classes of whirlers has been given? In order to obtain an answer to this question I have reclassified these individuals according to descent and direction of whirling.

INDIVIDUALS OF THE 200 LINE

RIGHT WHIRLERS LEFT WHIRLERS MIXED WHIRLERS TOTAL

Males 7 6 8 21 Females 5 8 8 21 12 14 16 42

INDIVIDUALS OF THE 400 LINE

RIGHT WHIRLERS LEFT WHIRLERS MIXED WHIRLERS TOTAL

Males 4 9 1 14 Females 6 9 4 19 10 18 5 33

INDIVIDUALS OF MIXED DESCENT

9 10 6 25

Three interesting facts are indicated by these results: first, the inheritance of a tendency to whirl to the left in the 400 line of descent; second, the lack of any definite whirling tendency in the 200 line; and third, the occurrence of right and left whirlers with equal frequency as a result of the crossing of these two lines of descent.

It is quite possible, and I am inclined to consider it probable, that the pure dancer regularly inherits a tendency to whirl to the left, and that this is obscured in the case of the 200 line by the influences of a cross with another variety of mouse. It is to be noted that the individuals of the 200 line were predominantly mixed whirlers, and I may add that many of them whirled so seldom that they might more appropriately be classed as circlers.

THE INHERITANCE OF INDIVIDUALLY ACQUIRED FORMS OF BEHAVIOR

The white-black discrimination experiments which were made in connection with the study of vision and the modifiability of behavior were so planned that they should furnish evidence of any possible tendency towards the inheritance of modifications in behavior. The problem may be stated thus. If a dancing mouse be thoroughly trained to avoid black, by being subjected to a disagreeable experience every time it enters a black box, will it transmit to its offspring a tendency to avoid black?

Systematic training experiments were carried on with individuals of both the 200 and 400 lines of descent. For each of these lines a male and a female were trained at the age of four weeks to discriminate between the white and the black electric-boxes and to choose the former. After they had been thoroughly trained these individuals were mated, and in course of time a male and female, chosen at random from their first litter, were similarly trained. All the individuals were trained in the same way and under as nearly the same conditions as could be maintained, and accurate records were kept of the behavior of each animal and of the number of errors of choice which it made in series after series of tests. What do these records indicate concerning the influence of individually acquired forms of behavior upon the behavior of the race?

TABLE 53

THE INHERITANCE OF THE HABIT OF WHITE-BLACK DISCRIMINATION

Number of Errors in Daily Series of Ten Tests

MALES FEMALES

SERIES FIRST SECOND THIRD FOURTH FIRST SECOND THIRD FOURTH GENERA- GENERA- GENERA- GENERA- GENERA- GENERA- GENERA- GENERA- TION TION TION TION TION TION TION TION

No. 210 No. 220 No. 230 No. 240 No. 215 No. 225 No. 235 No. 245

A 6 5 6 7 8 4 4 7 B 6 8 8 8 8 7 6 5

1 6 7 6 5 7 6 5 4

2 4 3 1 5 5 6 4 5

3 3 1 4 5 3 4 4 3

4 5 0 3 4 2 1 3 1

5 3 0 4 2 1 3 3 0

6 2 1 4 2 2 1 1 1

7 1 0 3 1 1 1 2 0

8 0 0 1 0 0 0 2 3

9 0 0 0 1 1 0 0 0

10 0 0 1 0 2 1 1

11 0 0 0 3 0 0

12 0 0 0 0 0

13 0 0 0 0

14 0

I have records for four generations in the 200 line and for three generations in the 400 line.[1] As the results are practically the same for each, I shall present the detailed records for the former group alone. In Table 53 are to be found the number of errors made in successive series of ten tests each by the various individuals of the 200 line which were trained in this experiment. The most careful examination fails to reveal any indication of the inheritance of a tendency to avoid the black box. No. 240, in fact, chose the black box more frequently in the preference series than did No. 210, and he required thirty more tests for the establishment of a perfect habit than did No. 210. Apparently descent from individuals which had thoroughly learned to avoid the black box gives the dancer no advantage in the formation of a white-black discrimination habit. There is absolutely no evidence of the inheritance of this particular individually acquired form of behavior in the dancer.

[Footnote 1: This experiment was interrupted by the death of the animals of both lines of descent.]

Printed in France by Amazon
Brétigny-sur-Orge, FR

27878715R00116